VEGAN
VEGETARIAN
OMNIVORE

ALSO BY ANNA THOMAS

Love Soup

The Vegetarian Epicure

The Vegetarian Epicure, Book Two

The New Vegetarian Epicure: Menus for Family and Friends

Fennel and Asparagus Ribbon Slaw (p. 138)

ANNA THOMAS

PHOTOGRAPHY BY VICTORIA PEARSON

VEGAN VEGETARIAN OMNIVORE

DINNER FOR EVERYONE AT THE TABLE

W. W. Norton & Company

Independent Publishers Since 1923

New York   London

For information about permission to reproduce selections from this book,
write to Permissions, W. W. Norton & Company, Inc.,
500 Fifth Avenue, New York, NY 10110

For information about special discounts for bulk purchases, please contact
W. W. Norton Special Sales at specialsales@wwnorton.com or 800-233-4830

Manufacturing by RR Donnelley Shenzhen
Book design by Caroline Clark Design
Production manager: Louise Mattarelliano

ISBN: 978-0-393-08301-9

W. W. Norton & Company, Inc.
500 Fifth Avenue, New York, N.Y. 10110
www.wwnorton.com

W. W. Norton & Company Ltd.
Castle House, 75/76 Wells Street, London W1T 3QT

1 2 3 4 5 6 7 8 9 0

To My Christmas Eve Family . . . Beginning with my own family, Chris and Teddy, Eve and Tomás . . . and including with open arms the families who became my larger tribe, the comrades in the kitchen, the cast of regulars, and the friends from far-off places who joined when they could. I love you all.

CONTENTS

CONTENTS

VEGAN
VEGETARIAN
OMNIVORE

INTRODUCTION

One of the joys of my life, from the time I first struck out on my own and learned to cook, has been to invite friends over and to cook for those I love. Small dinners in cramped student apartments at UCLA, big parties when I lived in a real house, family meals and holidays when I married and had children, and lavish events in honor of this or that—all joy.

I began to write about food at a young age; I wrote most of *The Vegetarian Epicure* before I was old enough to legally drink, so it's been many years now that I've cooked, and learned, and thought about food, and I know that what I put on the table is important. But there is something even more important:

Who is at the table?

So this is a book about hospitality. Because when it comes to food, the important thing in life is to be able to sit down with those we love and share food and drink in a companionable way.

When guests come to my table, I want to make them welcome and honor them. When we sit down together and share food, tell each other our stories and raise a glass, we are united in a profound way. Eating is survival, but sharing food—that's celebration, comfort, hail and farewell, friendship and love. I don't want to give that up because *we don't all eat exactly the same way.*

Not long after *Love Soup* was published, I was in New York visiting my editor, Maria Guarnaschelli. We were walking through the Union Square farmers' market, admiring the abundance of the harvest season, when we bumped into a friend of Maria's. Maria introduced me as someone who wrote about food, and at once the woman—a stranger to me until that moment—clutched my arm with a look of such desperation that I thought the zombie apocalypse might be upon us at last.

"I don't know what to do!" she cried. "I'm hosting Thanksgiving, and this one eats that and not this, and that one eats this and not that—" She went on in a torrent of anxiety, then sighed, shook her head. "I just want to give up. Cancel."

No! Don't cancel, I thought. This is your family, your holiday, your wonderful life. It should not be a food fight.

We were standing in the midst of such an extravaganza of beautiful food as she lamented that she didn't know how to feed her family. But I understood. I heard versions of her complaint from so many people. Holidays have the demands of tradition. This is when we gather with our extended families, our friends, the friends of our children—a group of people not necessarily selected for their shared preference in eating style!

The way we eat is changing. For some it happens gradually, for others in a sudden burst, perhaps on doctor's advice. And at any given moment we are in very different places on the larger curve, as the woman in Union Square observed.

There are so many questions: What's a healthy diet? What is sustainable? On the other hand: What do I *love*, or remember from childhood? What did I discover on my trip to Thailand? How can I lose five pounds? What's in the fridge?

Are we eating less meat, as a nation? I'm not sure, but in my college days, when I was writing my first book, being a vegetarian was still considered cranky and weird. I could hardly go to a restaurant—and I lived in California. In Munich once, I was actually laughed at by the restaurant staff when I asked for a meal without meat. Now vegetarians seem mainstream, and it is vegans who are reading labels with care. Vegan is the new vegetarian—but hey, something is always the new something.

Can we still sit down and enjoy dinner together?

At holidays these questions can reach a flash point, but they are with us all the time. We need a way, I thought, of approaching food that allows us to be inclusive. To relax, and be flexible.

Most of us grew up in a food culture with a fixed idea of how to plan a meal—a piece of meat in the center of the plate and vegetables or grains on the side. That's our default setting. And yes, we can adapt those familiar dishes, but we are immediately taking things away, substituting—compromising.

We're doing this backward, I thought. Why not start with the food everyone eats?

Everyone eats the watermelon at the picnic. It's not the vegan watermelon, it's just the watermelon. Everyone eats the minestrone and the ciabatta . . . the toasted almonds with the aperitif . . . the peanut butter sandwich of lunchbox fame! And a thousand other foods.

It seemed simple. Start with the foods that everyone eats, design a meal that works, then expand it, make it flexible—add butter or eggs or cheese in ways that pair well. Add fish or meat, perhaps as supporting players.

I did this years ago when I was hosting my own big Thanksgiving for extended family, friends, and assorted strays far from home, a mix of vegetarians and traditionalists. I designed a festive vegetarian meal with the familiar flavors of the season but made sure everything would also work beautifully with a turkey.

There were appetizers—a tapenade, fresh, spicy hummus, persimmon slices with walnut pesto—and then a rich golden cheese and polenta torta studded with sweet squash and pine nuts, surrounded by an array of vegetables. Green beans and pearl onions roasted to a burnished sheen. Baked yams, garlicky sautéed greens, braised fennel and onions. Cranberry relish with port. The spit-roasted turkey my husband prepared fit in seamlessly for those who wanted the traditional bird.

It was Thanksgiving for everyone. Wine flowed, we ate what we liked and gave thanks, the grandparents were happy, the vegetarians were happy, and we were all sharing the same meal.

It's actually easy to design a holiday meal for everyone; it's big and there are many dishes. But we eat every day. So this became my holy grail: to design meals at which the vegan, the vegetarian, and the omnivore could sit down together, toast each other, and eat dinner in my peaceable kingdom.

I made *chile verde* with white beans and added chicken to some of it. I made stuffed peppers and tomatoes Lebanese style, filled with an aromatic rice and lentil stuffing, then mixed sautéed, spiced lamb into part of that stuffing for another batch.

I served kabocha squash risotto with sage and pine nuts and passed the shavings of Parmigiano and the sautéed pancetta as optional garnishes. For antipasto we had cannellini salad with olives, and it could be eaten with or without the tuna in olive oil and capers.

My easy fish soup came back again and again, by popular request; it starts as a robust vegetable soup, and the fish is added in the last moments before serving, so it can easily be served in two versions.

In the summer, a tabbouleh with tomatoes and garbanzo beans could be eaten with prawns seared in garlic—or without them. In the winter, the big minestrone might take on slices of sautéed Italian sausage for the omnivores.

None of this was hard. It took a little thinking—the protein needs of a vegan diet had to be addressed, and things could not get too complicated—but I was having fun. I could have dinner with a group of friends or family without interrogating them in advance about what they did or didn't eat. We could all eat the same meal, varying it to taste. No one felt sidelined, no one felt guilty. Peace and prosperity reigned at my table. Or was it peace and hilarity?

This book is my way of inviting everyone to that easygoing table. I have tried to share practical information here; I hope it can be helpful.

There are 16 menus, and they range from lavish holiday menus, including the Thanksgiving menu that started it all, to casual dinner parties, to some ideas for the simple meals we rely on every day. Nearly every menu is designed to work as a vegan meal and to expand flexibly for vegetarians and omnivores.

And there are recipes—nearly 200, plenty of choices. The largest number are vegan, because really good vegan recipes are still harder to find than others. Many of these have variations that include dairy products. The vegan and vegetarian recipes are based on fresh raw materials, not on meat analogues; you won't find commercial "meat substitute" products here, not because I have anything against them but simply because that is not my style of cooking. I like food that is the best version of itself, not a copy of something else.

There are also recipes for egg dishes, fish and seafood, poultry, and meat—although there are fewer of these, as I feel these categories are solidly represented in the general repertoire. Meat recipes are kept simple for a reason—they are the elaboration of a dish or a menu, not the starting point or center of it.

I do not tell anyone what they *should* eat; I never have. We'll all eat what we like—but let's not be afraid to eat together. And if anything between these covers can help the traditional cook whose son or daughter is coming home from college with the vegan roommate, or help the blossoming vegetarian cook who wants to make her boyfriend's traditional parents feel welcome, or help the lady in Union Square whose entire family is descending on her with their nonnegotiable demands, then I'm happy.

We long for the social table. It draws us. It is a place of sharing, of stories and news, old jokes and comfort. It is a place of connection. When we sit down to eat together, we form the bonds that allow us to be a family. When families join together at Thanksgiving, Passover, Christmas, or a wake, they understand what it means to be a tribe. When tribes meet at the wedding feast, we know civilization is possible.

Sit down at that table with the people you love and have dinner together. Cook for them, eat with them, raise a glass. The world will be a better place.

PART ONE

HOLIDAYS AND CELEBRATIONS

Menus for the Big Occasions

THANKSGIVING FOR EVERYONE

That was my goal...

For many years I was the one with the great big kitchen and the spacious dining room, and I was happy to host a crowded table of extended family and friends for the holidays. There were different eating styles among us, but a warm sense of tradition and a desire to celebrate together. My own style was mainly vegetarian, and I could have said, "It's going to be a vegetarian Thanksgiving." Some of my guests would have been thrilled—but others would not have been entirely happy. Especially in the grandparent generation, some would have felt left behind. And I wanted everyone to feel welcome and honored at my table.

I set out to devise a menu that could stand alone as a robust celebratory meal for the vegan or vegetarian—and could also embrace the traditional turkey. It would be seasonal, fresh, and everything would go with everything. We would toast each other and all eat the same meal—in slightly different versions. No vegetarian would have to nibble around the edges of the plate, and no turkey-eater would feel deprived or guilty.

And it worked just that way—a wonderful time for everyone. Over the years that meal evolved and became its own tradition, redolent with flavors of the harvest, full of the spirit of hospitality. It's Thanksgiving for a crowd, the one when you pull the extra tables out of the garage and everyone pitches in. It begins with an abundance of vegan dishes, includes a few dishes with cheese or butter, and one big roasted turkey. And it's adaptable: the elegant polenta torta that is the centerpiece around which roasted and sautéed vegetables are arrayed can be made with or without cheese, a fruit crisp can be made with butter or as a vegan dessert. Favorite dishes from your family can be added, and the whole menu can be tilted to the desires of your table.

As for the turkey: I think a turkey roasts better with no stuffing in it, just handfuls of herbs, onions, and garlic to infuse it with aromatic flavor, and that's the recipe you'll find in this book. The stuffing is baked separately in two casseroles; it's easy to drizzle turkey drippings over one of them for that familiar flavor.

A Practical Note...

If you leave the cheese out of the appetizers, everything in this menu except the turkey is vegan or has a vegan option.

THANKSGIVING MENU

FOR 12 TO 14

Miniature Black Bean and Chipotle Quesadillas,
some with goat cheese

Crostini with Carrot-Top Pesto and crumbles of Gorgonzola

sugar snap peas with hummus

———

Polenta Torta with Roasted Squash *and onion marmalade*

Sautéed Kale with Garlic

Roasted Cipollini and Green Beans

Roast Turkey with Herbs
Turkey Giblet Sauce with Madeira

Harvest Bread Stuffing in a Casserole

Casserole of Roasted Yams with Green Chiles

Cranberry Sauce with Oranges and Wine

———

Pumpkin Gingerbread with Citrus and Spice Caramel Sauce

Apple Cranberry Crumble

THE GREAT PUMPKIN

A true story . . .

I had a gorgeous, huge pumpkin that a gardener friend had brought me, a cream-colored beauty with wide ridges. It sat like a marble sculpture on the kitchen counter for a few weeks—and then it was Thanksgiving. That year there were going to be just a few of us at the holiday table, and the group was tilting vegan. We decided to stuff that pumpkin, and we built a menu around it. My sons and I cooked together, casually, relaxed. Can you imagine that? It was such fun. We filled that giant pumpkin with a savory stuffing of grains, nuts, fall vegetables, herbs— the whole cornucopia. We roasted it in the oven for hours, and the house smelled heavenly. To serve it, we cut fat wedges and watched them fall away from the center, the stuffing spilling out and fragrant steam rising. There were relishes and a zesty salad alongside the great pumpkin—a lovely meal.

And there's no reason why the rich autumn flavors of our improvised vegan meal couldn't get along with a turkey . . .

For this lighter Thanksgiving menu, start with a glass of prosecco and crostini with one brilliantly spicy pesto and one creamy puree of cannellini and sweet peppers. Then the Great Pumpkin, served with ceremony at the table, full of grains and so many other vegetables that you only need a lemony-bright salad and a raw cranberry relish with it.

For the turkey lovers, I suggest a roast turkey breast or a pair of leg quarters in place of a whole turkey. This is a dramatic meal, with the slicing of the pumpkin at the table, but it is also a lighter menu than the traditional-style Thanksgiving, so a smaller roast may be just right, especially for a smaller group. (And on a practical note, you may not have room in your oven for two giant items.) To finish, juicy Winter Fruit Crumble with Gingersnap Topping, which can be made with butter or in a vegan version. See p. 24 for the Great Pumpkin Menu.

A Practical Note . . .

Everything in this menu except the turkey is vegan; even the dessert can be made either way, vegan or with butter, and both are excellent.

The Great Stuffed Pumpkin (p. 228)

THE GREAT PUMPKIN MENU

FOR 8 TO 10

Spicy Cilantro and Mint Pesto

Cannellini and Garlic Spread

Crostini or flatbread

The Great Stuffed Pumpkin
filled with Farro and Black Rice Pilaf and fall vegetables

Roast Turkey Breast or Leg Quarters with Garlic and Herbs

Chicory and Kale with Agave Vinaigrette

Raw Cranberry and Fuyu Persimmon Relish

Winter Fruit Crumble with Gingersnap Topping

MY CHRISTMAS EVE MENU

FOR 12 TO 14

Crostini with Raw Persimmon and Jalapeño Salsa
and creamy goat cheese

Teddy's favorite fresh hummus

Christmas Eve Porcini Soup

Christmas Eve Pierogi *two ways*

My Polish Chopped Vegetable Salad

dry-smoked salmon
gherkins, onions, capers, fresh dill

Roasted Beets and Beluga Lentils

The Dessert Table

Russian tea cakes, Larry's dried persimmons,
Dark Chocolate Almond Bark, Christmas cookies

Note: My Christmas Eve Porcini Soup is featured in *Love Soup*, so it is not repeated here.
Several versions of excellent fresh hummus are also included in that book.

MY CHRISTMAS EVE

How it changes, how it stays the same . . .

In our house, the big festivity takes place on Christmas Eve. The food we share is the story of my Polish family, of immigration, of new places and new desires, of families growing and coming together . . . of traditions evolving to stay alive. My Christmas Eve is a ritual. As I sit down to write out the menu, I realize that it was written over decades.

My family came to America a few years after World War II, with nothing. When my parents arrived in Michigan, their recent address had been a displaced persons camp, which was itself an improvement following the prisoner-of-war camp. I was a baby, and in my earliest Christmas memories I see a long, linen-draped table—I had to stand on tiptoe to see the top—and relatives coming in the door with blasts of icy, snowy air, carrying dishes of the elaborate foods that would mark the occasion. It was a close immigrant community, the recent arrivals struggling to build a life, but they found a way to celebrate the old customs. It is in immigrant communities that tradition is most fiercely honored. When every earthly possession has been lost, when the place called home has itself been taken away, tradition can still be brought to a new place—it can be cherished and carried forward.

So we had a Polish Christmas Eve, with the aunts and uncles and the close friends who were like a larger family. There were courses—always an odd number, seven or nine. Fish courses, because there was no meat on Christmas Eve; it was a day of abstinence in this Catholic celebration. Were there really seven fish courses? All right, there were some vegetables, too—Middle European winter food: cabbage baked in a sauce, beets in the clear soup, and an amazing, elaborate root vegetable salad. Most memorably, there were mushrooms—earthy, deep-flavored *Boletus* mushrooms, the gift of the forest. Thank heaven for the Italian market that provided my mother with those dried porcini.

When I went off to college and became a vegetarian, I was happy enough to come home and pick my way through that meal. By that time it had become less elaborate. I could eat the beet *barszcz*, and the sublime porcini-filled *uszki*, tiny dumplings that swam in the clear red soup. I loved the complex vegetable salad, and the many desserts. I was content.

Later, when I was married and we had a baby, my husband and I decided we needed to begin our own Christmas traditions. After some experimentation, I settled into a personal version of the Polish flavors of my childhood. I made a porcini soup and my own style of pierogi, but the vegetable salad was the exact one my mother made. We moved to a larger house, with a generous dining room, and I began to invite several families of close friends to share the evening with us. This became tradition, too; the children, as they grew to be teenagers, called these friends the Christmas Eve family.

One year my friend Dennis cured and smoked a side of salmon. It was such a hit that we dropped the Scottish smoked salmon and the pickled herrings from the menu; they could not compete. Dennis was tagged to cure and smoke salmon every year. In a sense, the menu was becoming simpler—if you can call something simple that requires days of simmering, baking, chopping, smoking, filling, and crimping.

We did always begin with something simple— crudités, nuts, and olives. Then the essential porcini soup was served with platters of pierogi, little turnovers of meltingly rich pastry wrapped around caramelized potato or cabbage. After the soup we ate Dennis's smoked salmon with all its garnishes, and my mother's chopped vegetable salad. Finally, the dessert table. My sister Eve's Russian tea cakes became legendary the first time she brought them, and always dominated the array of homemade cookies, confections, and dried fruits.

But a celebration is a living thing. My friend Larry Yee began drying persimmons from his tree, using the traditional Japanese method, which is insanely labor-intensive but results in a dried fruit of such soft, rich, flavorful intensity that people scramble to get on Larry's gift list. When he brought chocolate-dipped dried persimmons for Christmas Eve, the dessert table changed dramatically. Then one year

he made a persimmon salsa as well, from crisp, sweet Fuyu persimmons, lime juice, and jalapeño peppers, and the champagne hour got much more interesting!

Years rolled by. My younger son, Teddy, went off to college and came back a vegan, so the vegetable salad had to be veganized. I made two versions, and to my surprise, everyone preferred the vegan salad, so now that is the standard. A homemade hummus was added to the appetizer table because it's Chris and Teddy's favorite. And I brought the traditional beets back into the menu. How could I not have done it sooner? My roasted beet and beluga lentil salad is so alluring and dark red, so perfect with the flavors of the menu . . .

The power of tradition. My Polish relatives, the ones who came to America as war-bruised adults, would not know what to make of Japanese dried persimmons, a fresh salsa with jalapeño peppers, and a Middle Eastern hummus on Christmas Eve. Or perhaps they would. Perhaps they would see that it was the power of tradition, the honoring of family, friendship, and shared celebration, that pulled these things in with its gravitational force, so that the great communion of kindred spirits could continue. We adapt so that we can go on. We share food that has a past but also a future. The purpose of it is to be able to sit together with people we love, and celebrate.

Here's the menu for this year (p. 25). I like it. And my mom, who came as a refugee and overcame every obstacle to put on a true Polish Christmas Eve—she'd like it, too.

A Practical Note . . .

Most of this meal is vegan, including the crostini, persimmon salsa, hummus, and the porcini soup. The pierogi can be made two ways: with a butter pastry or a vegan pastry. The two big salads served with salmon are vegan, and the dessert table is mixed.

ITALIAN STYLE

For Christmas, New Year's, or any celebration

I love Italian food, the joyful, generous aesthetic of it, and I want that delicious joy on my table at the holidays. This festive five-course meal, full of big, extravagant flavors, is perfect for a sparkling, dressed-up Christmas Eve, an elegant sit-down New Year's Eve, or any other important occasion. Yet it is not fussy or overly formal. It's an approachable meal, elevated with celebratory ideas—the luxury of truffle honey drizzled on the rosemary flatbread, the sumptuous platter of roasted winter vegetables on the antipasto table, the panforte and the truffles in the array of sweets (I'll visit a good Italian grocery for those).

Of course it is flexible. The flatbreads are for everyone, served as the prosecco flows, and the antipasto table is a vegan's bounty, but also includes smoked tuna with capers and spoonfuls of fresh ricotta to be added to the jewel-like beet crostini. The exuberant pasta is all vegetables—I started with the spicy flavors of an *arrabiata*, added dark green sautéed rapini, and finished with crunchy toasted breadcrumbs for a robust dish. Does anyone have room for more? Steamed ling cod on aromatic fennel and onions is beautiful but not heavy. Lovers of seafood will be delighted with it, but I don't think anyone who stops after the pasta will go hungry.

Buone feste!

A Practical Note . . .

In this menu the vegan dishes are the rosemary flatbread, crostini with glazed beets, roasted vegetable antipasto, cannellini salad, penne rigate, candied peels, and tangerines. The panforte you buy is likely to be vegan, too.

ITALIAN MENU

FOR 8 TO 12

With a Glass of Prosecco

Rosemary Flatbread *with truffle honey*

The Antipasto Table

Crostini with Sweet-and-Sour Glazed Beets,
some with fresh ricotta

Roasted Winter Vegetable Antipasto

Marinated Cannellini with Olives and Roasted Peppers
smoked tuna in olive oil and capers

Penne Rigate with Garlic, Rapini, and Sautéed Breadcrumbs

Ling Cod Steamed on Fennel and Onions

The Sweets

panforte, candied peels, tangerines,
nougats, truffles, cookies

Italian Style, the Antipasto Table (clockwise from left): Roasted Winter Vegetable Antipasto (p. 272), smoked tuna in olive oil and capers, Sweet-and-Sour Glazed Beets on arugula (p. 83), Marinated Cannellini with Olives and Roasted Peppers (p. 132)

COCKTAILS ON NEW YEAR'S EVE

Big party, small plates . . .

On New Year's Eve, you may want to have a big, shiny, over-the-top party. A Party! With an exclamation point! Friends will mingle and drink, listen to music, dance, and kiss someone at midnight. We won't be sitting down much, and yet we will want to eat, so small plates and finger food are just right—bright kicks of flavor and texture, moments of pure pleasure, and plenty to eat if you're making it dinner. New Year's Eve comes at the dark dead of winter, so this is a selection of small plates for the cold season, with enough style and spice to wake us up and keep us lively into a new year.

For ease of serving, the menu leans to room-temperature dishes, but a few hot plates keep it interesting; pass them around at various points in the party, a delicious punctuation.

The food is from all over. The pumpkin-seed pesto and the quesadillas with their bite of chipotle are from Mexico. The black lentil puree is Armenian. The crisp-roasted potato wedges with *mojo verde* are Spanish, the pork meatballs Italian. Velvety parsnip soup, served in teacups, is as French as it can be without heavy cream. And dark chocolate bark comes straight from heaven. I love mixing foods from different cultures and traditions. World peace starts here. Happy New Year!

A Practical Note . . .

If you make one recipe of each dish listed in this menu, you will have enough food for 16 to 20, because of the number of dishes. But if you know that your friends love a particular dish, double up on that one. At my house, for example, there would have to be two Onion Agrodolce Galettes and *lots* of Mojo Verde . . .

All the cold plates except the trout and crème fraîche are vegan. In the hot plates, the soup can be served with or without pancetta, and the quesadillas with or without goat cheese. The potato wedges with *mojo verde* are vegan, as is the dark chocolate bark.

NEW YEAR'S EVE MENU

FOR 16 TO 20

The Cold Plates

marinated olives, spicy nuts

sliced radishes with sweet butter

Crostini with Pumpkin-Seed Pesto

Crostini with Beluga Lentil and Caramelized Onion Puree

Charred Red Pepper Crostini *two ways*

smoked trout with crème fraîche and crackers

Onion *Agrodolce* Galette

The Hot Plates

Parsnip and Apple Soup in teacups with crispy pancetta

Miniature Black Bean and Chipotle Quesadillas
some with goat cheese

Roasted Potato Wedges with Mojo Verde

Mint-Scented Pork and Pine Nut Meatballs

The Dessert Plates

Dark Chocolate Almond Bark *with cherries and ginger*

Galician Almond Cake with Citrus and Spice Caramel Sauce

Cocktails on New Year's Eve (clockwise from left): Crostini with Pumpkin-Seed Pesto and Charred Red Pepper Crostini (pp. 48 and 57), Mint-Scented Pork and Pine Nut Meatballs (p. 363), sliced radishes with sweet butter, Roasted Potato Wedges with Mojo Verde (p. 302)

EASTER BRUNCH

For many of us, Easter is indelibly connected to a single food: painted eggs, hot cross buns, or roasted spring lamb. And what is Easter without chocolate? But when we sit down to a meal, whether brunch, lunch, or dinner, it's a time to celebrate the greening of the earth: the bright shoots and leaves, the wild nettles, fennel fronds, sweet peas, asparagus, first tender lettuce, and feathery dill. Green is what gives it meaning.

When my children were small, Easter was a long, relaxed brunch on the terrace. It was kicked off by the egg hunt on the lawn and our own family tradition, the egg war. Painted Easter eggs were selected for the tournament and knocked together until we had a winner—and a big mess of cracked, colorful eggs. Then we could eat. There were more eggs on the table, in a roulade with asparagus or a green frittata. There might be smoked salmon, and often a creamy white cheese mixed with parsley and chives. Dense pumpernickel and sweet, yeasty baba. Leafy salads and strawberries from the nearby fields. Chocolates in the Easter baskets and eggy, buttery Polish *mazurek*. Eggs and butter were everywhere!

Not long ago, when I was invited to a potluck Easter brunch, I took a different approach. I made a farro salad full of bright spring produce: baby peas, asparagus, fennel, mint. It was an instant favorite. It makes a gorgeous centerpiece for a flexible brunch or lunch, a robust grain salad full of snappy, distinct flavors. Everyone eats it, from the purest vegan to the dedicated omnivore, who finds that a piece of salmon or a slice of smoked Easter ham goes very well with it. Here is an Easter Brunch menu built around that salad, a make-ahead meal, extravagant but easy to manage.

A Practical Note...

The vegan meal at the heart of the larger menu begins with fava bean puree and crostini, goes on to the robust spring market salad with farro and the fennel and asparagus slaw, and ends with strawberries and dark chocolate Easter eggs.

EASTER BRUNCH MENU

FOR 8 TO 12

mimosas

———

Fresh Fava Bean Puree *with garlic and mint*

Fresh Ricotta with Herbs

pumpernickel or Crostini

———

Spring Market Salad with Farro,
golden beets, wild herbs, and sweet peas

Chard and Parsley Frittata *with lemon, pepper, and goat cheese*

Fennel and Asparagus Ribbon Slaw

Gently Baked Salmon *with a parsley pesto coat*
capers and cornichons

hot cross buns

———

strawberries with whipped cream

dark chocolate Easter eggs

Easter Brunch (from left):
Fresh Fava Bean Puree (p. 61),
Spring Market Salad with Farro (p. 114),
and Gently Baked Salmon (p. 344)
coated with Parsley Pesto (p. 56)

PART TWO

RECIPES

And Everyday Menus

APPETIZERS, PESTOS, SPREADS, AND DIPS

DÉTENTE

An idyll in Provence—that was the magical summer we spent near the tiny village of Lumière in the Lubéron, surrounded by lavender fields and medieval hill towns. My husband and I had been working hard for several years with no break, and now we had a new baby, too. We were tired! But our next job allowed us to be where we liked, so we rented a small house on a restored estate, Beaureport. Centuries before, our whitewashed little place had been the bakery. Behind it was a meadow, and when we walked across it to hang the laundry on the line, the wild herbs under our feet sent their fragrance into the air. The proprietors were Jacques and Ginotte, a retired couple. One evening they invited us over for drinks. We sat on their terrace, the lavender spreading around us in the blue twilight. Jacques poured wine and red vermouth into glasses and handed them around, a simple kir.

"Un apéritif," he said, *"c'est la détente, entre la journée et le dîner . . ."* He passed his hand through the perfumed evening air: "The aperitif, it's the détente between the workday and the dinner . . ."

As it turned out, we were invited for drinks and a life lesson. In the South of France, dinner meant the whole evening, and Jacques felt we should not enter it rudely. This aperitif was the pause, the easing of tension. No wonder the French live long!

I haven't forgotten Jacques's lesson. It was with me as I concocted these appetizers, a few nibbles of sparkling flavor to accompany the glass of kir or the dry rosé. Mostly they are easy: crostini with charred red peppers, to put out on the counter with the olives and nuts, or a slice of Basque-Style Tortilla Española. A few are more elaborate, like Rosemary Flatbread with Truffle Honey. Make any occasion special by serving it.

And those spreads and dips—little flavor bursts. Mojo Verde, sparkling with chile and mint; *Muhamarra*, rich with walnuts and sweet peppers; or the simplest cannellini spread. I nearly always set out a pesto or spread with a chewy loaf or crostini for the aperitif moment when guests are arriving, whether they are dropping by in sneakers and jeans after a hike or arriving all dressed up for a party.

These spreads and dips have other lives, of course. They make sandwiches into instant marvels, leap into a bowl of pasta and become dinner, crown a piece of fish or an omelet.

But mostly this is casual counter or patio food. It suits perfectly Jacques's idea of détente. And these little dishes can serve a practical purpose as well: many involve legumes, nuts, or cheese and provide a welcome boost of protein for the vegan or vegetarian. And in their easygoing way, most of them can be prepared ahead and wait quietly in the refrigerator until that lovely moment.

Détente.

APPETIZERS

ROSEMARY FLATBREAD
WITH TRUFFLE HONEY

VEGETARIAN

When a friend brought me a jar of Italian truffle honey as a gift, I made this unexpectedly perfect appetizer. Truffle honey is a traditional Italian product, honey infused with the flavor of truffles—sweet and earthy at the same time, with the intense flavor of the truffles coming right through, so good with the savory flatbread. Tear off a piece of bread, best still warm from the oven, drizzle a bit of honey on it, and eat it as you sip your chilled prosecco. Pure delight.

1 large batch Olive Oil Bread Dough (p. 245)

extra-virgin olive oil for brushing

1½ Tbs. chopped fresh rosemary or 1 Tbs. dried rosemary

Maldon sea salt or other flaky sea salt, to taste

freshly grated Parmigiano-Reggiano cheese

freshly ground black pepper

truffle honey

Prepare the Olive Oil Bread Dough as usual, and when it is ready to roll out, cut the ball of dough in half and roll each half out to a circle or oblong, a bit thicker than a pizza.

Lay the rolled-out dough on 2 oiled baking sheets. With a sharp knife, cut a few slashes across right through the dough, several inches apart and stopping an inch or two short of the edge. Pull the ends of the dough gently to open up the cuts just a little. Cover the dough circles or oblongs with kitchen towels and leave them to rise again for about 45 minutes; they will puff up slightly.

Preheat the oven to 400°. Brush the flat loaves gently but generously with olive oil, then sprinkle them with the chopped rosemary, a little sea salt, and some grated Parmesan cheese. Grind on a little black pepper.

Bake the loaves for about 20 minutes, until they are golden on top and sound hollow when the bottom crust is tapped. Slide them from their pans onto racks to cool slightly.

Serve the flatbreads on a large cutting board, letting everyone tear off pieces and drizzle on some of that amazing honey.

Makes 2 medium flatbreads

In a Festive Menu . . .
Italian Style (p. 28) kicks off with this treat. But imagine this warm flatbread with its luxury upgrade on a weeknight, accompanied by toasted nuts, a few olives, a plate of roasted vegetables. That's dinner.

Rosemary Flatbread *with truffle honey* (p. 46)

CROSTINI,
PLAIN OR GARLIC

VEGAN

So simple, so right for so many moments—crostini, the thin slices of baguette, brushed with olive oil and grilled or oven-toasted to a crisp edge. They call out to all the savory pestos, spreads, and piquant dips.

See photo on p. 34.

8 oz. thin, rustic baguette (½ long baguette)

1 Tbs. extra-virgin olive oil, plus more to taste

sea salt

Preheat the oven to 375°. Slice the baguette on a slant, about ¼- or ⅓-inch thick; you'll have between 24 and 30 slices. Brush the slices lightly with olive oil on one side and sprinkle them with a little flaky sea salt. Arrange the bread slices on a baking sheet and toast them in the oven for 10 to 12 minutes. Finish the crostini by placing them under a hot broiler for 30 to 45 seconds, just until you see a brown edge blooming on the crust. This happens quickly, so watch them.

Makes 24 to 30 crostini, generally enough for 6 to 8

Basic Garlic Crostini
To make a garlicky variation, rub each slice of bread with the cut side of a garlic clove before brushing it with olive oil.

CHARRED RED PEPPER CROSTINI
TWO WAYS

VEGAN OR VEGETARIAN

A sweet-savory peperonata piled on goat cheese–smeared crostini—wonderful with a glass of red wine and a bowl of cured black olives. The vegan way can be done with Cannellini and Garlic Spread as a tasty layer under the charred sweet peppers. And charred peppers from a jar are a fine option in winter.

2 lbs. sweet red peppers

1–2 Tbs. extra-virgin olive oil

sea salt to taste

freshly ground black pepper to taste

1 Tbs. chopped fresh oregano or tarragon

8 oz. fresh white goat cheese, or Cannellini and Garlic Spread (p. 63), or any hummus

1 batch Crostini

Char the peppers under a broiler or on a grill, turning them frequently until they are blistered all over, about 15 minutes for large peppers. Put the peppers in a paper bag for a few minutes to steam, then slip off their skins, core and seed them, and cut them in ¼-inch strips. Toss the peppers with the olive oil, salt, black pepper, and chopped herb.

Shortly before serving, spread some goat cheese on each toasted baguette slice, then mound a few of the charred red pepper strips on top. Alternately, spread the crostini with the Cannellini and Garlic Spread or hummus, then mound the peppers over that.

Makes 24 to 30 crostini

CROSTINI WITH RICOTTA AND BLISTERED CHERRY TOMATOES

VEGETARIAN

My friend Dana dreamed these up once when we were cooking together, and we all just crowded around the kitchen counter and snatched them as fast as he made them. They are composed of crostini, ricotta with fresh herbs, pan-blistered cherry tomatoes, and a drip of pesto. Sounds complicated, but it isn't, and it makes the aperitif hour sublime.

1 cup fresh ricotta cheese

1 tsp. minced fresh garlic

2 Tbs. finely chopped fresh parsley

1 tsp. fresh lemon juice

sea salt

1 batch Crostini (p. 48)

1 recipe Blistered Cherry Tomatoes (p. 284)

¼ cup Basil Pesto (p. 56), thinned with olive oil, or any favorite pesto

Mix the ricotta with the minced garlic, chopped parsley, lemon juice, and enough sea salt to bring the flavors together.

Assemble the crostini as you serve them, or moments before, to preserve the distinct textures of crispy bread, cheese, and juicy tomatoes. Spread each toasted slice with a thin layer of ricotta, place a couple of blistered tomatoes on top, and finish it off with a drizzle of basil pesto. There you are, the most delicious little appetizer you could imagine.

Serves 6 to 8, in theory

CROSTINI WITH SWEET-AND-SOUR GLAZED BEETS
TWO WAYS

VEGAN OR VEGETARIAN

Jewel-like diced glazed beets make lovely crostini in the winter season. You will find these little beauties in Italian Style (p. 28).

1 recipe Sweet-and-Sour Glazed Beets (p. 83)

1 cup sliced arugula leaves, tossed with 2 tsp. extra-virgin olive oil and a pinch of salt

1 batch Crostini (p. 48)

OPTIONAL:

about 1 cup fresh ricotta cheese

Assemble these just before serving, to preserve texture. Top each toast with a spoonful of the shiny, ruby-colored beets and garnish with a few slivers of arugula. Or, for a richer appetizer, start with a smear of ricotta on the crostini, followed by the beets and arugula.

Makes 24 to 30 crostini, enough for 6 to 8

SKILLET-BLISTERED PADRÓN PEPPERS

VEGAN

Padrón peppers are a favorite bar tapa in Galicia, in northern Spain, where they are served hot from the grill, oily and dusted with salt. Pick one up by its stem and bite in: they are superbly flavorful and most are mild—but now and again you get a hot one! That's part of the fun. When peppers are in season, late spring through summer, I include them in any tapas party.

1 lb. Padrón peppers

2 Tbs. extra-virgin olive oil

¼ tsp. sea salt, plus more to taste

Wash the peppers and dry them. In an ample nonstick sauté pan, heat the oil over high heat until it shimmers. Add the peppers and immediately cover the pan with a spatter guard. Shake the pan occasionally, and lift the mesh lid to stir the peppers and turn them. In 7 or 8 minutes they should be blistered all over and showing brown spots.

Sprinkle a little salt over the peppers and slide them onto a warm platter.

Serves 8 to 10 as part of a tapa assortment

CHARD AND PARSLEY FRITTATA
WITH LEMON, PEPPER, AND GOAT CHEESE

VEGETARIAN

Chard and parsley make it green, but it's the lemon juice and that indispensable touch of lemon zest that give this cheese-rich frittata a special freshness. Cut it in squares and serve it as an appetizer, with a glass of wine, or include it in a *mezze* assortment.

2½ Tbs. extra-virgin olive oil

2 medium onions, coarsely chopped

1¼ tsp. sea salt, plus more to taste

1¼ lbs. chard, large stems removed (to yield about 12 oz. greens)

1 Tbs. fresh lemon juice

a pinch of crushed red chiles

1 cup coarsely chopped fresh flat-leaf parsley

8 extra-large eggs

½ tsp. finely grated lemon zest

freshly ground black pepper

4 oz. crumbled or mashed fresh white goat cheese

Heat 1½ tablespoons olive oil in a medium nonstick pan, add the onions and ¼ teaspoon salt, and stir over medium heat for 12 to 15 minutes, or until the onions are tender and beginning to color.

Preheat the oven to 325°. Steam the chard leaves just until they are wilted. When they have cooled, squeeze out the excess moisture, chop the greens coarsely, and add them to the onions with another pinch of salt. Toss over high heat for 3 to 4 minutes. Add the lemon juice, crushed red chiles, and parsley, toss to mix, then remove from the heat.

In a large bowl, whisk the eggs with the remaining teaspoon of salt and the lemon zest. Grind in plenty of black pepper and whisk in the goat cheese. Add the chard and onion mixture and stir well.

Add the remaining 1 tablespoon olive oil to a 9-inch gratin dish with a nonstick surface and heat it briefly in the oven. Pour in the egg mixture, give it a quick stir to distribute everything evenly, and put the pan in the oven. Bake the frittata for about 30 minutes, or until the eggs are completely set and lightly golden brown on top.

Allow the frittata to cool a bit, then slide a spatula under it gently to free it of its pan and slide or invert it onto a serving platter. Eat the frittata hot, warm, or at room temperature.

Serves 6 as a main dish, more when cut small for appetizers

An Easy and Flexible Meal . . .
For an easy family dinner or a casual evening with friends, pair this savory green frittata with one of the tabbouleh variations (p. 116), marinated olives, and a few sautéed prawns.

BASQUE-STYLE TORTILLA ESPAÑOLA

I have made the simple and delicious *tortilla española* for decades, since I first tasted one in Madrid as a student. The traditional omelet, found in every tapa bar in Spain, is made with onions and potatoes and plenty of good Spanish olive oil. But my Basque mother-in-law always added diced green peppers to hers, and I thought, Anything goes. Here it is, in honor of Betty Nava (born Loperena), her savory Basque version of Spanish tortilla.

4 medium Yukon gold potatoes (1½ lbs.)

2½ Tbs. extra-virgin olive oil

2 large onions, chopped medium

1½ tsp. sea salt, plus more to taste

freshly ground black pepper

2 medium green bell peppers, finely diced (2 cups)

1 bunch green onions, white and green parts, thinly sliced (1 cup)

2 tsp. chopped fresh oregano leaves

8–9 large eggs

Scrub the potatoes and cut them into ½-inch dice; you should have about 4 cups. Heat 1½ tablespoons of the oil in a 10- or 11-inch nonstick pan. Add the potatoes and the chopped onions, along with a teaspoon of sea salt and some freshly ground black pepper. Cook over medium heat, stirring often, until the potatoes and onions are beginning to color, about 15 minutes. Add the diced green peppers, green onions, and oregano and continue cooking and stirring until all the vegetables are tender, another 10 to 15 minutes. Taste and add salt if it's needed.

In a large bowl, whisk the eggs, adding the remaining ½ teaspoon salt and black pepper to taste. Quickly stir the cooked vegetables into the eggs. Wipe the pan clean and heat the remaining 1 tablespoon olive oil in it, then pour in the egg mixture, spreading it evenly. Turn the heat very low, cover the pan, and cook until the eggs are set, 10 to 15 minutes. Loosen the edges of the tortilla with a thin spatula, letting it slide freely in the pan. Cover the pan with a flat lid, grasp the pan and lid firmly with potholders, and invert, letting the tortilla drop onto the lid. Slide the tortilla back into the pan and cook it for another few minutes, enough to lightly brown the bottom, then slide it out onto a serving platter.

The tortilla can be served hot, warm, at room temperature, or cool. Cut it in thick wedges or in thin ones, depending on how much other food is being served.

Serves 6 as a center-of-the-plate dish, more as an appetizer with other small plates

Matchmaking . . .

No tapas party would be complete without a *tortilla española*, but whether it's a party or a simple meal of tortilla, crusty bread, and a salad, you can serve slices of *jamón serrano* with it; they pair up all the time in those Spanish bars.

The Classic Tortilla . . .

If you want the simple potato-and-onion tortilla, omit the green peppers, green onions, and oregano.

MINIATURE BLACK BEAN AND CHIPOTLE QUESADILLAS

VEGAN OR VEGETARIAN

These tasty morsels are the humble appetizers that steal the show. The beans are rich but mild, and spicy heat can be added with more of that marvelous chipotle and onion relish.

6–8 flour tortillas, white or whole wheat

2–3 cups Refried Black Beans (p. 311)

1 cup Chipotle Sauce (p. 75) or Chris's Sweet Onion and Chipotle Relish (p. 75)

OPTIONAL:

1 cup crumbled *queso fresco*, *queso cotija*, or goat cheese

extra-virgin olive oil for the pan

Use small flour tortillas for these miniatures. Warm the tortillas over medium-high heat in a large sauté pan, two at a time, turning them every 15 seconds or so until they are soft. Wrap the hot tortillas in a kitchen towel to keep them warm.

Spread about 1/2 cup refried black beans evenly over half a soft tortilla, then spread a spoonful or two of chipotle sauce or relish on the other half. If you want cheese, scatter a little cheese over the beans, but don't overdo it. Fold the tortilla in half over the fillings.

Toast the quesadillas two at a time in the hot pan or on a griddle, as many as will fit. Some cooks put a little olive oil in the pan to toast their quesadillas; I prefer a dry pan, but it's a matter of taste. Cook them about a minute on each side, then check to see that the beans are hot through and the cheese melted and give them a few more seconds on each side as needed. The tortillas should have golden brown spots.

Use a very sharp knife to cut the quesadillas into thin wedges. Arrange the wedges on a platter around a small bowl of salsa and serve at once with a glass of wine or a shot of tequila.

Makes 24 to 30 quesadilla wedges, enough for 6, or more if part of a spread

---

An Omnivore Way . . .
Add a heaping spoonful of Carnitas (p. 364) to the quesadillas.

In Festive Menus . . .
Thanksgiving for Everyone (p. 20) begins with these miniature quesadillas. See them also in Cocktails on New Year's Eve (p. 32).

PESTOS, SPREADS, AND DIPS

SPICY CILANTRO AND MINT PESTO

VEGAN

This refreshing pesto has the sting of fresh green serrano chile underlining lively cilantro and mint. You can moderate the level of heat from delicate to chile-head hot by adding more or less of the chile. Use this, or any variation, as a spread for crostini or a happy addition to a sandwich. I also like to smear a generous spoonful of the parsley pesto variation on a piece of salmon before I put it in the oven, then serve more of the pesto at the table.

1–2 cloves garlic

½–¾ tsp. flaky sea salt, less if using fine salt

½ cup (3 oz.) whole raw almonds

½ cup (2½ oz.) pine nuts

1 bunch fresh cilantro, chopped (1¼ cups, lightly packed; 1¼ oz.)

leaves from 1 small bunch fresh mint, chopped (about ½ cup, lightly packed; ½ oz.)

6 Tbs. extra-virgin olive oil, plus more to taste

1–2 Tbs. fresh lemon juice

½–1 fresh serrano chile, minced

Put the garlic cloves in the food processor and pulse them briefly to mince, then add ½ teaspoon salt, the almonds, and the pine nuts and pulse again. When the nuts are pretty well chopped, add the cilantro, mint, and olive oil and pulse until you have a coarse but even mixture.

Add some of the lemon juice and just a little bit of the minced chile. Pulse briefly and taste the pesto, then keep adding more lemon juice, salt, and chile, a bit at a time, pulsing briefly after each addition, until you have the balance you like. A hot chile must be respected—it can be nirvana or it can kill. And remember that sometimes a drop more lemon juice or another pinch of salt brings all the flavors into focus.

Makes about 1 cup

Other Ways . . .
For a deep-flavored winter pesto that still carries the sparkle of chile, mint, and cilantro, make a **Parsley Pesto**: add 2 cups packed fresh flat-leaf parsley leaves (about 3 ounces) to the herbs, and instead of almonds and pine nuts, use ¼ cup (1 ounce) walnuts, or more if you want a richer pesto.

And if you have fresh basil and a food processor, it is the work of a moment to make a **Basil Pesto**, and the fresh flavor is unbeatable. Instead of cilantro and mint, use 2 ounces clean, dry fresh basil leaves and skip the almonds, lemon juice, and chile. Pine nuts to taste.

PUMPKIN-SEED PESTO

VEGAN

The seductive flavors of toasted pumpkin seeds and tart tomatillos give a unique character to this dense pesto. Serve it with tortilla chips or crostini as an appetizer, as a condiment for roasted vegetables, or as a layer in a sandwich. Spread it on a black bean burger or a turkey burger. It brings excitement wherever it goes.

See photo on p. 34.

1 cup hulled green pumpkin seeds

1 lb. tomatillos

1–2 fresh serrano chiles

1 cup roughly chopped fresh cilantro

¼ cup fruity extra-virgin olive oil

1 tsp. sea salt, plus more to taste

2–3 Tbs. fresh lemon juice, plus more to taste

Toast the pumpkin seeds in a dry skillet, stirring them almost constantly over medium heat until they begin to turn golden brown and give off a toasty, nutty aroma, about 10 minutes. Move the seeds to a plate and allow them to cool.

Preheat the oven to 400°. Remove the papery husks from the tomatillos, rinse them, and if they are large cut them in half. Spread them in a single layer on a baking sheet lined with foil and roast them until they are soft, blistered, and spotted with brown, probably about 30 minutes, but it depends on their size and moisture. Scrape the roasted tomatillos gently into a mound, leaving behind skins if they stick to the foil. Don't worry about charred bits coming along—they're good.

Trim and chop the serrano chiles. Reserve 3 tablespoons of the toasted pumpkin seeds for a garnish, then put the rest in a food processor and pulse until they are coarsely chopped. Add the roasted tomatillos, cilantro, olive oil, salt, 2 tablespoons lemon juice, and ½ teaspoon chopped chiles. Pulse until you have a rough mixture. The pesto should be thick, but if it seems too stiff, add a tablespoon or two of water to loosen it.

Taste the pesto, and finish the seasoning: start adding more chopped chile, a little at a time, pulsing briefly with each addition. Chiles vary greatly in heat, so it is impossible to say what the right amount is, but you will find it. The chile is not meant to dominate the pumpkin seeds and tomatillos here, rather to liven them up. You can also add a touch more lemon juice now, and a pinch of salt if it is needed.

Makes about 2 cups

Roasted carrots with Carrot-Top Pesto (p. 59)

CARROT-TOP PESTO

How many times have you thrown away those bushy green tops? Me, too—but no more. Now I make this wonderfully peppery, textured pesto. Have it as a condiment with roasted carrots and parsnips or other winter vegetables. Be sure you have fresh, bushy, bright green carrot tops. And if you have no basil to add, try parsley or cilantro and a few fennel greens instead.

4 oz. trimmed carrot tops (from 1 or 2 bunches), big stems trimmed off

2 cloves garlic

¼ cup (1 oz.) walnuts

1 oz. fresh basil leaves, chopped (½ cup)

½ oz. fresh mint leaves, chopped (½ cup), plus more to taste

¾ tsp. sea salt

½ cup extra-virgin olive oil, plus more to taste

2 Tbs. fresh lemon juice

Pull the fronds of the carrot tops off the stems and discard the stems. Carrot tops have a firm, chewy texture, but the stems are tough. Wash and spin-dry the greens.

Pulse the garlic and walnuts briefly in a food processor, then add the various greens and the salt and pulse again, scraping down the sides of the container as needed, until the greens are finely chopped. Add the olive oil and lemon juice and process the pesto until it is smooth.

Makes about 2 cups

MOJO VERDE WITH MINT

VEGAN

This Spanish mixture, more than a sauce, is *divine* with crisp roasted potatoes—a knockout appetizer. But don't stop there. Spread it on a tomato sandwich, dip artichokes in it, spoon it over goat cheese on crackers. *Mojo verde* can become a habit.

6 medium cloves garlic

1/2 tsp. sea salt, plus more to taste

1 1/2 oz. cilantro, chopped (1 cup), long stems removed

1/2 oz. parsley, chopped (1/2 cup), long stems removed

1/2 oz. fresh mint leaves, chopped (1/2 cup)

1/2 green bell pepper (3 oz.), chopped

1/2–1 green serrano chile (1/4 oz.), minced

3 small slices of a baguette (1 1/2 oz.)

5 Tbs. extra-virgin olive oil

3 Tbs. wine vinegar

Mince the garlic in a food processor. Add the salt, cilantro, parsley, mint, and both peppers and pulse until everything is finely chopped. Cut the baguette slices into small pieces, add them, and pulse again. Finally, add the oil and vinegar, scrape down the sides of the container, and give it a final spin to blend. You should have a thick sauce, with a bit of texture.

Makes a little more than 1 cup

FRESH FAVA BEAN PUREE
WITH GARLIC AND MINT

VEGAN

Bright green, fresh, seductive . . . The work is in peeling all those fava beans, but it feels worth it for this springtime special. I love it, and serve it as part of Easter Brunch (p. 36).

See photo on p. 38.

1¼ lbs. fresh shelled fava beans

6 Tbs. extra-virgin olive oil

2 medium cloves garlic, chopped, or 2 Tbs. chopped green garlic

½–1 tsp. sea salt

4–5 Tbs. fresh lemon juice

¼ cup finely chopped fresh mint, plus more to taste

OPTIONAL:

1 tsp. finely chopped fresh jalapeño pepper

a pinch of cayenne

Drop the fava beans into a pan of boiling water for 2–4 minutes, depending on their size. Drain the favas, and while they are still warm peel off their skins. This is easy to do: pierce the skin with your fingernail and pop the tender fava bean out of its jacket. You should have about 2 cups of bright green peeled favas.

Heat 2 tablespoons olive oil in a nonstick pan and sauté the chopped garlic and the jalapeño, if you wish, for a minute or so, then add the peeled fava beans and ½ teaspoon salt. Toss the favas over medium heat for 4 to 5 minutes, until they show a few light brown spots. Remove them from the heat and add a tablespoon of lemon juice to deglaze the pan.

In the container of the food processor, combine the sautéed fava beans, the remaining 4 tablespoons olive oil, and 3 tablespoons lemon juice and pulse briefly. Add the mint and more salt as needed, and process until you have a smooth spread. Taste, and correct the seasoning with more salt, lemon, or a pinch of cayenne, if you wish.

Serve the fava bean puree with crostini, pita bread, or whole wheat crackers.

Makes 1¾ to 2 cups

Cannellini and Garlic Spread (p. 63)

CANNELLINI AND GARLIC SPREAD

VEGAN

One of the easiest and tastiest little spreads. When people drop by unexpectedly, I open a bottle of wine, put out a bowl of this creamy white bean spread, a plate of olives, and some crusty bread, and everyone is happy while we figure out the next step.

I prefer to use beans I have cooked myself. It is so simple to cook dried beans, and the flavor is so much better that it doesn't make sense to me to used canned beans. But in an emergency, you know what to do.

2 cloves garlic

3 cups cooked cannellini beans

1/4 cup extra-virgin olive oil, plus more for drizzling

3–4 Tbs. fresh lemon juice

1/2 teaspoon sea salt, plus more to taste

1 Tbs. chopped fresh oregano, plus whole leaves for garnish

plenty of freshly ground black pepper

Put the garlic cloves in the food processor and pulse until finely chopped. Add the remaining ingredients and pulse until smooth, or until the spread has the texture you like. If it seems too thick, you can add a few tablespoons of the cooking liquid from the beans or a dash of vegetable broth.

Serve the spread in a generous, shallow bowl and pour a few loops of olive oil on top, then sprinkle with some oregano leaves. This spread also makes a great layer for wraps or sandwiches.

Makes about 3 1/2 cups

Other Ways . . .
Add Kalamata olives cut in slivers, or add thin slices of marinated sun-dried tomatoes.

To Cook Cannellini . . .
In a soup pot, combine 1 1/4 cups dried cannellini beans with about 2 quarts water, a dozen sage leaves, and 6 to 8 whole peeled garlic cloves. Bring to a boil, then lower the heat and simmer the beans for an hour or longer, depending on their age, until they are completely tender. Add 1 teaspoon salt and simmer gently for another 10 minutes, then allow the beans to sit in their liquid for a little while before draining them. Reserve the liquid to use in a soup—it's a delicious broth.

BELUGA LENTIL AND CARAMELIZED ONION PUREE

VEGAN

This dusky spread of black lentils and slowly cooked onions seems too simple to be as good as it is—but it really is that good. My friend Haigaz, who showed me how to make this, puts his cooked lentils through a ricer and strains out the skins, but I use the whole lentils for a rougher-textured spread.

1 cup (7½ oz.) beluga lentils

1½ tsp. sea salt, plus more to taste

6–7 Tbs. extra-virgin olive oil, plus more for drizzling

2 lbs. yellow onions, coarsely chopped

1 Tbs. fresh thyme leaves or 2 tsp. dried thyme

½ cup of short-grain white rice, Arborio, or sushi rice

1 Tbs. fresh lemon juice

OPTIONAL:

1–2 tsp. hot red chile paste, such as sambal oelek

GARNISH:

chopped fresh flat-leaf parsley

Rinse the lentils and combine them in a pot with 3 cups boiling water and ½ teaspoon salt. Lower the heat to a simmer, cover the pot, and cook the lentils for 35 minutes. Turn off the heat and allow the lentils to cool in the remaining liquid, which will be very little.

Meanwhile, heat 3 tablespoons olive oil in a large skillet and add the chopped onions and ½ teaspoon salt. Cook the onions over high heat for 5 minutes, stirring. Lower the heat, add the thyme, then cover the pan and cook the onions slowly for an hour, stirring occasionally. The onions should be golden-brown, soft, and moist, like an onion jam.

At the same time, heat 1 cup water and ¼ tsp. salt in a small pot, add the rice, cover, and simmer over low heat for 25 minutes. Turn off the heat and leave the rice covered for 5 minutes more. All the water should be absorbed.

Drain the lentils through a sieve but reserve the liquid. Add the lentils and rice to the onions, stir, and taste. Stir in salt, a pinch at a time, until the mixture tastes alive—probably ¼ teaspoon or more. Stir in 3 to 4 tablespoons olive oil, the lemon juice, and the chile paste if you like.

Puree the mixture in a food processor until it is smooth, and add 2 or 3 tablespoons of the cooking liquid from the lentils if you need to soften the puree. Allow the puree to cool in the refrigerator.

To serve, spread the puree in a thick layer in a shallow bowl or on a beautiful platter. Run the back of a spoon over it to give it some shape, then drizzle it with olive oil and scatter the parsley over it. Serve with pita bread or crackers.

Makes about 3 cups

In a Mixed Menu . . .
No One Eats *Mezze* Alone (p. 118).

ROASTED EGGPLANT AND POBLANO CHILE SPREAD

VEGAN

Here's a Middle Eastern eggplant spread with a Southern California kick, full of flavor from beautifully cooked vegetables, plenty of garlic, and olive oil. Serve it with triangles of fresh soft pita bread, make it part of a *mezze* dinner, or roll it in a flatbread with sliced lettuce and chopped tomatoes for a great sandwich.

2 lbs. firm young eggplant

2 large fresh green poblano chiles
(10–12 oz.)

1 tsp. sea salt, plus more to taste

3–4 cloves garlic

5 Tbs. fresh lemon juice

2 Tbs. extra-virgin olive oil, plus
more for drizzling

2 Tbs. tahini

¼ cup chopped fresh flat-leaf
parsley

1 tsp. hot red chile paste, such
as sambal oelek, plus more to
taste

1 tsp. ground sumac

OPTIONAL:
3–4 Tbs. thick Greek-style yogurt

Preheat the oven to 400°. Roast the eggplants on a baking sheet for 40 minutes to an hour, until they are tender and collapse when pushed with a spoon. Let them cool, then split them, scrape out and discard any dark seed clumps, and pull the cooked flesh off the skins. Put the eggplant into a sieve and let it drain for 20 minutes or so, then chop it coarsely.

Char the chiles on a grill or under the broiler until they are blistered and browned all over (see "A Word About Charring and Peeling Peppers," p. 227, for details). Put them in a paper bag or a covered bowl to sweat for 10 minutes, then peel off the cellophane-like skins, pull out the stems, and take out the seeds. Chop the chiles coarsely, combine them with the eggplant, and add the salt.

Mince the garlic in a food processor, add the lemon juice, olive oil, and tahini, and pulse to combine. Add a third of the eggplant mixture and pulse briefly.

If you want a coarse mixture, scrape out the puree now and add it to the hand-chopped eggplant and peppers in the bowl. For a smoother spread, add the remaining eggplant and peppers to the food processor and pulse until you have the texture you like. Taste, and add salt if needed. Stir in the parsley and the red chile paste, adding as much paste as you want to get a nice hit of heat. Because poblanos are typically very mild, this is where the heat of the dish is adjusted. Stir in the yogurt if you like.

This dish benefits from an hour in the refrigerator. To serve, spread the mixture in a wide, shallow bowl, drizzle it with olive oil, and sprinkle with the sumac. Serve with any Middle Eastern flatbread or with crackers.

Makes about 3 cups

MUHAMARRA
WALNUT, RED PEPPER, AND POMEGRANATE SPREAD

VEGAN

If you've never had this Lebanese spread of walnuts, pomegranate molasses, and red peppers, you are in for a treat. Pomegranate molasses is a magical thing, the juice of the pomegranate seeds reduced to a syrup that contains all the sweetness and at the same time the exciting tartness of that fruit—wonderful with the rich walnuts in this traditional combination.

See photo on p. 120.

1 cup (4 oz.) walnut pieces

8 oz. roasted and peeled sweet red peppers

1–2 slices whole wheat bread, crusts removed

1¼ Tbs. pomegranate molasses

2 Tbs. extra-virgin olive oil

¼–½ tsp. crushed red chiles or 1 tsp. harissa

¼ tsp. sea salt, plus more to taste

½ tsp. toasted and ground cumin seeds

freshly ground black pepper to taste

2 Tbs. chopped fresh flat-leaf parsley

Pulse the walnut pieces in a food processor until they are coarsely chopped. If you are using peppers from a jar, be sure they are rinsed, well drained, and dried. Tear or chop the bread into small pieces. Add the roasted peppers, half the bread, and the pomegranate molasses, olive oil, ¼ teaspoon crushed red chiles or harissa, salt, and cumin to the walnuts and pulse until you have a rough mixture with no large pieces of red pepper left.

If the mixture looks a little too soupy to spread on a cracker, add as much more of the bread as you need to thicken it and pulse again. Now taste the spread and adjust the seasoning: a pinch more salt if needed, more crushed red chiles, and a few grinds of black pepper. The crushed chiles especially are very much a matter of taste, so add a pinch at a time until your taste buds sing.

Remove the spread to a bowl and stir in the chopped parsley.

Makes about 2 cups

In a Mixed Menu . . .
No One Eats *Mezze* Alone (p. 118).

GREEN OLIVE TAPENADE
WITH PINE NUTS

VEGAN

Spread this easy tapenade on crostini and top it with a blistered cherry tomato. Drop a spoonful on a piece of baked halibut. Or thin it with olive oil and broth to make a pasta sauce. Green olives are the main ingredient, so get the best—don't settle for something that tastes more like vinegar than olive.

1 clove garlic

¼ cup pine nuts, lightly toasted

1 cup marinated cracked green olives, pitted

2 Tbs. extra-virgin olive oil

¼ cup chopped fresh flat-leaf parsley

2 tsp. fresh lemon juice, plus more to taste

freshly ground black pepper to taste

Pulse the garlic clove in a food processor for a moment, then add the remaining ingredients and continue pulsing, scraping down the container when you need to, until you have a slightly chunky but well-blended paste, soft but thick enough to hold a shape. Taste, and adjust the seasoning with more lemon if needed.

Makes a little over 1 cup

FETA CHEESE AND YOGURT WITH HERBS

VEGETARIAN

Dab this on crostini and add a cherry tomato on top: delicious. It looks like the herb cheese in the deli case but tastes much better because you just chopped the fresh herbs.

1 cup (4 oz.) crumbled creamy feta cheese

½ cup (4 oz.) thick Greek-style yogurt

2 Tbs. finely chopped fresh chives

2 Tbs. minced fresh flat-leaf parsley

plenty of freshly ground black pepper

GARNISH:

extra-virgin olive oil

Mash the feta cheese with a fork until there are no large pieces, then stir in the yogurt. Add the chives, parsley, and as much freshly ground black pepper as you like. Spread the herbed cheese in a shallow bowl and drizzle with fruity olive oil.

Makes about 1¼ cups

Variation . . . Fresh Ricotta with Herbs
For a milder, richer version, replace the feta cheese and yogurt with 1 cup fresh ricotta cheese and ½ cup crumbled *queso fresco*, and add sea salt to taste.

CONDIMENTS

I AM NOT AFRAID OF FLAVOR

We were driving in the backcountry around Santa Fe and saw a roadside farm stand—chiles, nothing but chiles, hanging in beautiful brick-red *ristras* from the makeshift roof and piled in baskets on the table. They were still ripening and drying there in the autumn sun, the season's harvest. How could we resist? We pulled over. An old man with a weathered face appeared from somewhere in the shadows behind the stand. "Chiles," he said solemnly, nodding as he bagged them up. "Number-one food of the nation." And his face crinkled into a thousand pleats as he smiled.

I don't suppose he meant number one in quantity. I believe he meant that his chiles—dark red, sweet and hot at once—were the number-one best thing he'd ever tasted. It was an eloquent remark, and I understood it. I fell in love with chiles when I first went to Mexico, in my twenties, and I never fell out. For years I've been happily eating foods laced with chiles and making my salsas. I hasten to add, however, that I am not a chile-head. I do not engage in competitive chile-eating or count Scoville units. I like a little heat, sometimes a little more, but what I adore is the rich and complex *flavor* of the chiles.

I am not afraid of flavor!

I use spices, herbs, vinegars, and peppers of all kinds. I'm thrilled when I discover a special ingredient—pomegranate molasses from Lebanon or truffle honey from Tuscany—to enhance the flavors in my cooking. Sometimes I like a kick, a shout of excitement. I want to take a bite and feel it bite back. Or I want to let everyone at my table choose, mild or wild. Those are the times for relishes and condiments.

Chile salsas are only the beginning. I love the tang of a sour pickle—that's my Polish blood speaking up. The lift that a squeeze of lemon gives to food is magical. And the word *agrodolce* brings a smile to my face as I remember that winning combination of sweetness from a dried fruit or a well-caramelized onion mixed with the defining bite of a fine vinegar.

I love the giddy freshness of cilantro, mint, basil, parsley, chives . . . the taste of the green garden in my mouth. I love the snap of ginger, the pungent intensity of cured olives, the crazy sourness of tamarind, and the profound depth of an aged miso.

Here are the spikes of flavor, the happy high notes. They begin with a few chile salsas—number-one food!—some hot, others fruity and complex. Then there are the vinaigrettes, the raw relishes, the sweet-tart cranberry sauces, and yes, an easy pickle. Here are the punctuation marks of food—the spicy, the tangy, the sweet, the sour—the extra blast of *flavor*.

SALSAS, RELISHES, AND OTHER FLAVOR SPIKES

(Clockwise from top left) cumin seeds, tomatillos, garlic, and dried guajillo chiles for Guajillo Chile Salsa with Tomatillos (p. 73)

GUAJILLO CHILE SALSA WITH TOMATILLOS

VEGAN

Guajillos are among my favorite chiles, with just enough heat and so much bright and rich chile flavor. Toasting the dry pods for a moment in a hot pan brings it all out. Then the chiles are soaked to soften them and ground up with the other ingredients.

My salsa mentor, Guillermina, insisted that salsa had to be made in the volcanic stone *molcajete*, and I sometimes do use my Mexican *molcajete* to grind down the chiles and garlic, stone against stone. My *molcajete* is my favorite piece of low-tech kitchen equipment. But as I get older and lazier, I make adjustments. Now I usually drop the chiles into the food processor with some of the soaking liquid, pulse, then push the soft puree through a coarse sieve and toss out the skins and seeds that are left. My guajillo salsa is still screamingly good, but now it is easy as well.

7–10 dried guajillo chiles (2 oz.)

1 lb. tomatillos

2–3 cloves garlic

½ tsp. sea salt, plus more to taste

1 tsp. toasted and ground cumin seeds

⅓ cup thinly sliced green onions, white and green parts

½ cup chopped fresh cilantro

Toast the chiles over medium-high heat in a cast-iron or aluminum sauté pan, pressing them down with a spatula so the skins make good contact with the hot pan. After a minute or so on a side, you'll see brown and black spots forming on the reddish brown chiles—done. Put the chiles in a pot with hot water to cover them and simmer them over low heat for about 20 minutes.

Preheat the oven to 400°. Remove and discard the husks from the tomatillos, rinse the fruit, and cut them in half if they are larger than cherries. Arrange the tomatillos skin side down on a foil-lined baking sheet and roast them for 25 to 35 minutes, until they are charred on the bottom, collapsed, and soft. Scrape them into the container of a food processor.

Pull the stems out of the softened chiles, as well as any seeds that come along easily, and add them to the tomatillos in the food processor, along with about ½ cup of the soaking water, the garlic cloves, and the salt. Pulse for a few seconds at a time, stopping to scrape down the sides of the container, until you have a rough puree. If it feels stiff, add more of the soaking water.

recipe continues

Press the chile puree through a coarse sieve and discard the dry pulp of skins and seeds that remains. Stir the ground cumin into the salsa, taste, and correct the seasoning with more salt if needed. (At this point, the salsa can be kept in the refrigerator for up to a week.) Shortly before serving, stir in the sliced green onions and chopped cilantro.

Makes about 2 cups

OTHER SALSAS, LESS HEAT, MORE HEAT . . .

You can use the same method to make very different salsas by using different chiles, hotter or milder, or a mix of several. When you've done this a few times, you will find your own favorite blend and fall in love.

Salsa Roja

Use 1½ ounces dried New Mexico chiles and 2 or 3 chipotles. If you are a chile-head, add a few of the tiny very hot peppers, such as *chile pequin* or *chile Japones*. If you want a milder salsa, use a few *chile ancho* pods instead of the chipotles.

Salsa Negra

For a dark and deep-flavored salsa, use 7 or 8 dried *chile negro* pods and throw in a couple of guajillos for complexity. For a hint of sweeter, more vegetal flavor, simmer half an onion along with the chiles.

CHIPOTLE SAUCE

VEGAN

A simple chipotle sauce is something I like always to have in the refrigerator. It is an excellent salsa for a quesadilla, with tamales or with tortilla chips, fantastic with eggs, and it's amazing how it can improve a sandwich or a soup.

3–4 dried ancho chiles (about 2 oz.)

3 dried chipotle chiles

1 medium yellow onion, cut in large pieces

3–4 cloves garlic

½ tsp. sea salt, plus more to taste

2 Tbs. cumin seeds

Tear the stems out of the chile pods, remove the seeds, and rinse the pods under running water. In a nonreactive pot, cover the chiles with water and start them simmering. Add the onion, garlic cloves, and salt to the chiles and simmer for at least 30 minutes, adding more water if needed to keep everything covered.

Meanwhile, toast the cumin seeds in a pan over medium heat until they release an irresistible toasted aroma and begin to color, 2 or 3 minutes. Grind the seeds in a *molcajete* (a stone mortar) or a spice grinder.

When the vegetables are soft, add the ground cumin seeds and puree everything in a blender until the sauce is perfectly smooth. Add a drop more water as needed to get the right consistency: it should be a thick puree, but not stiff. Taste, and correct the seasoning with as much more salt as is needed to bring out the bright flavor of the chiles. This is important—chiles need salt.

Makes about 2 cups

An Easier Way . . . Chris's Sweet Onion and Chipotle Relish
If you don't have dried chipotles on hand, here's a wildly easy way to have a sweet and spicy, smoky chipotle relish using the chipotles in *adobo* sauce that are commonly available in small cans: To 1 cup of well-caramelized onions, add 2 to 3 tablespoons minced chipotles with their *adobo* sauce. Done and delicious.

PICO DE GALLO

VEGAN

A bowl of *pico de gallo* is always on the table in a Mexican kitchen, and this simplest raw salsa is now ubiquitous in the States as well, surpassing ketchup as the most popular condiment. When you make your own and taste the freshness, you will know why.

2 lbs. ripe red tomatoes

3 fresh serrano or jalapeño chiles (1 oz.)

½ mild or sweet onion (4 oz.), finely chopped

½ cup coarsely chopped fresh cilantro

1 tsp. sea salt, plus more to taste

OPTIONAL:

1–2 Tbs. fresh lemon juice

Cut the tomatoes in small dice, ½-inch or smaller. If your tomatoes are very, very juicy, drain them through a colander for a few moments. Trim the stems off the chiles, cut them in half, remove the ribs and most of the seeds, and chop them finely.

Combine everything in a bowl and mix, then taste and add more salt as needed. If your tomatoes are a low-acid variety, add a touch of lemon juice.

Makes about 4 cups

A Note About Chiles . . .
I used to make my *pico de gallo* with jalapeño peppers, but now that many jalapeños have had the heat bred out of them, I prefer to use serranos.

RAW PERSIMMON AND JALAPEÑO SALSA

VEGAN

The rich, mild flavors of persimmons and walnuts are spiked with chile, cumin, and lime for a superb relish. Have it on a tortilla chip, or with cream cheese or goat cheese on crostini. Or put a spoonful of this salsa in an endive leaf with a few chunks of Gorgonzola for a surprising appetizer.

1½ lbs. Fuyu persimmons (8 small persimmons; 4 cups diced)

2–3 large fresh jalapeño peppers, plus more to taste

1 Tbs. lightly toasted cumin seeds

1 bunch fresh cilantro, chopped (1 cup)

4 Tbs. fresh lime juice, plus more to taste

1 cup (4 oz.) chopped walnuts

a pinch of sea salt

Cut the persimmons by hand into ½-inch dice. Finely chop the jalapeños, discarding the seeds and ribs.

Toss together all the ingredients, then put the salsa in a food processor and pulse a few seconds only, just to give it a finishing touch. You do not want to make a paste. The hand-chopping is essential for best texture, which should be rough, with the nuts adding crunch and body. Taste the salsa after the first couple of pulses, adjust with more lime juice or jalapeño as needed, then pulse only until the salsa just begins to hold together.

Makes about 4 cups

Ingredient Notes . . .
Fuyu persimmons are the ones shaped like miniature pumpkins and eaten while still hard, like apples. Do not confuse them with the acorn-shaped Hachiyas.

Use persimmons that are firm but ripe; they should have a good, bright orange color and give *very slightly* when you press them. And jalapeños vary in their firepower, so you may want to adjust quantity up or down, or add a minced serrano for more heat. But remember that persimmons are sweet and will absorb a lot of heat.

SALSA VERDE

FRESH GREEN CHILE SALSA

VEGAN

The verve and freshness, the dancing heat of this green salsa, made with fresh, pan-blistered green chiles, will dazzle your taste buds.

1¼ lbs. tomatillos

8–9 fresh green serrano or 4–5 jalapeño chiles (4 oz.)

6 garlic cloves, unpeeled

¾ tsp. sea salt, plus more to taste

¼ cup chopped fresh cilantro

2–3 green onions, white and green parts, thinly sliced

Preheat the oven to 400°. Peel the husks off the tomatillos, cut the fruits in half, arrange them skin side down on a foil-lined baking sheet, and roast them for about 40 minutes, until they are soft and slightly charred. Let them cool a bit, then use a spoon to scrape them off their skins.

Toast the chiles in a hot pan, turning them until they are blistered all over, 5 or 6 minutes. Put them in a bowl and cover to sweat them for a few minutes, then slip off their skins and pull out the stems and seeds. (For detailed instructions, see "A Word About Charring and Peeling Peppers," p. 227.)

Toast the unpeeled garlic in the same pan, turning the cloves until they are charred on all sides and give when pressed down, 12 to 14 minutes. Cool the garlic and then peel it.

Combine the tomatillo pulp, the chiles, and the garlic in a food processor and pulse just until you have a rough puree. Add ¾ teaspoon salt, pulse again, and taste. Add more salt, a pinch at a time, until you have the flavor balance you like. Stir the cilantro and sliced green onions into the salsa and serve. Once the cilantro and onions are part of the salsa, it should be eaten within a day or so.

Makes about 1½ cups

Add Avocados for . . . Guacamole with Salsa Verde
Here's a superior version of the beloved mashed avocado that has accompanied so many tacos and bottles of Mexican beer. Choose 2 or 3 ripe—but not overripe—avocados. Cut them in half, spoon out the creamy gold flesh, and combine it with ¼ cup Salsa Verde, 2 tablespoons fresh lemon juice, and ¼ teaspoon salt. Mash until you have the texture you like. Add a handful of chopped cilantro and as much more salsa as you like, and there you are: about 1½ cups of perfect guacamole.

Salsa Verde (p. 78) with avocados

CRANBERRY SAUCE WITH ORANGES AND WINE

VEGAN

Cranberries with the sweetness of orange juice and the bite of zest—I never tire of this.

12 oz. fresh cranberries

1/2 cup fresh orange juice

1/4 cup water

1–2 tsp. finely grated orange zest

1/4 cup dry red wine

3/4 cup sugar, plus more to taste

1/2 tsp. ground cinnamon

1/8 tsp. ground cloves

a pinch of sea salt

OPTIONAL:

1–2 Tbs. finely chopped or grated
   fresh ginger

Wash the cranberries and pick them over, discarding any that are soft. Combine all the ingredients in an ample nonreactive pot and bring the liquid to a boil. Reduce the heat to a simmer, and stir as the cranberries pop and the sauce thickens. In about 10 minutes it should be thick and glossy. Have a taste, and add a bit more sugar if you want a sweeter sauce. Allow the sauce to cool, then stir it up and spoon it into a serving dish.

Makes about 2 1/4 cups

RAW CRANBERRY AND FUYU PERSIMMON RELISH

VEGAN

Tart cranberries meet their perfect match in persimmons, the glorious fruit that ripens in time for Thanksgiving. Use Fuyu persimmons, which are eaten while still hard, like apples. They are shaped like tiny orange pumpkins and have a well-developed bright orange color when ripe.

12 oz. fresh cranberries

1 large navel orange

2–3 Fuyu persimmons (8 oz.)

sea salt

⅓ cup sugar, plus more to taste

2–3 tsp. fresh lemon juice

Wash the cranberries well and pick them over, discarding soft ones. Scrub the orange and dry it. Use a microplane to grate off the zest and measure out 2 teaspoons, then peel the orange and remove the white pith, and break into segments. Wash the persimmons, trim out their stems and cores, and cut them into roughly 1-inch pieces.

Combine the cranberries, orange, grated zest, persimmons, and a pinch of sea salt in the container of the food processor and pulse briefly, just to break everything up. Add the sugar and 2 teaspoons lemon juice, pulse again, and taste. If you think you need more sweetness, add a tiny bit more sugar; if you need acid, add a drop of lemon juice.

Pulse once more to blend the seasonings, but do not overprocess. This relish should have a gravelly texture, with distinct pieces of golden persimmon showing among the cranberries.

Makes about 2½ cups

Crostini (p. 48) with Sweet-and-Sour Glazed Beets (p. 83)

SWEET-AND-SOUR GLAZED BEETS

VEGAN

Pickled beets are in my DNA—I'm Polish. But here are pickled beets with an upgrade, glazed and perfumed with orange zest and pomegranate. Have them as a relish with any roasted winter vegetables, or spoon them onto crisp crostini for an alluring appetizer.

See photo of Sweet-and-Sour Glazed Beets over arugula on p. 31.

1¼ lbs. beets

½ cup red wine vinegar

3 Tbs. brown sugar, light or dark

½ tsp. dried thyme

pinch of cayenne

¼ tsp. sea salt, plus more to taste

½ Tbs. pomegranate molasses

½ tsp. finely grated orange zest

Preheat the oven to 400°. Trim and scrub the beets, and wrap them in heavy-duty aluminum foil while they are still damp. Roast the beets for 45 minutes to an hour, or until tender. Allow them to cool, then slip off their skins and cut them in ¼-inch dice. You'll have about 2 cups.

Combine the vinegar, brown sugar, thyme, cayenne, salt, and ¼ cup water in a stainless steel pot and bring it to a boil. Add the diced beets and simmer briskly over medium heat for 10 minutes, until the liquid is down to a smear of bright pink glaze in the bottom of the pan and the beets are coated with the syrup. Add the pomegranate molasses and the orange zest, stir, and allow to cool. Taste the beets, and correct the seasoning with a pinch more salt if needed.

Makes about 2 cups

QUICK PICKLED ONIONS

VEGAN

Two-minute pickles—really. Barely cooked, barely pickled, these onions are a bright, still-crunchy addition to many salads. I've found them habit-forming. And so simple!

1 large red onion (10 oz.)

½ cup water

¼ cup cider vinegar

3 Tbs. sugar

½ tsp. salt

Peel the onion, cut it in quarters, and slice it thinly. Combine the water, vinegar, sugar, and salt in a small nonreactive pot and bring the liquid to a boil, then lower the heat to a simmer and stir until the sugar dissolves.

Add the sliced onions to the liquid and push them down to make sure they are all submerged; add a tablespoon of water if needed. Cover and simmer the onions 2 minutes, then remove from the heat and allow them to cool. If you're in a hurry, put them in the refrigerator. They are ready to use immediately or can be kept in the refrigerator in their pickling liquid in a covered glass jar.

Makes about 1½ cups

SAUCES, VINAIGRETTES, AND MARINADES

BASIC TOMATO SAUCE

VEGAN

When you have a supply of ripe tomatoes on hand, cook up a pot of this easy sauce. Use it right away or tuck it into the freezer, where it will be a treasure to find on some chilly day in the future.

5 lbs. tomatoes

2 Tbs. extra-virgin olive oil

6–8 large cloves garlic, chopped

1 tsp. kosher salt or fine sea salt

Peel the tomatoes: cut a cross in the bottom of each one with a sharp knife, drop them into boiling water for 60 seconds, then transfer them with a slotted spoon to a bowl of cold water. Slip off their skins, core them, and cut them into wedges or chunks, keeping all the juice.

Heat the olive oil in a large sauté pan and sear the chopped garlic in it for a minute, until it releases its fragrance and begins to color. Add the tomatoes with their juice and the salt. Simmer over low heat until the tomatoes turn a deep red and you have the consistency you want, 20 to 30 minutes, a little longer if you want a thick sauce.

Makes about 7 cups, a little more or less depending on how much you reduce the tomatoes

Other Flavors . . .
Add a handful of slivered basil to the cooked tomatoes to make a good fresh pasta sauce. Add oregano, tarragon, or flat-leaf parsley for a more complex herbal flavor.

Variation . . . Cumin-Scented Tomato Sauce
The addition of toasted cumin seeds and oregano makes the perfect condiment for Poblano Chiles Stuffed with Quinoa and Corn (p. 224). Put about 3 cups of Basic Tomato Sauce into a blender and puree briefly. Lightly toast and grind 1½ teaspoons cumin seeds, and chop up 1 to 2 teaspoons fresh oregano leaves. Stir the cumin and oregano into the tomato sauce.

SIMPLE TOMATO AND MEAT SAUCE FOR PASTA

An easy meat sauce can be made by using some of the Basic Tomato Sauce (p. 86) as a base. It's not much work, and you can have a spaghetti dinner for a mixed crowd, everybody happy.

1 medium onion, finely chopped

1–2 Tbs. extra-virgin olive oil

1 tsp. sea salt

2 medium carrots (4 oz.), finely diced

2 medium stalks celery (3 oz.), finely diced

½ lb. ground pork sausage

½ lb. lean ground beef

2½ cups Basic Tomato Sauce (p. 86), plus more to taste

freshly ground black pepper to taste

2 tsp. chopped fresh oregano

crushed red chiles

In a large pan, sauté the onion in the olive oil with a big pinch of salt, stirring over high heat for 6 to 7 minutes, until it begins to color. Add the diced carrots and celery, lower the heat to medium, cover the pan, and cook, stirring occasionally for 10 to 12 minutes.

Meanwhile, in another pan, brown the ground pork sausage and the ground beef with ½ teaspoon salt, breaking the meat up into bits as you stir it around, until it is cooked through and slightly browned, 8 to 9 minutes. Pour off the excess fat and add the meat to the vegetables, along with the tomato sauce. Season with freshly ground black pepper, the oregano, and a pinch of crushed red chiles, and simmer gently for 10 minutes. Taste, and correct the seasoning with more salt or pepper if needed.

Makes about 4½ cups, enough for 1 lb. pasta

JALAPEÑO-SPIKED ROASTED TOMATO SAUCE

VEGAN

A roasted tomato sauce is an indulgence of concentrated summer flavor. This chile-spiked version can be used in any dish where you want a little kick with your tomatoes, or as an all-purpose mild table salsa.

1¼ lbs. ripe red tomatoes

2 fresh jalapeño peppers

2 tsp. extra-virgin olive oil

½ small onion, finely chopped

3 cloves garlic, finely chopped

sea salt

OPTIONAL:

1–2 Tbs. red wine vinegar

Preheat the oven to 375°. Quarter the tomatoes and arrange them skin side down on a baking sheet. Put the jalapeños at one end of the pan. Roast the vegetables until they are soft and charred around the edges, about an hour, or more if the tomatoes are juicy.

Allow the vegetables to cool a bit, then scoop the tomato pulp off the skins, reserving the pulp and juice. Pull the stems and seeds out of the peppers and pull off and discard their skins.

Combine the tomato pulp with half the roasted jalapeños in a blender and puree. Taste, and add more jalapeño until you like the flavor; the heat of jalapeños can vary greatly.

Heat the olive oil in a nonstick skillet and cook the onion and garlic in it gently until the onion is golden and soft, 20 minutes or so. Stir in the tomato and chile puree and ½ teaspoon salt. Simmer the sauce for about 5 minutes to blend flavors, and taste. Add more salt as needed, and a bit of wine vinegar if you want your sauce on the tart side.

Makes about 1½ cups

Another Way . . .
Add roasted garlic to this sauce for another deep layer of flavor. Cut the top off a head of garlic, drizzle a bit of olive oil on it, wrap it in aluminum foil, and place it on the baking sheet with the other vegetables. Roast the garlic for 45 minutes or longer, until it is soft, then cool the garlic, squeeze it out of its husks, and add it to the tomato sauce.

And Just Plain Roasted Summer Tomatoes . . .
Tomatoes on their own, with just a splash of olive oil and a sprinkle of sea salt, can be a wonderful accompaniment to polenta, a tasty filling for an omelet, or an amazingly flavorful layer in a sandwich. When tomatoes are abundant at the end of summer, I cut a big batch into halves or quarters and roast as many as will fit on the pan in a single layer.

SALSA ROMESCO

VEGAN

Romesco sauce is a gift from the province of Tarragona in Spain. It seems to improve anything it touches—steamed or roasted potatoes, green vegetables, a simply cooked fish, a bowl of cooked bulgur—and it's easy. It is based on roasted pimiento peppers, almonds, and olive oil, with a little spice to keep things interesting. And yes, you can use a jar of good-quality roasted and peeled pimiento peppers.

2 large pimiento peppers (about 9 oz.), roasted and peeled, or 1 jar roasted red peppers

2 cloves garlic

⅓ cup (2 oz.) lightly toasted almonds, or ¼ cup almond butter

10 hazelnuts, lightly toasted, peeled or unpeeled

½ tsp. sea salt, plus more to taste

½ tsp. spicy smoked paprika, such as pimentón de la vera

⅓ cup chopped fresh flat-leaf parsley

2 Tbs. wine vinegar

¾–1 tsp. crushed red chiles

6 Tbs. extra-virgin olive oil

Remove the stems and seeds from the roasted red peppers and cut the peppers in pieces. If you are using roasted peppers from a jar, rinse them and drain them well.

Mince the garlic in a food processor, then add the almonds or almond butter and the hazelnuts and process until you have a coarse paste. Add the peppers, salt, paprika, parsley, wine vinegar, and ½ teaspoon crushed red chiles, and blend until the sauce is fairly smooth.

With the food processor running, add the olive oil in a stream. The sauce will develop a creamier texture and color. Taste, and correct the salt if needed, then blend in more crushed red chile, a pinch at a time, until you have the level of spiciness you like. Remember that to get a true sense of how much salt or chile you have added, you need to pause for a few moments between additions, which allows the seasoning to permeate the sauce.

Makes about 1½ cups

FRESH CRANBERRY VINAIGRETTE

I'm usually a minimalist with salad dressings—a sheen of fruity extra-virgin olive oil, a discreet splash of good vinegar, and I leave it at that. But one Thanksgiving, with fresh cranberries in front of me, I got an idea to throw some of them in the blender with a lemony vinaigrette. I added a bit of agave nectar to balance the tart berries and lemon, a little orange zest, and *bang:* a bright-flavored dressing that I now make all winter.

4 Tbs. extra-virgin olive oil

2 Tbs. fresh lemon juice

3 Tbs. agave nectar

a pinch of sea salt

freshly ground black pepper to taste

1/2 cup fresh or frozen cranberries

freshly grated zest of 1 small orange (about 1 tsp.)

Combine all the ingredients in the container of a blender and pulse briefly, just until the cranberries are almost pureed. It's nice to have a little texture, so don't overblend. The recipe can easily be doubled and will keep for a week or so in the refrigerator in a tightly sealed jar.

Makes about 3/4 cup

FRESH GINGER AND CITRUS VINAIGRETTE

Pungent, tart, sweet, spicy, salty . . . This dressing is perfect with Asian greens.

1 Tbs. freshly grated ginger

3 cloves garlic, minced

1/3 cup peanut oil

1 tsp. dark sesame oil

1/3 cup fresh lemon juice

1 Tbs. tamari or soy sauce

1 1/2 Tbs. rice vinegar

1 1/2 Tbs. agave nectar

Combine all the ingredients in a blender and pulse until a smooth sauce forms. This dressing will separate after a while, so give it a shake before using.

Makes about 1 cup

Variation . . . Ginger, Citrus, and Chile Vinaigrette
For a salad dressing with a brighter and spicier personality, drop out the tamari or soy sauce and garlic and add 1 small fresh green serrano chile, sliced, or a big pinch of crushed red chiles. For this version, increase the amount of both the rice vinegar and the agave nectar to 2 tablespoons, and blast it in the blender just as described above.

(Clockwise from left) Fresh Ginger and Citrus Vinaigrette (p. 90), Fresh Cranberry Vinaigrette (p. 90), and Agave Lemon Vinaigrette (p. 92)

AGAVE LEMON VINAIGRETTE

VEGAN

I used this simple formula to marinate kale—lots of lemon, less olive oil, and a little agave to balance the acid—and I liked it so much that I began using it as a dressing for all kinds of salads. The fresh taste of the lemon juice just knocks me out—I love it.

See photo on p. 91.

5 Tbs. fresh lemon juice

3 Tbs. extra-virgin olive oil

2 Tbs. agave nectar

1 tsp. sea salt

Whisk together all the ingredients, or shake them well in a jar.

Makes about 2/3 cup

Variation . . . Agave Lime Vinaigrette
Here's a milder version, with lime juice, which is not as acidic: use 4 tablespoons each fresh lime juice and extra-virgin olive oil, a single tablespoon agave nectar, 1/2 teaspoon grated lime zest, and salt and freshly ground black pepper to taste.

And Another . . . Citrus Glaze
The same delicious idea, adjusted to make a glaze for roasted root vegetables or a tart-sweet dressing to bring out the best in the spicy or bitter cold-season greens. Reduce the lemon juice to 2 tablespoons, add 1 tablespoon of sherry vinegar and at least 1 teaspoon finely grated orange zest, and go easy on the salt.

MISO MARINADE

VEGAN

This deep-flavored marinade can be used to prepare fish or tofu for the grill or the oven. Leftover marinade can be easily dressed up to become a savory miso vinaigrette.

½ cup red miso paste

2 Tbs. rice vinegar

2 Tbs. tamari or soy sauce

1 tsp. dark sesame oil

¼ cup mirin (rice wine)

2 cloves garlic, minced

1 Tbs. grated fresh ginger

½ cup fresh orange juice

2 Tbs. fresh lemon juice

Whisk together all the ingredients and taste for salt. If the marinade seems too salty, dilute it with a little water, adding 1 tablespoon at a time until it tastes good.

Makes 1¾ cups

Variation . . . Miso Vinaigrette
Whisk together 1 cup Miso Marinade with 2 tablespoons chopped fresh cilantro, 2 more tablespoons lemon juice, and ¼ cup extra-virgin olive oil. Taste, and add more lemon juice if needed.
Makes about 1⅓ cups

SALADS

CENTER-OF-THE-PLATE SALADS

―――――

COMPANION SALADS

―――――

SALADS

A warm summer evening. The sun is low, the afternoon heat easing at last, and the patio is in shade. I open the refrigerator and take out a container of Summer Farro Salad with Tomatoes, Seared Onions, and Fennel. It's fragrant with the juicy ripeness of summer vegetables, the smoky touch of the seared onions, the pungent black olives, all buried in toasty farro flecked with shreds of arugula and basil and glistening with olive oil. I spoon it out onto plates and push a bottle of crisp, dry rosé into an ice bucket. Friendly hands reach out to carry it all to the table in my backyard.

Is there anything more welcome on those balmy evenings than to sit outside and have a beautiful salad for supper? A salad that was ready, waiting for you in the refrigerator? I live in California, where we enjoy warm weather for much of the year, so I am an enthusiastic consumer of the salad that is a meal, that needs only a good bread and a glass of wine and that sunset . . .

Many, like the Summer Farro Salad or Tabbouleh in all its colorful variations, are based on vegetables and grains. They are ready to carry you through the dog days, at home or at the beach. Others are built on legumes, like Roasted Beets and Beluga Lentils, or grains and legumes together, like Succotash with Scarlet Quinoa, full of fresh lima beans and sweet summer corn.

And there are salads for all seasons. Some of my favorites are the robust salads I make in the cold season, like Kabocha Squash and Tuscan Kale Salad with Mixed Grains. Kale was ignored for so long, then rocketed to stardom and became overused, and as a result we saw some mediocre treatments of that warrior green. But I marinate and lightly massage my kale in sweet and tart Agave Vinaigrette, until it is gleaming, tenderized, and supple. It's the new black—dress it up with anything.

Most of my salads begin as vegan dishes and then happily take on other ingredients—anything from shavings of an aged cheese to slices of grilled lobster or steak. They are salads, after all—the definition of flexibility.

And salads are here as supporting players, too, ready to add what is needed to make a meal lovely and complete—invaluable when you are designing a meal for different tastes. They add flavorful surprise, like the easy Carrot and Cilantro Slaw with cumin seeds. They add elegance, like Fennel and Asparagus Ribbon Slaw. They add a whiff of exotic taste, like Moroccan Yam Salad with Preserved Lemon. And they add pure, happy refreshment, like Watermelon and Cucumber Salad with quick pickled onions.

So many salads, so little time . . .

CENTER-OF-THE-PLATE SALADS

WINTER KALE SALAD WITH ASIAN PEARS AND CELERY ROOT

Crisp, sweet Asian pears and roasted celery root set off earthy kale beautifully in one of my favorite salads for autumn.

2 bunches curly kale (1½ lbs.)

1 recipe Agave Lemon Vinaigrette (p. 92)

1 large celery root (about l lb.)

extra-virgin olive oil

sea salt

2 medium Asian pears (1 lb.), cored and thinly sliced or diced

1 cup (6 oz.) red flame grapes, halved or sliced

2/3 cup (2½ oz.) walnuts, coarsely chopped

fresh lemon juice

OPTIONAL:

about 4 oz. Stilton or Gorgonzola cheese, crumbled

Strip the kale off of its tough stems and tear it into bite-sized pieces. Wash the kale, spin it in a salad spinner to get rid of all excess water, and put it in your largest bowl or pot. Pour at least half the agave vinaigrette over the kale, then use your clean hands to massage the kale, kneading it as if it were bread dough for about 2 minutes. This gentle kneading starts the process of tenderizing the kale, which will shrink dramatically in volume. Taste, and add as much more of the vinaigrette as you like.

Preheat the oven to 425°. Peel the celery root and cut it into ½-inch dice. Toss the diced celery root with 1 tablespoon olive oil and ½ teaspoon salt, spread it on a baking sheet, and roast for 30 to 40 minutes, turning and mixing at least twice during that time. The pieces will be golden brown and crisp at the edges.

Toss the marinated kale with the diced pears, grapes, and walnuts. Add more vinaigrette, or adjust the dressing with more olive oil and lemon juice to taste. If the celery root is still warm and crisp, scatter some over each serving; otherwise simply mix it in. Pass the crumbled blue cheese, if you are using it, at the table.

Serves 5 to 6 as a center-of-the-plate salad

Another Way . . . Try Fuyu Persimmons

Fuyu persimmons make a spectacular fall pairing with kale. Sweet, crisp Fuyus are ripe when still hard, like apples. They look beautiful against the bright green kale, and taste heavenly—a seasonal splendor. Use 3 or 4 Fuyu persimmons instead of the Asian pears, and omit the red grapes. But throw in some fresh pomegranate seeds if you have them.

And for Another Season . . . Kale with Nectarines

For a summertime version of the fruit and kale marriage, toss your marinated kale with a pound of firm-ripe yellow nectarines cut in thin wedges and a sliced cucumber, along with a handful of chopped pecans, a smaller handful of slivered basil, and some chopped pickled onions.

Omnivore Ways . . .

I like this salad with a few crumbles of Gorgonzola cheese on top, but it would also be appealing with a smoked cheese, sliced smoked chicken breast, or a smoked sausage.

For the Fuyu persimmon variation, try a seafood match: toss cooked crabmeat or lobster with fresh lime juice, finely chopped jalapeño pepper, and a bit of mayonnaise, and put a spoonful of that concoction on top of a serving of the salad.

And for the summer salad with nectarines and cucumbers, serve slices of pan-roasted pork tenderloin on the side.

SUMMER CHOP SALAD WITH CORN AND PEPPER SALSA

VEGAN

This is a robust and cheery salad. Paired with some crusty bread and your favorite hummus, it makes a perfect summer meal. I have also served Farro and Black Rice Pilaf (p. 212) mounded in the center of a platter with this salad glistening all around it—a very successful supper, with a glass of chilled sauvignon blanc. You can add a bit of teriyaki tofu or grilled chicken for a heartier salad, or some tangy Maytag Blue. And see the menu that follows for yet another pairing, with strips of pan-grilled swordfish.

2 bunches Tuscan kale (about 1 lb.)

1 recipe Agave Lemon Vinaigrette (p. 92)

3 ears fresh sweet corn (2 cups kernels)

2 Tbs. extra-virgin olive oil, plus more to taste

1 large red onion (12 oz.), quartered and sliced

1 tsp. sea salt, plus more to taste

2 cloves garlic, chopped

2 cups (about 10 oz.) diced sweet red bell peppers

3 Tbs. balsamic vinegar, plus more to taste

2 cups halved cherry tomatoes

3 Tbs. chopped fresh mint

3 Tbs. chopped fresh basil

a pinch of crushed red chile

OPTIONAL:

6–8 oz. diced Teriyaki Grilled Tofu (p. 324) or diced, grilled chicken, or crumbled Maytag Blue cheese

Slice the kale: stack 10 or 12 leaves at a time, roll them up lengthwise, then slice them crosswise into thin ribbons; stop short of the last inch or two and discard the thickest bottom part of the ribs. Toss the slivered kale with the agave vinaigrette and massage it with your hands for 1 or 2 minutes to soften it. Slice the kernels off the corn.

Heat the olive oil in a large sauté pan and sauté the onion with $\frac{1}{2}$ teaspoon salt over medium-high heat for 6 to 7 minutes, tossing often, until it is limp and showing charred edges. Add the corn kernels and continue tossing and stirring for another 2 to 3 minutes, until the corn is also showing brown spots. Add the garlic and diced peppers, stir for another minute, then add the balsamic vinegar and toss until it has cooked away, about 30 seconds. Remove the salsa from the heat.

Combine the tomatoes, fresh herbs, crushed red chile, and the remaining $\frac{1}{2}$ teaspoon salt. Pour the corn and pepper salsa over the kale and toss, then add the tomato mixture and toss again. Taste. Enough salt? Vinegar? Oil? Correct the seasoning if needed, and mix well one more time. Now customize: toss crumbles of blue cheese or some grilled tofu or chicken into all or part of the salad, or pass them separately at the table.

Serves 4 to 6 as a center-of-the-plate salad, more as a side salad

Summer Chop
Salad with Corn
and Pepper Salsa
(p. 102)

A SALAD SUPPER FOR THE HEAT WAVE

A summer evening is a time to linger in the easing warmth, with a cool drink and food that is refreshing yet satisfying. At my house it may be a chop salad with marinated kale, dressed for summer in a colorful salsa of sweet corn, red peppers, and tomatoes. Spoon the salad over a room-temperature pilaf of farro and black rice. Done and done.

But strips of garlicky pan-grilled fish can be added to the salad as a robust, warm garnish. The strong character of kale can handle the strong flavor of grilled swordfish—power with power. I drizzle the fish with some of the same marinade I use for the kale, slice it thinly, fan the slices out on a plate, and pass it at the table. And that chilled soup! It's a concoction of cucumbers and grapes, with garlic and serrano chile to give it a spine, and it makes this meal a dinner party. Is it really a gazpacho? Do we care? It's almost effortless and tastes fabulous.

This menu is a template, and works just as well with other robust salads. Summer Farro Salad with Tomatoes, Seared Onions, and Fennel, for example, is another one I love to bring out to the patio on a summer evening. It already incorporates a satisfying grain, it pairs up beautifully with the gazpacho, and I think it only improves with a few hours in the refrigerator, all the deep and pungent flavors of the vegetables saturating the farro—ready to come out and make life easy at the end of a warm day.

The heat wave can stay around if we're eating like this.

A Practical Note . . .

The starting point is an easy vegan supper: a plate of cured olives, the center-of-the-plate summer chop salad, farro and black rice pilaf, and berries for dessert. The white gazpacho is vegetarian.

SALAD SUPPER MENU

FOR 6

a plate of cured olives
White Gazpacho *with cucumbers and grapes*

Summer Chop Salad with Corn and Pepper Salsa

Farro and Black Rice Pilaf

sliced Pan-Grilled Swordfish with Garlic

fresh berries

RAW CHARD AND FENNEL SALAD
WITH CANNELLINI

VEGETARIAN

I never thought of raw chard for a salad until a Mexican friend made one for me—and instantly converted me. If the chard is fresh and tender, it's wonderful; the lemon gives it an acidic zing, and ripe tomatoes add sweetness. Be sure to get good oil-cured olives—their taste is essential to the balance of flavors—and use a Montrachet-type chevre or Maytag Blue cheese.

12 cups thinly sliced chard (1½ lbs., untrimmed)

1 medium fennel bulb (5–6 oz.)

¼ cup pine nuts or slivered almonds

15 oil-cured black olives, pitted and sliced

2 medium tomatoes, diced, or 1½ cups halved cherry tomatoes (8–10 oz.)

3–4 oz. fresh white goat cheese or Maytag Blue cheese, broken up

1½ cups cooked cannellini

2 Tbs. extra-virgin olive oil

2 Tbs. fresh lemon juice

sea salt

freshly ground black pepper

Wash the chard and trim off the thickest bottoms of the stems, leaving the thinner ribs. Cut the large leaves in half lengthwise. Stack the leaves and slice them thinly about ⅓-inch wide. You should have about 12 cups of shredded chard (it will settle down, don't worry). Wash and trim the fennel bulb, cut it in quarters lengthwise, and slice it paper-thin with a mandoline.

Toast the pine nuts in a skillet over medium heat for just a few minutes, and watch them, or they'll burn. They're done when they begin to color and give off a toasty scent.

Combine the chard, fennel, sliced olives, tomatoes, cheese, pine nuts, and cannellini in a large bowl. Drizzle on the olive oil and lemon juice and toss. Taste, add salt and pepper as needed, and toss again.

Serves 5 to 6 as a center-of-the-plate salad, 6 to 8 as a small plate

An Omnivore Idea . . .
Raw chard has a pleasantly forward flavor, and the same can be said of tomatoes, goat cheese, and olives. Make both your vegetarians and your beef eaters happy with this robust salad: serve an accompaniment of grilled or Herb-Rubbed, Pan-Roasted Flank Steak (p. 368), thinly sliced and fanned out along the edge of the plate.

SUMMER FARRO SALAD WITH TOMATOES, SEARED ONIONS, AND FENNEL

VEGAN

This grain salad sings with robust Mediterranean flavors. The onions and fennel are seared together, tart with vinegar, mixed with sweet tomatoes and agave and pungent olives. The combination is irresistible and can be served as a vegan main course. Add a piece of focaccia and some cheese for a heartier vegetarian meal, and a glass of wine for a meal that feels like a vacation, especially if you take it outside on a warm day.

2 medium red onions (1 lb.)

1 large fennel bulb (about 12 oz. trimmed)

4 Tbs. extra-virgin olive oil, plus more to taste

sea salt

3 Tbs. balsamic vinegar

1½ Tbs. agave nectar

4 cups cooked farro, from 1½ cups semipearled farro (p. 211)

1 lb. ripe red tomatoes, diced (about 2 cups)

12 Kalamata olives, pitted and quartered

½ cup (2 oz.) pine nuts, pecans, or walnuts, lightly toasted

3 Tbs. slivered basil leaves

2 Tbs. slivered mint leaves, or 1 Tbs. chopped fresh tarragon

freshly ground black pepper to taste

1 bunch arugula (about 6 oz.), sliced

Quarter and thinly slice the red onions, and trim, quarter, and thinly slice the fennel bulb. You should have 3 to 4 cups sliced onion and about 2½ cups sliced fennel.

Heat 2 tablespoons olive oil in a large nonstick pan, add the onion and fennel and a big pinch of sea salt, and sauté over high heat, stirring, until the vegetables soften and begin to color, 6 to 7 minutes. Turn the heat down to medium and continue stirring as the vegetables become tender and spotted with brown, perhaps another 7 minutes. Add the vinegar and agave nectar and toss quickly as they cook away. The onions and fennel will be limp, dark, and glistening with their sweet-and-sour glaze. Stir the cooked farro into the onions and fennel, transfer the mixture to a large mixing bowl, and stir in all the remaining ingredients except the arugula, which should be added just before serving. Serve the salad warm, at room temperature, or cool.

Serves 4 to 5 as a center-of-the-plate salad for vegans, more if served with accompaniments

Make an Omnivore Meal . . .
The bold flavors of this salad can take bold accompaniments. It's another good match for Herb-Rubbed, Pan-Roasted Flank Steak (p. 368). The steak is rubbed with a chile and herb pesto, then grilled and sliced into thin strips, ready to layer on top or place alongside the salad for the omnivores in the family. Or, for 4 to 6 people, treat about 1 pound of pork tenderloin with a similar rub, pan-roast it, then cut it into medallions.

My Polish Chopped
Vegetable Salad (p. 109)

MY POLISH CHOPPED VEGETABLE SALAD

VEGAN

This is the chopped vegetable salad that my family has eaten on Christmas Eve since I can remember. It has a mild-mannered look but tastes like a wow, with the snap of raw apple, the crunch of celery, and the tang of pickled mushrooms. We often have a dozen people at the table for Christmas, so it is a holiday-scaled recipe. Leftovers keep well for several days afterward. The year my son Teddy began eating vegan, I made two versions, one traditional, including hard-cooked eggs, and one vegan. Everyone tried both, and everyone liked the eggless salad better. Now I make this new, improved version. Recipes keep evolving.

½ lb. small brown mushrooms

½ cup cider vinegar plus ½ cup water

1 tsp. pickling spices

1½ tsp. sea salt, plus more to taste

8 medium Yukon Gold potatoes (4 lbs.)

1 lb. carrots (2 cups diced)

8 oz. celery (2 cups diced)

4 large crisp, tart apples (2 lbs.; 5½ cups diced)

2 cups (12 oz.) fresh or frozen green peas

2½ cups finely diced dill pickles (1 lb. 2 oz. drained weight)

1 cup finely diced pickled onions (one 7-oz. jar)

freshly ground black pepper

¼ cup extra-virgin olive oil, plus more to taste

2 Tbs. fresh lemon juice, plus more to taste

The secret to this salad is the chop: fine and uniform. Aim to make everything you chop the size of a large pea. This will get you the magic flavor blend in each bite.

Clean the mushrooms and cut them in ½-inch dice. In a small stainless steel (nonreactive) pot, heat the cider vinegar and water. Put the pickling spices in a tea ball or wrap them in a coffee filter, making a packet similar to a tea bag, and drop them into the vinegar mixture, along with ½ teaspoon salt. Add the diced mushrooms and bring the liquid to a boil, then lower the heat and simmer for 2 to 3 minutes. Turn off the heat, cover the pot, and let the mushrooms steep in the vinegar for at least an hour, longer if you have more time.

Cook the whole, unpeeled potatoes in a large pot in well-salted water, starting cold and bringing the water to a simmer. Allow about 35 to 40 minutes, but cooking time will depend on the size of the potatoes. Test one with a fork after 30 minutes, and as soon as you can pierce a potato fairly easily, drain them. Allow the potatoes to cool completely; I usually give them some refrigerator time to make them easier to handle. Peel the potatoes and cut them no larger than ½-inch dice.

Peel the carrots and cook them in a large pot in salted water until they are barely tender. Cooking time will vary with the thickness of the carrots, but 6 to 8 minutes should be plenty. Allow them to cool and cut them into pea-sized dice. Trim the celery stalks, peel and core the apples, and dice both to the same size. Drain the mushrooms and discard the spices and liquid. If using fresh peas, drop them into boiling

recipe continues

OPTIONAL:

¼ cup Vegenaise or other vegan mayonnaise

1 tsp. Dijon mustard

finely chopped fresh dill

sprigs of fresh dill or parsley

thinly sliced radishes

water in a medium pan for 30 seconds, then drain. If using frozen peas, drop them into boiling salted water, and when the water returns to a boil, drain the peas.

In a very large mixing bowl, combine the potatoes, carrots, celery, apples, peas, pickles, onions, and mushrooms. Add the remaining 1 teaspoon sea salt, plenty of freshly ground black pepper, the olive oil, and the lemon juice and mix gently with your clean hands, lifting and turning until all the ingredients are well combined and the oil and lemon juice are evenly distributed. Wait a few minutes, then taste. More salt, or oil, or lemon? Only tasting will let you know. The pickles, mushrooms, and onions provide plenty of acid, but you might need more salt, or another spoonful of olive oil. And always wait 2 or 3 minutes before tasting again, to give salt a chance to be absorbed (and your taste buds a rest).

If you want to decorate this salad, mix together the vegan mayonnaise, mustard, and some finely chopped dill to make a sauce for the top. For years we always packed the salad into a beautiful serving bowl, smoothed the top flat, and spread a mayonnaise sauce over it like a glaze. Then we decorated according to inspiration with parsley sprigs, radish roses, whatever . . . Now I sometimes leave the salad undecorated, more rustic. You can also make a richer salad by doubling the amount of the mayonnaise mixture and adding some to the dressing when you mix the salad.

Any way you do it, I think you'll love it. Christmas comes once a year, and to tell the truth, I'd rather chop than shop.

Makes about 4 quarts, enough for 16 to 20. People do go back for seconds of this.

In a Festive Flexible Menu . . .
In My Christmas Eve (p. 25), this traditional salad shares the table with my friend Dennis's smoked salmon. Any smoked salmon, or any smoked fish, would be happy in that spot. Figure on about 3 to 4 ounces per serving for an excellent omnivore accompaniment.

BULGUR SALAD WITH ROMESCO SAUCE
AND MARINATED HEIRLOOM TOMATOES

If you want to fancy it up for a party, make this Spanish salad as a stuffed tomato dish: scoop out the tomatoes, fill them with the seasoned bulgur, and garnish to taste—very pretty. But for most days I prefer the rustic-elegant version: sliced heirlooms tomatoes arranged on a platter drizzled with good olive oil, and Bulgur Salad mounded on top of them. Use the vine-ripe summer tomatoes that are best in your area; if you can get heirlooms in a variety of colors, fabulous! And scatter some sweet cherry tomatoes into the mix as well.

½ tsp. sea salt, plus more to taste

1 cup (6½ oz.) dry whole-grain bulgur

½ cup (2 oz.) currants

½ cup (2¼ oz.) pine nuts, lightly toasted

2½ lbs. mixed heirloom tomatoes

2/3 cup Salsa Romesco (p. 89), plus more to taste

¾ cup fresh flat-leaf parsley, whole leaves or roughly chopped

3 green onions, white and green parts, sliced (¾ cup)

extra-virgin olive oil for drizzling

balsamic vinegar for drizzling

2 Tbs. slivered basil leaves

Heat 1¼ cups water with ½ teaspoon salt. When the water comes to a simmer, stir in the bulgur and the currants and cover the pot. Simmer for 1 minute, then turn off the heat and leave the pot covered for 40 minutes. Fluff the bulgur up with a fork, and break up clumps with your fingers. You'll have 3 to 3½ cups of bulgur. If you want to use it right away, you can cool it quickly by spreading it out on a platter or baking sheet.

Toast the pine nuts in a dry pan over medium heat, stirring constantly after the first 2 or 3 minutes, until they are pale amber with a few brown spots here and there, 7 to 8 minutes. Dice 8 ounces of the tomatoes, enough for 1½ cups.

Mix the Salsa Romesco into the bulgur and currants, then add the pine nuts, parsley, sliced green onions, diced tomatoes, and a big pinch of sea salt. Toss together gently and taste for seasoning. Add a little more Romesco, or more salt if needed.

Slice the remaining tomatoes and arrange them on a large platter. Drizzle them with a bit of olive oil and balsamic vinegar, sprinkle them lightly with sea salt, and scatter the slivered basil leaves over them. Push the tomatoes out a bit to the edges of the platter, making some space in the center. Mound the bulgur salad in the middle and serve.

Serves 5 to 6

recipe continues

Vegan, Vegetarian...

Toss a cup of cooked garbanzo beans into the salad. I like the beans I simmer with a chile de árbol pod and garlic cloves; they have a subtle warmth in their flavor and go perfectly in this bulgur-Romesco mix. And while these forward flavors don't require a salty cheese, they won't say no if you offer. Scatter a few slivers of ricotta salata—or chunks of feta—over the top of the salad, or pass a plate of cheese at the table.

And Omnivore Ways...

In Spain, Romesco sauce is often served with seafood; adding cold steamed shrimp or other shellfish to this salad is a natural choice and will make your seafood-eaters happy. For the luxury version, get freshly cooked lobster at your fish market, 1½ to 2 pounds for 6 servings. Take the lobster meat out of the shells and cut it into bite-sized pieces. Combine the diced lobster with part of the prepared Bulgur Salad or all of it, depending on how many lobster-eaters you have at the table, and taste. Add a little more Romesco or salt if needed, and proceed to mound the salad or salads on the tomatoes.

Bulgur Salad with Romesco Sauce (p. 111)
and steamed lobster

SPRING MARKET SALAD WITH FARRO

VEGAN

This is the centerpiece of my Easter brunch, full of bright spring flavors and satisfying texture. I wanted to use all the new vegetables that called to me at the farmers' market—asparagus, golden beets, and tender sweet peas—so I did. I tossed in fresh dill, mint, and a good squeeze of lemon for zing, and pecans for a touch of crunch.

Bonus points: This salad can be made a day in advance; it keeps well in a tightly covered container in the refrigerator. It's a big batch because I designed it as a party dish, but leftovers travel easily for a springtime lunch at the office.

See photo on p. 38.

1 lb. golden beets (trimmed weight)

4 Tbs. extra-virgin olive oil

1 medium yellow onion, coarsely chopped

3/4 tsp. sea salt, plus more to taste

1 large fennel bulb (8 oz. trimmed), diced

6 cups cooked farro, from 2 cups semipearled farro (p. 211)

1 1/2 lbs. green asparagus

1 cup shelled sweet peas

1 cup (3 1/2 oz.) chopped toasted pecans or pistachios

1 oz. fresh dill weed, coarsely chopped (1/3 cup)

2 Tbs. slivered fresh mint leaves

3 Tbs. fresh lemon juice

1 Tbs. agave nectar or honey

freshly ground black pepper

Preheat the oven to 375°. Scrub the beets, trim off the stems to 1 inch, and wrap the damp beets in heavy-duty aluminum foil, crimping the foil together to make a packet. Roast the beets for an hour, or longer if needed, depending on the size of the beets. They should be tender enough to be pierced through easily with a fork. Allow the beets to cool, then slip off their skins and cut them into 1/2-inch dice or slender wedges.

Heat 2 tablespoons olive oil in a large nonstick pan and sauté the onion with a pinch of salt over medium heat, stirring often, for about 10 minutes. Add the diced fennel, cover the pan, and stir occasionally for 20 to 25 minutes longer, until both the onion and the fennel are tender and light gold in color. Remove from the heat, stir in the cooked farro, and transfer to a large mixing bowl.

Snap off the tough ends of the asparagus and cut them on a slant in pieces about 1 inch in length. Steam the asparagus for 2 to 3 minutes, until just barely tender. Steam the peas for about 45 seconds, then refresh with cold water.

Add the beets, asparagus, peas, chopped pecans or pistachios, and herbs to the farro mixture and toss until everything is well combined.

Whisk together the remaining 2 tablespoons olive oil, the lemon juice, agave nectar or honey, and 1/2 teaspoon sea salt and drizzle over the farro mixture. Grind in as much black pepper as you like, then immediately toss again to distribute the dressing throughout. Serve the salad at cool room temperature.

Serves 8 as a main dish, 10 to 12 in a menu with other foods

In a Mixed Menu for Easter . . .
A flexible Easter Brunch (p. 36) is designed around this centerpiece salad. Gently Baked Salmon accompanies it, as do other foods that celebrate the season: fava bean puree, fennel and asparagus slaw, and a frittata. It's a beautiful spread on your dining room table, but if the weather allows, it's also perfect outdoor fare—everything can be prepared ahead and served at room temperature. Set up a table in the garden and welcome spring.

And Another Omnivore Meal . . .
Not a fan of salmon? Go to the very best deli you know and buy some good duck pâté to go with this salad.

TABBOULEH VARIATIONS

VEGAN, VEGETARIAN, OR OMNIVORE

In the summer heat, when evenings are languid, I often think I could eat a bowl of tabbouleh every day, sitting in the garden and sipping a glass of chilled rosé. And tabbouleh is so adaptable that I'd never get bored. Have it as a light lunch or supper, or let it take its place on the *mezze* table with the sunny food of the Middle East.
    See photo on p. 121.

SIMPLE TABBOULEH

Chewy bulgur with fresh green herbs and a lemony dressing, a bit of cumin for a subtle depth of flavor, and that touch of cinnamon, on advice from my friend Haigaz.

1½ cups (10 oz.) whole-grain bulgur

1½ tsp. sea salt, plus more to taste

1½ cups chopped fresh flat-leaf parsley (3 oz.—a big bunch!)

½ cup chopped fresh mint

½ cup thinly sliced green onions, white and green parts

¾ tsp. toasted and ground cumin seeds

½ tsp. ground cinnamon

4 Tbs. fresh lemon juice, plus more to taste

freshly ground black pepper

3–4 Tbs. extra-virgin olive oil, plus more to taste

Pour 3 cups boiling water over the bulgur in a large bowl, stir in ½ tsp. salt, cover the bowl, and let it stand for 30 minutes. Drain the bulgur through a fine sieve and press down on it firmly with the back of a large spoon or a small bowl to squeeze out any excess moisture. Allow the bulgur to cool.

In a large mixing bowl, combine the well-drained bulgur with the chopped parsley and mint, sliced green onions, cumin, cinnamon, the remaining 1 teaspoon salt, and the lemon juice. Mix it all together, then taste and add more salt, a pinch at a time, as needed. Grind in some black pepper. Add 3 tablespoons olive oil, toss lightly, and taste again. Add more salt, oil, or lemon juice if you like.

Makes about 5 cups, enough to serve 5 to 6 as a light main dish

---

Make an Omnivore Meal . . .

Tabbouleh is a high-protein grain salad that makes a fine vegan main dish, and for your omnivore friends you can add Spicy Lamb Meatballs (p. 370) or grilled lamb kabobs. Shellfish are also a good choice with the tomato and cucumber variation: accompany the tabbouleh with a plate of Prawns Sautéed with Garlic (p. 349) and let those who like shrimp have at it. If you live in Maine, have lobster—but you know that. And see Tabbouleh with Chickpeas and Preserved Lemon in the abundant *mezze* menu that follows.

Tabbouleh with Tomatoes and Cucumbers

My version of a classic. To the Simple Tabbouleh, add 1½ pounds cucumbers and 1 pound ripe summer tomatoes. Peel and seed the cucumbers, cut them in ½-inch dice, toss them in a bowl with a teaspoon of salt, and leave them for about 45 minutes; you should have about 2 cups. Drain the cucumbers, give them a quick rinse, then press them in a sieve with the heel of your hand until the excess moisture is squeezed out. Dice the tomatoes to about the same size as the cucumbers (again, about 2 cups) and allow them to drain a few minutes in a sieve; you don't need to salt them. Stir the cucumbers and tomatoes into the tabbouleh, and before serving taste again. This is the point at which the tabbouleh speaks to you, and you really will know what to do—perhaps add another pinch of salt, or more oil and lemon juice for a more pungent salad. This variation serves 6 to 8.

Tabbouleh with Chickpeas and Preserved Lemon

To Simple Tabbouleh, or to Tabbouleh with Tomatoes and Cucumbers, add about 1½ cups sprouted or cooked garbanzo beans (chickpeas). I also like to add a tablespoon of minced, salt-preserved lemon: I rinse it first, squeeze it dry, and chop it finely, then mix it in. It's not enough to announce itself but just enough to make the salad more interesting. A little extra oil and lemon is good to balance the chickpeas, and this version is a powerhouse protein dish. It serves 6 to 8.

Tabbouleh with Olives and Peppers

To Simple Tabbouleh or to Tabbouleh with Tomatoes and Cucumbers, add about ½ cup sliced black or green cured olives. Roasted red peppers, peeled and cut in chunks or strips, go beautifully with them, and I like to add a spoonful of harissa and an extra dash of lemon juice. For your omnivores, add thinly shaved slices of prosciutto alongside. And of course some crumbled feta cheese added here would make another classic variation.

Tabbouleh with Kumquats, Pine Nuts, and Olives

To Simple Tabbouleh, add about 1 cup thinly sliced kumquats, ½ cup pine nuts, and a few olives cut in thin slices or slivers. Kumquats have a natural acidity—their inside is like a lemon—so in this variation the lemon juice could be taken down a notch. The kumquat skin is sweet and orangelike, the pine nuts add richness, and a few olives are perfect against the sweetness of the kumquat zest. Make this variation with the simplest tabbouleh, no tomatoes.

NO ONE EATS *MEZZE* ALONE

The *mezze* table, an array of sun-drenched flavors, tart and sweet, spicy and rich, is the most sociable kind of eating, and the definition of flexibility. It can include pungent dips, crunchy salads, herbs that explode with flavor in your mouth, roasted vegetables smothered in olive oil, mint-scented meatballs, briny cheeses, garlicky prawns, cured olives, flaky pastries—the whole world in a well-spiced Middle Eastern mosaic.

In the world of *mezze*, the menu suggested here is a modest one: the dishes are simple, and there are not too many of them. A more elaborate *mezze* party could include the traditional stuffed peppers and tomatoes of Turkey and Lebanon; they are served warm or at room temperature, and they can be made two ways, with a lentil and rice filling, and also with lamb. Or you might add *taramasalata*, the creamy spread of fish roe; or perfectly simple cucumbers in yogurt and mint; or a carrot salad with cumin seeds and cilantro; or grilled halloumi cheese; or yam salad with preserved lemon . . . The *mezze* table is an ever-expanding universe.

But what I love most about *mezze* is that this food is about hospitality. It's about gathering around a table and sharing. *Mezze* are not so much a type of food as a great tradition of conviviality. No one eats *mezze* alone! This food calls us to gather at one big table of abundance and variety, something for everyone and everyone together. It is how we became civilized. How we are happy together. I want my life to be a big ongoing *mezze* table, with my pals around it. Everyone tastes, reaches across, offers and samples, argues and insists, shares, has a drink, eats some more . . .

A Practical Note . . .

This menu makes for an easy evening with friends. Most of the food is perfect at room temperature, so it can be prepared ahead, and there is plenty of choice for all: vegans will eat the radishes and olives, the flatbreads with three savory spreads, the hearty tabbouleh with chickpeas, and the fattoush with purslane. Charred zucchini can be served with or without yogurt.

And remember, it is *not* cheating to visit the Armenian or Greek deli for stuffed vine leaves or baklava, or fresh, fresh hummus if you don't want to make it yourself. It is collaboration of the best kind.

THE *MEZZE* TABLE

FOR 12 TO 15

radishes and fresh herbs
cured olives
feta cheese

flatbreads with three spreads:
Beluga Lentil and Caramelized Onion Puree
Roasted Eggplant and Poblano Chile Spread
Muhamarra

Tabbouleh with Chickpeas and Preserved Lemon

Baked Kibbeh Wedges

Fattoush with Purslane

Charred Zucchini with Lemon and Mint

baklava

On the *mezze* table (clockwise from bottom left): cured olives, Charred Zucchini with Lemon and Mint (p. 288), hummus, Baked Kibbeh Wedges (p. 366), feta cheese with herbs, Tabbouleh with Chickpeas and Preserved Lemon (p. 117), Muhamarra (p. 66), a tapenade

KABOCHA SQUASH AND TUSCAN KALE SALAD WITH MIXED GRAINS

VEGAN

Take this to any potluck party and be prepared to send around the recipe the next day. It combines some of my favorite things—sweet winter squash, slightly bitter Tuscan kale, and chewy, nutty grains—in a salad that is a meal. Winter squashes like kabocha and butternut actually start to show up in the markets in late summer and stay through winter, and kale has become a year-round green, so it's a season-crossing dish.

See photo on p. 359.

1 medium kabocha squash (about 3 lbs.)

7 Tbs. extra-virgin olive oil

5 Tbs. fresh lemon juice, plus more to taste

3 Tbs. agave nectar

1½ tsp. sea salt, plus more to taste

2 medium bunches Tuscan kale (1 lb.)

1 small head radicchio

2/3 cup raisins

1 large Fuji apple

1 medium yellow onion

3 Tbs. balsamic vinegar

2 cups cooked farro, from 3/4 cup semipearled farro (p. 211)

3/4 cup cooked black or red rice

2 oz. (about ½ cup) pecan pieces

freshly ground black pepper

Scrub the exterior of the kabocha squash under running water; kabocha does not need to be peeled, so be sure it's clean. Cut the squash in half, scrape out the seeds and strings, slice it into thin wedges, and cut those into ¾-inch dice cutting with the blade always pointing away from your hand.

Preheat the oven to 400°. Whisk together 5 tablespoons olive oil, the lemon juice, the agave nectar, and 1 teaspoon sea salt. Toss the diced squash with half of this dressing, spread it on a baking sheet, and roast it for at least an hour, more if needed, turning a few times, until the squash cubes have brown spots and crispy edges.

Meanwhile, wash the kale and cut the leaves into ¼-inch strips, leaving off only the thickest bottom parts of the ribs. In a large bowl, toss the kale with the remaining dressing, then use your clean hands to massage the kale, kneading it lightly as if it were bread dough for about 2 minutes. This gentle kneading works the marinade into the greens and starts the process of tenderizing the kale, which will shrink dramatically in volume. Leave it to marinate for at least 30 minutes or up to 2 hours.

Wash the radicchio, shake it dry, quarter it lengthwise, and cut into thin strips. In a small bowl, douse the raisins with about ½ cup boiling water and leave them to soak for at least 20 minutes, then drain well. Core and trim the apple and cut it into ½-inch dice.

Peel the onion, cut it in half crosswise, then slice lengthwise into very thin wedges. Heat the remaining 2 tablespoons olive oil in a nonstick pan and toss the onion slices in it with the remaning ½ teaspoon salt, over high heat, for 5 to 6 minutes, or until it is showing dark brown spots and streaks. Lower the heat and continue cooking the onion another few minutes, stirring often, as it darkens more evenly—don't be shy here! Add the balsamic vinegar all at once and toss the onion quickly as the vinegar sizzles away.

Add the squash, shredded radicchio, plumped raisins, apple, balsamic onion, farro, rice, and pecan pieces to the kale and toss everything together well. Grind in some black pepper, then taste and correct the seasoning with more salt, lemon juice, or pepper, to your taste.

Serves 6 in meal-sized portions

Matchmaking . . .
Build a warming meal for fall or winter by starting with gorgeous, delicately spiced, and protein-rich Red Lentil Soup with Japanese Yams and Carrots (p. 177). Then pair the salad with Easiest Roast Chicken *stuffed with lemons* (p. 357). If you are pressed for time, pick up a good rotisserie chicken on your way home from work, tear some into strips, and toss it into individual servings of the salad for those who raise their hands.

SUCCOTASH WITH SCARLET QUINOA

VEGAN

Summer sweet corn, vine-ripe tomatoes, and bright green lima beans—this salad is a seasonal farmers' market joy. Prepare it ahead, then take it on a picnic, or eat it on the patio. Delicious ready food is the secret to beating the heat. (If you cannot get fresh green lima beans, you can substitute steamed edamame, which are now widely available both fresh and frozen.)

3–4 ears sweet corn

1 cup fresh green lima beans

sea salt

2 Tbs. extra-virgin olive oil

2 cloves garlic, minced

1 cup finely diced sweet red bell pepper

1½ cups diced tomatoes, drained in a colander

½ cup chopped fresh cilantro

1 tsp. finely chopped fresh hot green chile

2 Tbs. fresh lemon juice

3 cups cooked scarlet (red) quinoa (from 1 generous cup uncooked quinoa; see p. 211)

OPTIONAL GARNISH:

lightly toasted pine nuts

AND FOR VEGETARIANS AND OMNIVORES:

crumbled *cotija* cheese or diced toasted haloumi

Slice the kernels off the corn and measure out about 1½ cups. Drop the fresh lima beans into a pot of boiling salted water for 3 minutes, then drain them.

Heat 1 tablespoon olive oil in a medium nonstick pan and sauté the minced garlic in it for a minute, then add the lima beans and a big pinch of salt and sauté for 4 or 5 minutes over medium heat, until the beans are beginning to show spots of color. Add the corn kernels and toss for another 2 minutes. Allow the mixture to cool.

In a large bowl, toss together the corn and bean mixture, diced red pepper, tomatoes, cilantro, minced chile, lemon juice, the remaining 1 tablespoon olive oil, and ½ teaspoon salt. Taste and correct the seasoning with a pinch more salt if needed, then add the quinoa and toss it gently with the vegetables. Serve at room temperature or cool, alone or over mixed lettuces, with or without pine nuts, crumbled *cotija* cheese, or haloumi on top.

Serves 5 to 6 as a center-of-the-plate salad

An Omnivore Meal . . .

It's summer, so you might be grilling. The smoky touch in Charcoal-Grilled Marinated Chicken (p. 360), bathed in olive oil, garlic, and rosemary, will be just right with this juicy salad. Or slice cold leftover grilled chicken into strips and mix it into part of the salad. The salad is substantial, so about 3 ounces per person will be plenty. Pan Grilled Swordfish (p. 347) is another great match; slice it thinly and pass it at the table.

Succotash with Scarlet Quinoa
(p. 124), paired with Pan Grilled
Swordfish with Garlic (p. 347)

Winter Quinoa Salad *with smoked cheese and walnuts* (p. 127), paired with caramelized sausage

WINTER QUINOA SALAD
WITH SMOKED CHEESE AND WALNUTS

VEGETARIAN

Hearty, high in protein, and rich in flavor, this fall or winter salad is a vegetarian main dish for lunch, perhaps served on a bed of mixed greens, or the first course of a larger meal. If you want to be fancy, serve it nested in radicchio or endive leaves. If you want to take it to work, pack it into a container; it will hold up just fine.

The smoked cheese adds richness and a dominant flavor; it's best to add it just before serving. If you have vegans at the table, pass the cheese separately.

1 large red onion

5 Tbs. extra-virgin olive oil, plus more to taste

sea salt

2 Tbs. balsamic vinegar

5 cups cooked red quinoa (from 1²/3 cups uncooked quinoa; see p. 211)

3/4 cup dried cranberries

1 cup (4 oz.) coarsely chopped walnuts

1 large, crisp apple, such as Fuji or Pink Lady, cut into 1/2-inch dice

1 cup finely diced fennel bulb

1 1/2 cups thinly sliced celery (about 3 stalks)

4 oz. wild arugula cut into 2-inch pieces

3–4 Tbs. sherry vinegar

freshly ground black pepper to taste

3–4 oz. smoked Gouda or smoked cheddar cheese, finely diced

Peel the red onion, quarter it lengthwise, then slice it thinly crosswise. Heat 2 tablespoons olive oil in a nonstick skillet and add the sliced onion with a pinch of salt. Stir and toss the onion constantly over high heat for 6 to 8 minutes; it will become limp and develop seared brown edges and spots. Add the 2 tablespoons balsamic vinegar and quickly toss again as the vinegar cooks away.

Combine the cooked quinoa, cranberries, chopped walnuts, diced apple, diced fennel bulb, sliced celery, arugula, and seared onion in a large bowl and toss together.

Whisk together the remaining 3 tablespoons olive oil, the sherry vinegar, about 1/2 teaspoon sea salt, and a few grinds of black pepper. Add the dressing to the salad and mix it in gently, wait a moment, then taste and add more salt and pepper if needed, as well as more olive oil if the salad still seems dry.

Before serving, scatter the diced smoked cheese over the salad in its serving dish, or over each individual serving.

Serves 6 as a center-of-the-plate dish

An Omnivore Meal . . .
This is a salad that can take on some smoked sausage, either along with the cheese or in place of it. See the Note for Sausage Lovers that follows this recipe.

A NOTE FOR SAUSAGE LOVERS

The Winter Quinoa Salad on p. 127, full of autumn flavors and already calling out a smoky touch with the cheese, is an ideal dish to pair with a few slices of your favorite smoked sausage.

I am an infrequent meat eater, but there is a history of kielbasa in my family, so I do have a bite of sausage now and then, especially now that so many new and interesting kinds of sausage are available. Some years back, as we became more health-conscious (at least, my West Coast world did), lower-fat sausages began appearing in upmarket delis. Some are made with chicken or turkey instead of beef and pork. There are sausages made with cranberries, sausages studded with red peppers and basil, sausages with apples . . . And small, artisanal producers are competing with the larger, established companies, finding their markets online, in specialty shops, or at farmers' markets.

It may seem that the fashion for adding all sorts of unexpected ingredients to sausage is a new thing, but that is not so. Remember, the *whole idea* of sausage is to put a load of different things together, with plenty of spices and aromatic elements. I think that what we are experiencing now is a new burst of creativity in an old tradition.

And if you love sausage, it is only good news that you can have a lot of flavor without an overload of unhealthy fats. It is reassuring as well to buy anything from a small producer who sources ingredients carefully and knows where everything came from. Of course, you have to seek out the sausage that is your own ideal, and know that many of them are still just as loaded with fat and mystery as ever they have been. But with a little investigation, you can enjoy that smoky, spicy kick now and then without dying for it.

Sautéed Sausage Coins

Use your favorite smoked sausage, one that is already fully cooked. To garnish the Winter Quinoa Salad for 5 or 6 people, you could use about a pound of lean sausage, slightly more if your omnivores are big eaters. Slice it into disks about 1/4-inch thick, and if it is a low-fat sausage, heat 1 tablespoon of olive oil in your large pan. Sauté the sausage slices over medium heat for about 3 minutes on each side, just enough to brown them, then transfer them to a plate lined with paper towels to absorb excess fat. There you are. Drop those disks on top of individual servings of the salad, or mix them in if everyone at the table eats meat.

ROASTED BEETS
AND BELUGA LENTILS

VEGAN

The wine-red color of this salad is alluring, darkly mysterious, and the taste is fabulous. Earthy black lentils and deep red beets, mixed with shreds of beet greens and seared red onions, make a salad hearty enough to be the centerpiece of a meal; mound it on a bed of tender leaves and accompany with a chewy whole-grain roll.

2 lbs. beets

2¼ tsp. sea salt, plus more to taste

9 oz. (1¼ cups) Beluga lentils

4 oz. carrots, finely diced

3 cloves garlic

1 dried chile de árbol

6–8 oz. tender beet greens or rainbow chard

2 Tbs. extra-virgin olive oil

1 large red onion (8–9 oz.), quartered and thinly sliced

1½ Tbs. balsamic vinegar

1 recipe Agave Lemon Vinaigrette (p. 92)

plenty of freshly ground black pepper

OPTIONAL:

½–1 tsp. finely grated orange zest

Preheat the oven to 400°. Scrub the beets and trim off the greens, leaving an inch of the stalks. Wrap the damp beets in heavy-duty aluminum foil, crimping it to make a sealed packet, and roast them for 45 minutes to an hour, depending on their size. They should be tender enough to be easily pierced with a fork. Let them cool a bit, then slip off their skins, trim off the stalks, and cut them into ½-inch dice; you should have about 3½ cups.

Bring 7 to 8 cups water to a boil with 2 teaspoons salt and add the lentils, diced carrots, garlic cloves, and chile. Simmer the lentils for 25 minutes, until they are tender but still firm. Drain the lentils (and keep the broth for soup). Discard the chile and garlic. Spread the lentils and carrots on a baking sheet to cool and set them aside.

Wash the beet greens or chard, trim off only the thick lower stalks, cut the leaves in half lengthwise if they are large, then cut them in ¼-inch strips.

Heat 1 tablespoon olive oil in a nonstick skillet and sear the onion in it with ¼ teaspoon salt, tossing over high heat until the onion is softened, blistered, and shows brown spots, 6 to 7 minutes. Add the balsamic vinegar, turn off the heat, and stir quickly as the vinegar sizzles away. Add the onions to the diced beets in a large mixing bowl. In the same pan, heat the remaining 1 tablespoon olive oil and sauté the damp beet greens in it with a pinch of salt, tossing them over high heat just until they are completely wilted, 3 to 4 minutes. Add the beet greens to the beet mixture.

recipe continues

Pour all but 2 tablespoons of the vinaigrette over the salad, along with the pepper and orange zest, and mix. Now add the lentils to the bowl and mix again, gently. Taste, and add more lemon juice or salt if needed, but once you have added the lentils, do not overmix. Add the remaining dressing just before serving the salad to get that lovely, glistening look. Serve the salad on its own or piled on a bed of bright green watercress or baby arugula.

Serves 6 to 7 as a vegan center-of-the-plate dish

Vegetarian and Omnivore Ways . . .
For a flexible everyday meal, this salad could be accompanied by something easy from the deli—smoked fish or a sliced smoked duck leg. Or keep the smoky idea with a bit of diced, sautéed pancetta as a garnish. Another option: scatter slivers of ricotta salata or aged jack cheese over the top, or chunks of creamy Gorgonzola.

In a Festive Mixed Menu . . .
Beets came back into My Christmas Eve (p. 25) with this dark, earthy salad, served along with My Polish Chopped Vegetable Salad and Dennis's dry-smoked salmon.

Variation . . . Le Puy Lentils and Beets *with green beans, mint, and salt-preserved lemon*

Spikes of bright green beans and mint leaves and the exotic aromatic touch of salt-preserved lemons give the salad a wholly different personality. Salt-preserved lemons are a Moroccan condiment, available at markets that stock Middle Eastern foods.

For this version, use green Le Puy lentils, which also hold their shape, and eliminate the sautéed beet greens and the orange zest in the dressing. Make the salad as above, and while the lentils are simmering, cut ½ pound of tender green beans into 1-inch pieces and drop them into boiling salted water for 3 to 4 minutes, until tender-crisp. Drain the beans and rinse them with cold water. Cut a small handful of mint leaves into slivers.

Rinse the crusted salt off a small piece of preserved lemon, pat it dry with a paper towel, then cut it into fine dice; you should have 1 to 2 tablespoons. Add the green beans, slivered mint, and diced preserved lemon when you are tossing everything together. Garnish this salad with a few flakes of ricotta salata.

Roasted Beets and Beluga Lentils (p. 129), served with dry-smoked salmon

MARINATED CANNELLINI WITH OLIVES AND ROASTED PEPPERS

VEGAN

Cannellini marry perfectly with the vibrant, pungent flavors of lemon, fresh parsley, olives, and roasted red peppers. They are a beautiful and easy appetizer—with crostini, over a few arugula leaves, or as part of an antipasto assortment. And if you're adding grilled chicken or a slice of sausage to a salad for the omnivores, this is just the kind of thing to have on hand for the vegans.

See photo on p. 31.

12 oz. (a scant 2 cups) dried cannellini beans

10 fresh sage leaves or 2 Tbs. crumbled dried sage

6 garlic cloves

2 tsp. sea salt, plus more for the dressing

4–5 Tbs. extra-virgin olive oil

3 Tbs. fresh lemon juice, plus more to taste

3/4 cup coarsely chopped fresh flat-leaf parsley

1 tsp. minced fresh oregano or 1/2 tsp. crushed dried oregano

1–2 Tbs. minced shallots

plenty of freshly ground black pepper

10–15 cured black olives, pitted and sliced or chopped

1 large fire-roasted pimiento pepper, 1/2 cup diced (peppers from a jar are fine)

Rinse the cannellini and put them in a large pot with about 2½ quarts water, the sage leaves, and the garlic cloves. Bring the water to a boil, lower the heat, cover the pot, and simmer the beans for 1 to 1½ hours, longer if needed, until they are tender but not falling apart. The beans should always be covered by at least an inch of water; add more water if it is cooking away too quickly. Be sure to test a few beans after an hour, as cooking time for dried beans varies with the size and age of the beans.

When the beans are just tender, add the salt and allow the beans to simmer very gently for another 10 minutes or so. They should have a creamy texture but hold their shape. Drain the beans, handling them gently so as not to turn them into a mush. (Reserve the liquid to use in a soup or broth—it's delicious.)

In a large mixing bowl, drizzle the beans with the olive oil and lemon juice, mix them gently, then add the remaining ingredients and mix again. Taste, and add as much salt as needed, or another splash of lemon. Allow the beans to marinate in the dressing for about 30 minutes, then taste and adjust the seasoning a final time.

Serves 6 to 8 as an appetizer. A larger serving of this salad—about 3/4 cup—turns a vegetable salad into a vegan main course.

In Flexible Menus . . .

This salad is the starter in one of the first flexible menus I tried when I began thinking about this book, Risotto As You Like It (p. 198), which remains one of my favorites. With the cannellini, serve Tuna in Olive Oil and Capers (p. 351). It's a classic antipasto combination; see it again as part of a larger antipasto in Italian Style (p. 28).

And Other Omnivore Pairings . . .

The spicy chickpea version given below would make a good combination with Spanish chorizo, a hard, cured sausage similar in texture to dry salami. Chorizo is a popular tapa in Spanish bars, cut in thin slices and served with chunks of bread to accompany a *vino tinto*. You could serve it that way, alongside the salad, or dice it finely and stir it in; use 3 to 4 ounces (about ¾ cup) diced chorizo for half this salad, or pass 6 to 8 ounces of thinly sliced chorizo on a platter.

Other Beans, Other Ways . . . Spicy Marinated Chickpeas

Garbanzo beans (chickpeas) can be prepared in just the same way, or in this variation: omit the olives and roasted pimiento pepper and instead add ¼ teaspoon crushed red chiles and about 2 tablespoons chopped or slivered fresh mint leaves.

WARM LENTIL AND ROOT VEGETABLE SALAD
WITH MUSTARD VINAIGRETTE

VEGAN

This richly flavored lentil dish starts with a base of sweet and earthy root vegetables, adds a tangy, mustardy dressing, and finishes with handfuls of flat-leaf parsley. I like it best served still warm, over a bed of wild arugula lightly bathed in olive oil, lemon juice, and sea salt. Alongside, I have pan-grilled olive oil toast made with rustic whole-grain bread. The combination of the warm, savory lentils, the bite of raw arugula, the chewy, crunchy pan toast . . . heaven.

5 Tbs. extra-virgin olive oil

1 cup finely diced carrots

1 cup finely diced celery root

1 cup finely diced turnips

1 tsp. sea salt, plus more to taste

1³/4 cups (12¹/2 oz.) Le Puy lentils

1 bay leaf

1 tsp. chopped fresh thyme

¹/3 cup red wine vinegar, plus more to taste

1¹/2 Tbs. grainy Dijon mustard

1¹/2 Tbs. agave nectar or sugar

freshly ground black pepper

1¹/2 cups (about 6 oz.) chopped fennel bulb

1¹/2 cups (about 8 oz.) chopped shallots

1 large clove garlic, finely chopped

1 cup chopped fresh flat-leaf parsley

Heat 2 tablespoons olive oil in an ample sauté pan and sauté the diced carrots, celery root, and turnips with ¹/2 teaspoon salt, tossing the vegetables over high heat for 6 to 7 minutes. Rinse the lentils and combine them in a pot with 3 cups water, the remaining ¹/2 teaspoon salt, the bay leaf, and the thyme. Bring the water to a boil, then lower the heat to simmer, cover the pot, and cook the lentils gently for 20 to 25 minutes. Check them at 20 minutes, to be sure the liquid has not cooked away. The lentils should be tender but not mushy, and almost all the liquid should be absorbed.

Meanwhile, whisk together the vinegar, mustard, agave nectar or sugar, some freshly ground black pepper, and a pinch of sea salt.

Heat 1 tablespoon olive oil in a nonstick skillet and sauté the fennel, shallots, and garlic, tossing over high heat for 5 to 6 minutes. The vegetables should be tender-crunchy and just lightly colored. Stir in the vinaigrette, and keep stirring over medium-high heat for a moment as it boils up, then turn off the heat and add the vegetables and dressing to the lentils. Stir in the remaining 2 tablespoons olive oil and the parsley, as well as more salt or vinegar to taste, and toss gently to combine. Serve the salad warm or cool, over spicy greens or on its own, with pan toast or without.

Serves 6 as a center-of-the-plate dish, more if served as an appetizer

SERVE WITH:

wild arugula or other greens, in oil and lemon juice

pan-grilled whole-grain olive oil toast (technique follows)

Omnivore Pairings . . .

Meat-eaters will enjoy these lentils with sautéed slices of kielbasa or crisp bits of pancetta scattered over the top. I'm Polish, so I'm partial to the kielbasa. For about 6 servings, cut ½ to ¾ pound sausage on a slant into ½-inch slices and brown the slices in a hot, dry skillet for a couple minutes on each side. If you are using a lower-fat sausage, you might have to prime the pan with a bit of olive oil. Keep the sausage slices warm, and layer them alongside individual servings of lentil salad.

To Make Pan-Grilled Olive Oil Toast . . .

It is as easy as it sounds. Cut slices from your rustic whole-grain loaf and brush them generously on both sides with extra-virgin olive oil. Sprinkle the slices with sea salt, then grill them in a hot pan for 2 to 3 minutes, until golden brown. Turn them over and do the same on the other side. They should have crunchy edges. Eat while hot.

COMPANION SALADS

FATTOUSH WITH PURSLANE

VEGAN

Fattoush is the Lebanese version of *panzanella*, the lovely Italian bread salad—an idea too good to belong to just one cuisine. It's made with pita crisps and crunchy purslane sprigs, for a wonderful texture. Tossed with juicy summer vegetables and herbs, the bread gradually soaks up the dressing of olive oil, lemon, and tangy sumac. The salad changes during the course of a meal; at first the textures are distinct, the pita is crunchy, but later it softens, infused with the juice of the tomatoes and the dressing.

2 or 3 medium-sized whole wheat
    pita breads, quartered

about 6 Tbs. extra-virgin olive oil

3 cups sliced or diced cucumber
    (1½–2 lbs.)

1 tsp. sea salt, plus more to taste

1½ lbs. tomatoes

2 medium bell peppers (8 oz.)

½ cup coarsely chopped fresh
    flat-leaf parsley

⅓ cup coarsely chopped fresh
    mint leaves

2 Tbs. fresh lemon juice

1½ Tbs. ground sumac

2 cups purslane sprigs

Preheat the oven to 375°. Brush the pita breads with 2 tablespoons of the olive oil. Pull the layers apart and arrange them on a baking sheet. Bake the pita triangles for about 10 minutes, until golden on the edges and crisped. Allow them to cool, then break them into pieces.

Toss the cucumbers with 1 teaspoon salt and leave them to drain for an hour, then rinse them in a colander and press out the excess moisture. Cut the tomatoes in large dice; you should have 3 cups. Quarter and core the peppers and slice thinly crosswise; you should have 1½ cups.

Mix the vegetables with the parsley, mint, remaining 4 tablespoons olive oil, lemon juice, and 1 tablespoon sumac. Add sea salt, a pinch at a time, until the salad tastes perfect. Shortly before serving, gently mix in the purslane sprigs and the pita chips. Sprinkle the remaining sumac on top.

Serves 6

A Simpler Way . . . Armenian Summer Salad
To make a refreshing salad without the purslane and the toasted pita bread, reduce the olive oil to 3 tablespoons and the ground sumac to 1 to 2 teaspoons, then prepare the ingredients, toss gently, and taste. Correct the seasoning with more lemon or oil if you like, and serve.

In a Party Menu for Everyone . . .
No One Eats *Mezze* Alone (p. 118) is the menu where Middle Eastern vegetable dishes mix it up with Baked Kibbeh Wedges and Chard and Parsley Frittata.

FENNEL AND ASPARAGUS RIBBON SLAW

VEGAN

Shaved fennel and raw asparagus make a palate-brightening slaw for spring. Use a mandoline to shave the fennel, and watch a hard bulb turn into thin, translucent ribbons.

2–3 large fennel bulbs (about 1 lb.)

3 Tbs. fresh lemon juice, plus more to taste

1¼ lbs. fresh asparagus (about 2 bunches)

¼ cup chopped fennel fronds

¼ cup dill weed, pulled off the stems

⅓ cup (1½ oz.) lightly toasted pine nuts

2 Tbs. extra-virgin olive oil

½ Tbs. agave nectar

½ tsp. sea salt, plus more to taste

Trim the fennel bulbs, peeling down the tough outer layer, and cut the green stalks down to about 2 inches, just enough to hold on to as you slice. Use a mandoline to shave the fennel into paper-thin ribbons. You should have at least 4 cups, loosely packed. Pour the lemon juice over the shaved fennel to keep it from turning brown.

Rinse the asparagus and snap off the tough bottoms of the stalks. You should have about 12 ounces of trimmed asparagus, to yield about 3 cups when sliced. Use your sharpest knife to slice the stalks thinly on a deep slant, and reserve the tips.

Combine all the ingredients in an ample bowl and toss gently. Taste, and adjust the salt or lemon if needed. Scatter the reserved asparagus tips over the top as a pretty garnish, or mix them into the salad.

Serves 6 to 8 as a first course or side salad

In a Festive Mixed Menu . . .
This delicate slaw is on the menu for Easter Brunch (p. 36).

Fennel and Asparagus Ribbon Slaw (p. 138)

FARMERS' MARKET TOMATO SALAD

VEGAN

What are your favorites? Brandywine? Black Krim? Oaxacan Jewel? How about Mortgage Lifter? The names themselves are a treat, conjuring up not only the flavors and textures but the history of these heirloom plants. I hope the Mortgage Lifter did pay off the farm.

When gorgeous tomatoes flood the farmers' market all summer and fall, I choose Purple Cherokees and Brandywines, along with Early Girls, an abiding favorite. Find the tomatoes that do best in your area, the tomatoes you love, and then make this simple salad, a celebration of ripe summer flavor. Throw a few cherry or grape tomatoes on top for sheer visual fun.

1½ lbs. mixed tomatoes, heirlooms and others, all colors

½ oz. fresh basil leaves

a few thin slices of red or sweet onion

3 Tbs. fruity extra-virgin olive oil

1 Tbs. red wine vinegar

½ tsp. sea salt, plus more to taste

freshly ground black pepper

OPTIONAL:

cured black olives

large shavings of Parmigiano-Reggiano or thin slices of ricotta salata

Cut the tomatoes in wedges or fat slices. Small cherry tomatoes can be left whole. Tear the basil leaves into large pieces or slice them in a chiffonade. (To make a chiffonade, roll the large leaves into a tight cylinder and then cut in very thin strips.) You should have about ⅓ cup.

Combine half the basil with the tomatoes, onion slices, olive oil, vinegar, salt, and black pepper to taste, and mix very gently. Use your hands so the tomatoes do not get bruised. Arrange the salad on a platter, scatter the remaining basil over the top, and garnish with shavings of cheese or a few olives if you like.

Serves 4

In a Mixed Menu . . .
Vegetables in the Center (p. 265) is a meal for a summer evening. Tomato salad starts the party, with fresh goat cheese and perhaps some duck pâté. Grilled Ratatouille follows, paired with an option of Garlic-and-Herb-Rubbed Lamb Chops.

But I have to admit that on some hot evenings, I like the simplest meal of all: this heirloom tomato salad, a wedge of cheese, my favorite bread, and a glass of wine.

Farmers' Market Tomato Salad (p. 140)

CARROT AND CILANTRO SLAW

VEGAN

One of the most refreshing carrot salads, and so simple. Carrots, with their sweetness and slightly minty zing, are perfect with loads of cilantro and lemon juice and the surprise of whole cumin seeds. When buying carrots, look for the bunches that have their tops; those fresh-looking greens are your best guarantee of sweet, fresh-tasting carrots.

2 lbs. carrots

1 Tbs. whole cumin seeds

1 Tbs. extra-virgin olive oil

2–3 Tbs. fresh lemon juice

scant ½ tsp. sea salt

½ cup (about 2 oz.) chopped
   fresh cilantro

½ cup raisins

OPTIONAL GARNISHES:

½ cup (2 oz.) chopped walnuts

a pinch of chopped green
   serrano chile

a big spoonful of chopped mint

Peel and trim the carrots, then either grate them on the coarse side of a box grater or cut them in 3-inch pieces and feed them into the tube of a food processor fitted with a grating disk. I prefer the texture of the salad when the carrots are grated by hand on the box grater; the slightly larger pieces hold up better, and this only takes a few minutes.

Toast the whole cumin seeds in a small, dry skillet, stirring them over medium heat until they are fragrant, only a couple of minutes. Immediately remove to a cool dish.

Toss the grated carrots in a bowl with the remaining ingredients, mixing everything together very thoroughly, then let the salad rest for an hour or so as the flavors marry and the raisins plump up. I like the salad with finely chopped walnuts mixed in, but any of the optional garnishes are tasty.

Serves 8 as a side salad

Everyday Matchmaking . . .
Combine this salad with a chewy grain, such as Farro and Black Rice Pilaf (p. 212), for an easy vegan meal, or serve it with roasted poultry in an omnivore meal; it's crunchy, sweet, and lemony, an ideal companion to richer or milder dishes.

WATERMELON AND CUCUMBER SALAD

WITH LIME VINAIGRETTE, PICKLED RED ONIONS, AND FETA CHEESE

VEGAN OR VEGETARIAN

I remember the first time I ate this salad. It was a hot evening, and I was sitting outside with a couple of friends. I thought, I want another bowl . . . *I want another bowl every evening for the rest of the summer.* How cool and refreshing it was, how lively and flavorful with its combination of sweet, salty, tart, and herbal notes.

FOR THE SALAD:

1½ lbs. salad cucumbers

1 tsp. sea salt, plus more to taste

½ red onion

¼ cup red wine vinegar

1 Tbs. agave nectar

4–5 lbs. chilled watermelon, to yield 2 lbs. trimmed

2 cups yellow and red cherry tomatoes

1 medium fennel bulb

½ cup fresh mint leaves cut in strips

½ cup green fennel tops torn into small fronds

about ⅓ cup lime vinaigrette (recipe follows), plus more to taste

Peel the cucumbers and taste their ends for bitterness, trimming them down as needed. Cut them in quarters lengthwise and trim out the seeds. Cut the long pieces into 1-inch-long sticks. You should have just shy of 3 cups cut-up cukes. Add ½ teaspoon salt, toss well, and leave the cucumbers in a colander over a bowl in the refrigerator to drain for at least 30 minutes and up to 2 hours.

Thinly slice the red onion. In a small stainless steel pot, combine the wine vinegar, ¼ cup water, the agave nectar, and a big pinch of salt. Heat the liquid until it simmers, add the onion, and stir over medium-high heat for 60 seconds as the slices soften. Remove the pot from the heat, let everything cool slightly, then refrigerate for 20 minutes or so.

Cut the watermelon in ¾-inch slices, trim off and discard the rind, and cut the slices into ¾-inch cubes. You should have 6 cups of cut-up watermelon. Trim the stems from the cherry tomatoes, cut them in half with a serrated knife, and toss them with ½ teaspoon sea salt.

Trim, quarter, and shave the fennel bulb, using a mandoline if possible. You want paper-thin, flexible, almost translucent slices. Drain the pickled onions through a sieve.

In a large, shallow salad bowl, combine the drained cucumbers, cherry tomatoes, watermelon, shaved fennel, pickled onions, mint leaves, and fennel tops. Whisk together all the ingredients for the lime vinaigrette

recipe continues

FOR THE LIME VINAIGRETTE:

¼ cup fresh lime juice

½ tsp. finely grated lime zest

¼ cup extra-virgin olive oil

1 Tbs. agave nectar

¼ tsp. sea salt

plenty of freshly ground black
  pepper

OPTIONAL GARNISH:

4 oz. crumbled feta cheese,
  shaved ricotta salata, or mild
  blue cheese

until you have a smooth sauce, and drizzle 5 to 6 tablespoons of it over the salad. Use your hands to lift and turn the salad very gently until everything is mixed and evenly coated. Taste, and add more vinaigrette or more salt if needed. At this point the salad is ready to serve, but it benefits from 20 minutes or so in the refrigerator for everything to regain its chill.

Cheese can be scattered over the top of the salad or simply passed in a bowl at the table.

Serves 6 as a first course

Pairings . . .

This juicy salad seems the perfect starter for any grain-based meal. Have it with Barlotto with Braised Greens, Currants, and Pine Nuts (p. 205) or any tabbouleh variation (pp. 116–17)

Watermelon and Cucumber
Salad *with lime vinaigrette,
pickled red onions, and feta
cheese* (p. 143)

TATSOI AND RADICCHIO SALAD

WITH FRESH CRANBERRY VINAIGRETTE

VEGAN

Flavorful and firm-textured greens match up with sweet-tart cranberry dressing for a tasty winter salad. When I looked at my original notes, I saw in the margin "Make a lot of this, it goes fast."

Tatsoi is a dark Asian green with a white stem; the leaves resemble small chard leaves, but the head they form is flat and open, a large rosette. Tatsoi is available in Asian markets most of the year and in my farmers' market from early spring through late fall.

½ lb. baby tatsoi

5 oz. radicchio (1 medium head)

4 oz. wild arugula

⅓ cup coarsely chopped pecans

1 medium Fuji apple or Asian pear, cored and diced

¼ cup Fresh Cranberry Vinaigrette (p. 90)

sea salt to taste

Wash the greens and spin them dry in a salad spinner. If the tatsoi leaves are tiny, leave them alone; if larger, cut them into 1-inch strips. Quarter and slice the radicchio, and cut the arugula into bite-sized pieces.

Toss together all the ingredients and taste. Correct the seasoning with a pinch of salt if needed.

Serves 4 to 6

Other Ways . . .
To go fancy, substitute lightly caramelized pecans for the plain ones. This salad would also be good with roasted squash pieces in it.

In a Mixed Menu . . .
Pilaf and Friends (p. 217): This intriguing salad is the opening act for Red Quinoa and Pumpkin-Seed Pilaf, with Citrus-Glazed Roasted Root Vegetables, in a meal that could expand to include pork tenderloin medallions.

WATERCRESS AND CHICORY
WITH PUMPKIN SEEDS

VEGAN

Pumpkin-seed oil has a rich, nutty flavor, and apple balsamic vinegar is the most subtle and gentle of vinegars. Both are marvelous with the peppery watercress and bitter greens, but feel free to substitute a good extra-virgin olive oil and a delicate sherry vinegar if that is what's available in the cupboard.

3 cups torn fresh watercress

1 large head red radicchio

3 medium Belgian endives

1½ Tbs. pumpkin-seed oil

3–4 tsp. apple balsamic vinegar

sea salt

freshly ground black pepper

3 Tbs. toasted, salted pumpkin seeds

Wash the watercress thoroughly, as it can be muddy, and remove thick stems, then tear it into pieces. Wash and tear the radicchio, and slice the endives crosswise. Spin all the salad greens to remove excess water, or dry them by rolling them up in a kitchen towel.

Toss the salad with the pumpkin-seed oil until all leaves are glistening. Add the vinegar and salt and pepper to taste and toss again, then sprinkle on the pumpkin seeds.

Serves 6 to 8 as a side salad

Variation . . . Chicory and Kale with Agave Vinaigrette

Earthy kale takes the place of peppery watercress in this version with agave vinaigrette.

1 bunch curly kale (8 oz.)

1 head radicchio (4–5 oz.)

3 cups torn hearts of curly endive (3 oz.)

4–6 Tbs. Agave Lemon Vinaigrette (p. 92)

Strip the kale from its stems, tear it into bite-sized pieces, wash it, and spin it dry in a salad spinner. Cut the radicchio into quarters and then slice it crosswise in ¼-inch strips. Toss everything together and add as much of the dressing as you like.

In a Mixed Menu . . .
This is the bright, leafy salad that so many winter meals need, ideal with a pasta or polenta. And see A Soup Supper for All of Us (p. 166), where it is paired with Easy Fish Soup in a lovely, uncomplicated little dinner party.

Parsley and Radish Salad (p. 149)

PARSLEY AND RADISH SALAD

VEGETARIAN

Invigorating and refreshing, this is an ideal winter salad: great handfuls of dark green flat-leaf parsley, sliced radishes and celery for crunch, radicchio for color, salty capers, and a few dried cherries and walnuts. If you don't have daikon radish, use French breakfast radishes, or any fairly mild radishes that are available.

⅓ cup (1½ oz.) dried tart cherries or cranberries

8 oz. fresh flat-leaf parsley

1 head radicchio (5–6 oz.)

1 cup thinly sliced daikon radish (4 oz.)

1¼ cups thinly sliced celery (5–6 oz.)

2 Tbs. capers, salt-packed if you can get them

½ cup (2 oz.) coarsely chopped walnuts

½ tsp. sea salt, plus more to taste

2 Tbs. extra-virgin olive oil

2 Tbs. fresh lemon juice, plus more to taste

1 Tbs. agave nectar

freshly ground black pepper to taste

OPTIONAL:

3 oz. Jarlsberg or aged Gouda cheese, coarsely grated or cut in small dice

Pour about ½ cup of boiling water over the dried cherries or cranberries and leave them to soak for about 30 minutes. Take the parsley leaves off the large stems; small sprigs of 3 leaves are fine. You should have 5 to 6 cups. Wash the parsley well and spin it in a salad spinner. Wash the radicchio, quarter it lengthwise and core it, and cut the quarters in ½-inch strips.

Toss together the parsley, radicchio, sliced radish and celery, capers, and walnuts. Drain the fruit, and add it to the salad. Shortly before serving, sprinkle the salad with the sea salt and toss gently. Then add the olive oil, lemon juice, and agave, and toss again. Taste, add more lemon juice or salt if you like, and grind on some black pepper.

Grated or finely diced cheese can be added now and tossed with the whole salad, or it can be passed at the table as a garnish.

Serves 6 to 8 as an appetizer or side salad

In a Mixed Menu . . .
Let's Have a Pie (p. 246): This terrific salad is paired with a hearty Kabocha Squash and Kale Galette, the savory vegan pie that can be made an omnivore pie at the drop of a smoked sausage.

YAM SALAD WITH CUMIN AND MINT

VEGAN

This irresistible potato salad is made with Japanese yams, which have purple skins and are pure white inside. (Use sweet potatoes if you can't get Japanese yams.) Take it on a picnic, or serve it as an opener for a dinner party, piled on lightly dressed watercress or mizuna. Yams are perfectly set off by peppery or bitter greens. And see the amazing variation below, with Moroccan salt-preserved lemon.

2½–3 lbs. Japanese yams (4 medium yams)

4 Tbs. extra-virgin olive oil

¾ tsp. sea salt, plus more to taste

1 medium yellow onion, quartered and thinly sliced

2 Tbs. sherry vinegar

1 Tbs. lightly toasted cumin seeds

freshly ground black pepper

2–3 Tbs. slivered fresh mint leaves or chopped fresh cilantro

Preheat the oven to 375°. Scrub the yams, rub them with a little olive oil and salt, and roast them for 45 minutes to an hour, depending on how thick they are. They should give a little when pressed with a spoon and be easy to pierce with a fork—tender but not mushy.

Let the yams cool slightly, then peel them; the skins should pull off easily. Cut them in thick slices and cut large slices in halves or in quarters. Sprinkle the yams with ½ teaspoon sea salt and mix very gently.

While the yams are roasting, heat 1 tablespoon olive oil in a nonstick pan, add the onions and a big pinch of salt, and toss over high heat for 7 to 8 minutes, until the onions are limp and speckled with brown spots. Add 1 tablespoon sherry vinegar, toss as it steams away, add the cumin seeds, toss again, then remove the onions from the heat.

Add the seared onions to the yams, along with the remaining 3 tablespoons olive oil and 1 tablespoon vinegar. Grind in some black pepper and gently mix it all together. Your clean hands are best for this job—you want potato salad, not mashed potatoes. Taste for salt.

This salad is good warm, cool, or chilled. Pile it on a platter, alone or on a bed of peppery greens, and sprinkle the slivered mint leaves or chopped cilantro over the top.

Serves 6 to 8 as a side salad or part of a buffet

Another Way . . . Moroccan Yam Salad with Preserved Lemon
Make it a Moroccan salad by adding a tablespoon of finely diced salt-preserved lemon, a few marinated green olives, pitted and sliced, and a heaping tablespoon of grated fresh ginger. Use lemon juice instead of vinegar for this version.

SHAVED BRUSSELS SPROUT AND PEANUT SALAD

A drop of truffle oil and a handful of peanuts play so well together with Brussels sprouts. If you don't have good truffle oil—and be careful, because many so-called truffle oils have never seen a truffle—try a little walnut oil instead for this appealing way with sprouts.

1½ lbs. fresh Brussels sprouts

¼ cup extra-virgin olive oil

1 tsp. black truffle oil, plus more to taste

3 Tbs. fresh lemon juice, plus more to taste

½ tsp. sea salt, plus more to taste

½ Tbs. coarse-grain mustard

freshly ground black pepper

¾ cup roasted peanuts (if salted, go easy on salt in the dressing)

½ cup coarsely chopped fresh flat-leaf parsley

Trim the Brussels sprouts, pulling off any discolored leaves. Wash them well, checking for little pockets of grit. Slice the Brussel sprouts very thinly, using a mandoline, cutting them by hand with a sharp knife, or using the slicing blade of a food processor. The slices should be almost paper-thin, and you'll have about 6 cups.

In a small bowl, whisk together the olive oil, truffle oil, lemon juice, salt, and mustard. Pour the dressing over the Brussels sprouts and toss until well combined. Grind on some black pepper. Taste, and add lemon juice or salt if needed.

Shortly before serving, mix in the peanuts and the chopped parsley.

Serves 8 as a side salad

SOUP

A MEAL IN A BOWL

In my house, a bowl of soup means friendship, welcome, warmth—and nourishment, of course. A pot of soup simmering on the stove means all is well. It is no secret that I love soup; a few years ago I wrote a book about it, *Love Soup*. It's full of my enduring favorites: the green soups that became a crazy little cult, the porcini soup I make for Christmas, the barley and vegetable soup that gained fame as Pickle Soup, and about a hundred others. I learned that I could cook in a postage-stamp kitchen and still have fresh, delicious food, that soup can be a meal. And it can be a meal for *everyone*, because soup is so blessedly adaptable. It makes it easy to sit down around a convivial table with family, friends, or casual drop-in guests, whatever their eating preference.

A hearty minestrone or *pistou*, a loaf of crusty, chewy bread, and a salad—this is a meal that anyone can love, and anyone can make. Take that minestrone and add slices of sautéed Italian sausage to the bowl for your omnivore. Or garnish it with chunks of fresh farmer cheese, pesto, or croutons for the vegans and vegtarians. Make each bowl to order. My Easy Fish Soup works the same way, designed for flexibility from the ground up. It starts as a hearty vegetable soup; the fish is added at the last moment, so the soup can be served in different versions at the same meal with no trouble at all.

This chapter begins with an assortment of these robust entries, the soups that want to be everything to you. Each of these satisfying soups begins as a vegan bowl, and each can be elaborated for the hungry omnivore. They are followed by a quartet of what I think of as companion soups, lighter soups that can begin a dinner party in just the right way, or make a perfect pairing with a good salad or a wedge of savory galette for the simplest lunch.

Soups aim to please—and they succeed! So start a pot of soup and make your table a happier place.

A MEAL IN A BOWL

My Best Tortilla Soup (p. 157), served
with *tostaditos*, fried panella cheese,
roast chicken, and Salsa Roja (p. 74)

MY BEST TORTILLA SOUP
WITH BLACK BEANS AND AVOCADOS

VEGAN, VEGETARIAN, OR OMNIVORE

Every ingredient is distinct in this savory broth—seared onions, toasted panella cheese, pieces of tomato, slices of avocado . . . and of course those crisp *tostaditos*, the fried tortilla strips. But that broth . . . I've been making tortilla soup for years, always tinkering with the broth. One day, cooking black beans, I tasted the liquid— Eureka! I combined my simple vegetable broth with a few cups of black bean broth, infused it with chiles, added seared onions and garlicky tomatoes, and there it was—the perfect soup base, aromatic, flavorful, mysterious.

1 recipe Super-Simple Vegetable Broth (recipe follows)

1 dried ancho chile, stemmed and seeded

1 dried chile de árbol, stemmed and seeded

1 cup dried black beans

4–5 fresh epazote leaves or 1 Tbs. crumbled dried epazote

10 cloves garlic, 4 of them sliced

2 tsp. sea salt, plus more to taste

3 Tbs. extra-virgin olive oil, plus more for brushing the *tostaditos*

2 large onions (1¼ lbs.), quartered and sliced

1 Tbs. wine vinegar

1½ lbs. ripe red tomatoes, peeled and cut up (2½ cups)

12 corn tortillas

12 oz. panella cheese

2 firm-ripe avocados

6–8 oz. roasted chicken, torn or cut in strips

If you are making vegetable broth, add the ancho and chile de árbol pods to the pot. These chiles are not very spicy, but they add lovely warmth and flavor. If your broth is already made, simmer it with the chiles for 20 minutes, then strain.

Combine the black beans in a pot with the epazote leaves, the 6 whole cloves garlic, and enough water to cover the beans by at least 2 inches. Bring to a boil, then lower the heat and simmer, covered, until the beans are tender, usually an hour or a little more. Add 1 teaspoon salt and simmer another 20 minutes. Strain the beans out of the broth and discard the epazote leaves. Taste the broth and add salt if needed, or dilute it with a bit of water if it has become too concentrated. You should have about 3 cups of dark, savory broth. Add the bean broth to the vegetable broth, along with half the beans.

Heat 1½ tablespoons olive oil in a large nonstick pan and sauté the sliced onions on high heat with ½ teaspoon salt, stirring frequently, for 5 to 6 minutes, until they are limp and speckled with brown spots. Turn down the heat, cover the pan, and stir the onions occasionally for another 5 minutes. Add the wine vinegar, stir quickly as it cooks away, then turn off the heat and add the onions to the broth. In the same pan, heat the remaining 1½ tablespoons olive oil over medium heat and add the sliced garlic. Stir it for a minute, just until it loses its raw edge, then add the tomatoes and ½ teaspoon salt. Simmer the tomatoes with the garlic for 5 minutes, and add them to the soup.

Preheat the oven to 400°. Prepare the *tostaditos*, the crisp tortilla chips that are essential to this soup: brush the tortillas with olive oil on both

recipe continues

about 1 cup of your favorite spicy chile salsa

1 bunch fresh cilantro, roughly chopped

lime wedges

sides, sprinkle them with salt, then stack them and cut them in strips ½-inch wide and 2 inches long. Spread the strips out on a couple of large baking sheets and bake them for 10 to 12 minutes, until they turn a deeper shade of gold. Slide them onto paper towels to cool; they will crisp up as they cool.

Not long before serving, cut the panella cheese in ½-inch-thick slices. Heat a large nonstick pan and arrange the cheese slices in it so that they are not touching. Brown the slices over medium heat for 2 or 3 minutes—lift an edge with a spatula to check for the golden brown color—then turn them and brown the other side for about 2 minutes. Cut the cheese slices in ½-inch strips and put them in a serving bowl.

Just before serving, peel and slice the avocados. To serve the soup, put the tortilla chips, toasted cheese slices, roasted chicken, sliced avocados, salsa, cilantro, lime wedges, and the remaining black beans into individual serving bowls and arrange them on a tray or in the middle of your table. The cheese, chicken, and black beans are better warm, but don't fret if they are at room temperature. Bring the soup up to a gentle boil—it needs to be very hot—and ladle it into warm bowls. Let everyone at the table take it from there.

Serves 6 to 8

Easier Ways . . .
Yes, you can buy the tortilla strips, but get good restaurant-style chips made from real tortillas. And in the winter feel free to use top-quality canned tomatoes, but nothing with herbs and spices. You're in charge of the seasoning here, not someone else.

Don't cheat on the broth; that simple vegetable broth really is simple. And don't even think about canned beans, as that would defeat the purpose; the beans are a by-product of the wonderful broth you are making.

An Easy Mixed Menu . . .
This soup is always a flexible menu, because it's finished at the table. The various elements are lined up, the steaming broth is poured, and everyone makes their marvelous bowls, vegan, vegetarian, or omnivore. So it makes sense to keep the rest of the meal simple—a refreshing salad, and a dessert with a touch of fruit, like coconut rice pudding with mangoes.

SUPER-SIMPLE VEGETABLE BROTH

VEGAN

This easy broth, made with five common vegetables and three herbs, is an excellent base for many soups. Elaborate with other vegetables if you have them on hand, but this basic version works, and I hope it gives every home cook the confidence to keep good homemade broth ready.

6 medium carrots (10 oz.)

1 large onion (8 oz.)

3 stalks celery (6 oz.)

1 medium leek (6 oz.), white and green parts

2–3 small potatoes (8 oz.)

½ cup (1 oz.) coarsely chopped fresh flat-leaf parsley

2 tsp. fresh thyme leaves or 1 tsp. dried thyme

1 bay leaf

1 tsp. sea salt, plus more to taste

1 tsp. black peppercorns

Peel the carrots and onion, wash the celery, trim and thoroughly wash the leek, and scrub the potatoes but do not peel them. Cut up all the vegetables roughly except the potatoes—leave those whole. Combine all the ingredients in a soup pot with 2 quarts water.

Bring the water to a boil, lower the heat, and allow the broth to simmer for 50 minutes to an hour. Strain the broth through a colander, then once more through a fine sieve.

If the broth tastes weak, simmer it in an uncovered pot for another 20 minutes or so, or until reduced to a concentration you prefer.

You should have 6 to 7 cups of delicate, savory broth

Tomato Soup with
Chickpeas and Moroccan
Spices (p. 161), served with
Spicy Lamb Meatballs (p. 370)

TOMATO SOUP WITH CHICKPEAS AND MOROCCAN SPICES

VEGAN

This robust and slightly exotic tomato soup is one of those discoveries that came as a result of leftovers in the fridge. A container of cooked garbanzo beans in their garlic-scented broth was beckoning to me. I combined the beans with ripe summer tomatoes and just enough garlic, cumin, and cinnamon to evoke a Moroccan flavor.

1 cup dried garbanzo beans (chickpeas)

12 cloves garlic

1 dried chile de árbol

1 bay leaf

1 carrot, cut in 3 pieces

2 tsp. sea salt, plus more to taste

3½–4 lbs. ripe tomatoes

4 Tbs. extra-virgin olive oil, plus more for garnish

⅓ cup coarsely chopped fresh basil

2 large red onions (1 lb.)

2 cups vegetable broth

¼ cup short- or medium-grain white rice

2 Tbs. chopped fresh mint leaves

¼ tsp. ground cinnamon

1 tsp. lightly toasted cumin seeds

1 Tbs. fresh lemon juice, plus more to taste

In a soup pot, combine the garbanzo beans, 2½ quarts water, 6 peeled garlic cloves, and the chile de árbol, bay leaf, and carrot. Bring the water to a boil and skim off the foam that collects on top. After 2 minutes, lower the heat and allow the beans to simmer gently, partly covered, until they are tender, anywhere from 1 to 2½ hours, depending on the age of the beans. Add ¾ teaspoon salt and simmer another 10 minutes. Taste a bean, taste the broth, and add a pinch more salt if it is needed.

Drain the beans through a colander, saving all the liquid. Discard the chile pod, bay leaf, and carrot. Measure the broth; you need about 6 cups. If you're a little short, add water to make it up. Measure out 2 cups of beans, and reserve the rest for another use.

Peel the tomatoes: Cut a cross in the bottom of each one with a sharp knife and drop them into boiling water for 45 to 60 seconds. Transfer the tomatoes to a bowl of cold water, then take them out, slip off their skins, and trim out the stem ends. Coarsely chop the tomatoes, saving the juice. You should have about 6 cups of tomatoes with the juice.

Chop the remaining 6 cloves garlic. Heat 2 tablespoons olive oil in a large sauté pan, add the chopped garlic, and stir it over medium-high heat for about a minute, until it just begins to color. Add the diced tomatoes with their liquid and 1 teaspoon of salt. Simmer the tomatoes 20 minutes, until their color darkens and the juice is somewhat reduced. Stir in the basil.

Peel the red onions, cut them in half, and slice them. In a medium nonstick pan, heat the remaining 2 tablespoons olive oil and add the sliced onions and ¼ teaspoon salt. Toss the onions over high heat for about 10 minutes, until they are limp and showing brown spots. Turn the heat down, cover the pan, and cook the onions slowly another 15 minutes, stirring occasionally. They should be tender and brown.

recipe continues

Heat the vegetable broth in a soup pot and simmer the rice in it for 15 minutes. Add the cooked tomatoes and the caramelized red onions and simmer 5 minutes. Add the 2 cups garbanzo beans and the bean broth to the soup, along with the chopped mint leaves, cinnamon, toasted cumin seeds, and lemon juice. Simmer the soup for another 5 minutes, then taste. Add a pinch more salt or a little more lemon juice if needed.

Drizzle a little extra-virgin olive oil on top of each serving.

Serves 8

An Omnivore Meal . . .
Mint, cinnamon, cumin, garbanzo beans—all the things that give this tomato soup its special flavor evoke Middle Eastern foods, and if you want to add meat to individual servings, you can't do better than the tiny Spicy Lamb Meatballs (p. 370), which also use mint as an aromatic.

EASY FISH SOUP
FROM EASY VEGETABLE SOUP

VEGAN, VEGETARIAN, OR OMNIVORE

This is the easiest fish soup or stew I know. It begins as an easy vegetable soup; five minutes before serving, you add the fish. The result is a fresh and lively flavor. And because it is not based on a fish stock, it is an ideal dish for flexible eating. You can remove some of the vegetable soup into another pot for the vegans and vegetarians at the table, and serve that with a toasted cheese crouton, or a big spoonful of cooked cannellini stirred into the vegetables, or straight up. See the menu that follows, A Soup Supper for All of Us (p. 166).

Use the fish that look best at the market that day, and mix several kinds. I've had good results with cod, halibut, sea bass, red snapper (watch for bones), monkfish, scallops, prawns, clams . . .

3–4 stalks celery (8 oz.), sliced

1 lb. small potatoes, cut in wedges or diced

4–5 medium carrots (12 oz.), sliced

3 cups peeled tomatoes, cut up (canned are okay)

2 fennel bulbs (12 oz.), quartered and sliced

1 large red bell pepper (5 oz.), quartered and thinly sliced

2 bay leaves

2 tsp. dried tarragon or 1 Tbs. fresh tarragon

2–3 tsp. chopped or fresh thyme

6 cups light vegetable broth

1 tsp. sea salt, plus more to taste

freshly ground black pepper

¾ cup (1½ oz.) fresh flat-leaf parsley leaves

Combine the first 6 vegetables in a large pot with 5 cups water, the bay leaves, tarragon, thyme, vegetable broth, salt, and pepper to taste. Simmer for 30 minutes, or until the vegetables are just tender, and add the fresh parsley.

Meanwhile, heat 2 tablespoons olive oil in a large nonstick pan and sauté the onions in it over medium heat for 10 minutes, until they are limp and beginning to color. Add the leeks and continue sautéing over medium heat for 8 to 10 minutes, stirring often, until everything is soft and golden. Push the onions and leeks to the edges of the pan, add the remaining 1 tablespoon olive oil in the middle, and when it is hot add the garlic and sizzle it for about a minute. Add this mixture to the soup, deglazing the pan with a bit of the broth. Add the white wine, bring the soup back to a simmer for 10 minutes, taste, and correct the seasoning with salt and pepper if needed, and crushed red chiles if you like.

Trim your fish if it needs trimming, and cut fillets into cubes or slices. Wash shellfish thoroughly. Do not peel shrimp.

No more than 5 minutes before you want to serve the soup, bring it back to a simmer, remove and discard the bay leaves, and add the fish—denser fish first, more delicate fish last. Simmer only until the fish is opaque and

recipe continues

3 Tbs. extra-virgin olive oil

2 large onions, quartered and sliced

1 large leek (5 oz.), white part only, sliced

6–7 cloves garlic, chopped

1 cup dry white wine, plus more to taste

about 3 lbs. assorted fish and shellfish

OPTIONAL:

crushed red chiles

croutons

GARNISH:

extra-virgin olive oil

flaking and the shrimp are pink, 3 to 5 minutes. Serve the soup at once, in large bowls, and drizzle olive oil on top of each serving. Add croutons if you like, or have plenty of fresh sourdough bread or garlic toast for dipping.

Serves 8 to 10 as a meal

A Practical Note . . .

This recipe is scaled for a dinner party, enough for 8 to 10. If you are 4 or 5 at the table and planning on leftovers, add half the amount of fish to half the vegetable soup, and repeat this on another night for fresh-tasting soup.

Another Way . . . with a Cheese Crouton

The hearty vegan vegetable soup that is the base for my fish soup is delicious on its own, but can also be dressed up with a cheese crouton for the vegetarians at the table. For each crouton: brush a thick slice of baguette with olive oil and toast it in a hot pan, a couple of minutes on each side, until it has golden brown edges. (This can be done in advance.) Top each crouton with a heaping spoonful of shredded Gruyere or a thick smear of fresh goat cheese, and toast under the broiler just until the cheese is hot and melty, 1 or 2 minutes. Drop a crouton on top of a generous bowl of vegetable soup, and serve.

Easy Fish Soup *from Easy Vegetable Soup*
(p. 163)

A SOUP SUPPER
FOR ALL OF US

My easy fish soup is a crowd-pleasing meal, and because it begins as a delicious vegetable soup, and the fish is added at the last minute, it adapts perfectly for vegetarians and vegans. I realized this in an unplanned moment when I told my dinner guests, as we were sitting down, that the menu featured fish soup. One of my friends apologetically told me that she was allergic to fish, then hastened to assure me she'd be fine with the appetizers. I stopped her. No fish? No problem. I served her a big bowl of the savory vegetarian soup with a toasty cheese crouton floating in it, then added fish to the pot for my other guests. Awkwardness vanished, deliciousness prevailed, and we all ate the same meal—in variations.

Soups are so adept this way, shifting style as they take on ingredients. My Best Tortilla Soup is another choice for a meal in a bowl—each bowl is assembled to taste at the table. Any hearty minestrone is equally flexible—I'll have mine straight up, you drop some crispy pancetta in yours, all good.

These are big soups; they carry the meal. My fish soup is almost a stew, so you don't need much with it. That fresh, zesty salad of watercress and chicory is a perfect foil. But any lighter salad will work with this soup; try Parsley and Radish Salad in the winter, or a simple Farmers' Market Tomato Salad in the summer—because this is a soup for all seasons. And in any season you can start with an appetizer of crostini with a savory bean spread—it's a tasty way to begin, and a protein-rich boon for the vegans at the table. Everyone is happy.

A Practical Note . . .
The vegan meal here begins with cannellini and garlic spread with crostini, goes on to watercress and chicory salad, a big bowl of vegetable soup, and lemon sorbet for dessert.

SOUP SUPPER MENU

FOR 6 TO 8

Crostini with
Cannellini and Garlic Spread

Watercress and Chicory *with pumpkin seeds*

Easy Fish Soup
from Easy Vegetable Soup

Lemon Sorbet

OLD-FASHIONED WINTER MINESTRONE

VEGAN

This comforting winter soup is the quintessential meal in a bowl. Root vegetables, winter squash, and kale are cooked quickly, to remain distinct, then added to slowly simmered white beans, garlic, and herbs for a beautiful flavor combination. And like any minestrone worth its name, it can be elaborated with garnishes—crusty garlic croutons, a spoonful of cooked farro, or shavings of Parmigiano-Reggiano to taste.

1 cup (6½ oz.) dried cannellini beans

5 fresh or dried sage leaves

5–6 cloves garlic

2½ tsp. sea salt, plus more to taste

2 Tbs. extra-virgin olive oil, plus more for garnish

1 large yellow onion (10 oz.), coarsely chopped

1 small kabocha squash (1½ lb.)

1 small bunch Tuscan kale (7–8 oz.)

1 medium leek (4 oz.), white part only, sliced

2 small turnips (6 oz.), peeled and diced

2 large stalks celery (5 oz.), sliced

2 carrots (5 oz.), peeled and sliced

3½ cups vegetable broth

crushed red chiles

Rinse the cannellini and put them in a large pot with 2 quarts water, the sage leaves, and the garlic cloves. Bring the water to a boil, lower the heat, cover, and simmer the beans gently for an hour, longer if needed, until they are tender. Add 2 teaspoons salt to the water.

While the beans are cooking, heat the olive oil in a nonstick pan and sauté the onions over high heat with a generous pinch of salt, until they begin to color, 6 to 7 minutes. Turn the heat to low, cover the pan, and allow the onions to cook slowly, stirring occasionally, until they are soft and caramel-colored, at least another 20 minutes. Add the onions to the cooked beans.

Wash the kabocha squash, cut it in half, and scrape out the seeds. Cut each half into thick slices and cut the slices into 1-inch dice. (Kabocha squash does not have to be peeled.) Rinse the kale, trim out the hard ribs, and slice the kale or cut it into 2-inch pieces.

In a large soup pot, combine the diced squash, kale, leek, turnips, celery, and carrots. Add 2½ cups water, the vegetable broth, and the remaining ½ teaspoon salt. Bring the liquid to a boil, lower the heat, and cook the vegetables for 12 minutes, until all are just tender.

Add the cooked beans with all their broth to the vegetables, as well as a pinch of crushed red chiles, the parsley, and the oregano. Simmer everything together for 6 or 7 minutes to marry the flavors. Add the lemon juice and some freshly ground black pepper and taste. Correct the seasoning with more salt, pepper, and lemon juice as needed.

½ cup coarsely chopped fresh flat-leaf parsley

1 Tbs. chopped fresh oregano or 1 tsp. dried oregano

2 Tbs. fresh lemon juice, plus more to taste

freshly ground black pepper

OPTIONAL GARNISH:

basil or parsley pesto

Drizzle olive oil over each serving, or garnish with a spoonful of basil or parsley pesto.

Serves 8

The Omnivore Way . . .

For your meat-eating friends, add slices of sautéed Italian sausage, either a traditional sausage or a lower-fat turkey sausage. And if sausage isn't your thing, Mint-Scented Pork and Pine Nut Meatballs (p. 363) would be a fine match for this wintry potage.

ASIAN-STYLE NOODLE BOWL

<u>VEGAN</u>

Noodle shops in Asian countries or neighborhoods all over the world make an art of these bowls, with endless combinations of ingredients. Here is a simplified version for your kitchen: thick udon noodles coiled in a nest of tender-crisp vegetables, all submerged in a steaming, fragrant broth.

The broth is infused with ginger, lemongrass, and kombu, a sea vegetable that gives many Asian soups their characteristic flavor; it can be found in any Asian market as well as in many supermarkets. Once you have made this noodle bowl part of your repertoire, you may want to vary the vegetables; try edamame, baby bok choy, broccolini, cubes of sweet squash, sliced turnips . . . just keep in mind the idea of contrasting colors and flavors.

10 cups Super-Simple Vegetable Broth (p. 159; 1½ recipes)

1½ oz. dried shiitake mushrooms

2 stalks lemongrass

4 oz. fresh ginger, peeled and sliced

1½ cups coarsely chopped fresh cilantro, with stems

two 6-inch strips dried kombu

2 tsp. tamari or soy sauce, plus more for serving

1 tsp. rice vinegar

sea salt

12 oz. Napa or savoy cabbage (½ large head)

12 oz. yams (2 medium)

8 oz. snow peas (about 2 cups)

8 oz. slender carrots (about 8), different colors if available

4 oz. green onions (1 bunch), white and green parts

1 lb. Japanese-style udon noodles or soba noodles

Heat the vegetable broth in an ample soup pot (6 quarts) and add 3 cups water. Give the dried shiitakes a quick rinse to remove any dust. Peel the lemongrass down to the pale green part and trim away the dry tops of the stalks. Thinly slice the tender part of the stalks.

Add the shiitakes, lemongrass, 3 ounces of the sliced ginger, and the chopped cilantro to the diluted vegetable broth and simmer, covered, for 30 minutes. Give the kombu a quick wipe with a damp cloth or paper towel and add it to the simmering broth for 1 minute (longer than this and the kombu will dominate other flavors). Remove the broth from the heat and strain it through a colander lined with 3 layers of cheesecloth. Reserve the shiitake mushrooms. Season the broth with the tamari or soy sauce and rice vinegar, taste, and add a pinch of salt if needed. It should be savory and delicious to sip, not overly salty.

Trim out the core and thick ribs from the cabbage and slice the leaves into ½-inch strips about 3 inches long. Peel the yams and cut them into ½-inch dice. Trim the snow peas if they have stem ends. Peel the carrots and slice them thinly on an angle. Trim and thinly slice the green onions. Cut the cooked shiitake mushrooms into thick strips. Slice the remaining 1 ounce ginger into matchsticks.

The fresh vegetables should remain slightly crunchy, to contrast with the soft noodles, so they should be blanched individually. To do this easily and quickly, use two medium-sized pots. Fill one about halfway with salted water and have the second one ready with a colander in it. Bring the water to a boil, drop in the yams, and let them cook over medium-high heat for about 3½ minutes, until tender-crisp. Drain them

OPTIONAL:

6–8 oz. firm tofu

GARNISHES:

sambal oelek (chile paste) or hot
  sauce

tamari or soy sauce

through the colander, catching the hot water in the second pot. Bring the water back to a boil—a matter of seconds—and drop in the carrot slices. Continue going back and forth between pots, cooking the carrots for 1 to 1½ minutes, the cabbage for 1½ minutes, and the snow peas for 20 seconds. Arrange the blanched vegetables on a platter as they are ready, and keep them slightly warm if possible.

Have your table set and your generous bowls ready. (Treat this as a pasta dish, not a soup that simmers patiently on the stove.) Add water to the vegetable cooking liquid to bring it up to about 6 quarts, bring it back to a boil, and cook the udon noodles according to package directions, probably about 8 to 10 minutes. While the noodles are cooking, add the matchsticks of ginger and the sliced green onions to the prepared broth and bring the broth to a simmer.

In each soup bowl, arrange a heaping tablespoon of cabbage, the same of yams, 8 to 10 snow peas, a few carrot slices, and a few shiitake slices, alternating colors.

As soon as the noodles are tender, drain them and give them a quick rinse with tap water. Using a pasta fork, drop a serving of noodles in the center of each bowl. Ladle the simmering broth over the noodles and vegetables—about 1½ cups into each bowl—and serve at once. Pass tamari or soy sauce and sambal oelek at the table for additional seasoning.

Serves 6 to 8

Omnivore Ideas . . .
It's a noodle bowl, so anything goes. Add shreds of cooked pork or chicken or a few quickly seared scallops, customizing individual bowls.

Noodle Bowl Two Ways . . .
If you want to make this soup in two prepared versions for one meal, you can divide the broth and add thin strips of beef to one batch. Simmer the beef in the broth for a minute or two only, then continue as in the recipe, assembling the two soups with all their vegetables and the udon noodles.

SMOKY SPLIT PEA SOUP
WITH GARNISHES

VEGAN

I loved my recipe for split pea soup. Then my old friend Roger Ebert asked me to contribute a soup for his book, *The Pot and How to Use It*. The thesis of this hilarious little book is that the only pot you'll ever need is a rice cooker. I told him this was ridiculous, but Roger was a dear friend and I wanted to make him happy, so I adapted my pea soup for his Pot. In adapting, I couldn't help tweaking—I caramelized the onion, added a touch of smoky pimentón and a little parsley, and there it was: a new, improved pea soup. I make it the sensible, conventional stovetop way, of course, and I love it.

1 lb. green split peas, rinsed

1 bay leaf

2 tsp. chopped fresh thyme or 1 tsp. dried thyme

¼ tsp. spicy smoked paprika, such as pimentón de la Vera

1½ tsp. sea salt, plus more to taste

¼ cup finely chopped fresh flat-leaf parsley

2 cups light vegetable broth

2 Tbs. extra-virgin olive oil

1 large yellow onion (10 oz.), chopped

3 stalks celery (6 oz.), chopped

3–4 carrots (6–8 oz.), chopped

freshly ground black pepper

OPTIONAL GARNISHES:

garlic croutons

crumbled cheddar cheese

crispy pancetta

diced ham

sausage coins

In an ample soup pot, combine the split peas, 2 quarts water, and the bay leaf, thyme, and smoked paprika. Bring the water to a boil and cook briskly over medium-high heat for 20 minutes. Lower the heat, add 1¼ teaspoons salt, the parsley, and the vegetable broth, and simmer, covered, for 40 to 45 minutes. The peas should be completely soft.

Meanwhile, heat the oil in a sauté pan, add the onion with ¼ teaspoon salt, and stir occasionally over medium heat for about 10 minutes. Lower the heat, cover the pan, and let the onion cook gently for another 20 minutes, until soft and amber. Add the celery and carrots and cook 15 minutes, stirring often. Add the cooked vegetables to the soup.

When the peas and vegetables are all tender, remove the bay leaf and puree the soup with an immersion blender. Make it velvety smooth. Now try a spoonful and use those taste buds. Add a few grinds of black pepper. Correct the seasoning with another pinch of salt or a little more paprika. You'll know when it's just right.

Serve the soup steaming hot, with a swirl of extra-virgin olive oil in each bowl and any garnish that appeals. To reheat, stir often, adding a drop of water or broth if needed.

Serves 6 to 8

Pea Soup for Omnivores . . .
Split pea soup seems made for garnishes, so it is the model of adaptability. Keep it vegan with crusty garlic croutons, scatter it with shreds of sharp cheddar cheese, or drop cubes of crispy sautéed pancetta, diced ham, or sausage coins on top.

COMPANION SOUPS

ROASTED RED PEPPER SOUP WITH TOMATOES

VEGAN

I first made this rosy, intensely flavored soup when the September farmers' market served up a mix of sun-ripened red and yellow peppers and some turned out to have a little heat—bonus! The soup was gorgeous, and we all loved it. But I can't start a recipe by saying, Just go to the market and *get lucky*. So I made the soup again, using sweet red peppers and adding jalapeños for heat, but carefully, so I could control the balance. Works just fine.

1 lb. yellow onions

4 Tbs. extra-virgin olive oil, plus more for garnish

1¼ tsp. sea salt, plus more as needed

3 lbs. ripe tomatoes, peeled and cored, with their juice

4 cloves garlic, chopped

2½ lbs. red bell peppers (6–7 large peppers)

4–5 fresh jalapeño peppers

3–4 cups vegetable broth

½ tsp. toasted and ground cumin seeds

OPTIONAL GARNISHES:

chopped cilantro

garlic croutons

Chop the onions and sauté them in 2 tablespoons olive oil with a pinch of salt, tossing and stirring often over high heat for about 5 minutes, or just until they show the first few flecks of color. Cover the pan, lower the heat, and cook gently for at least 45 minutes, stirring occasionally, until the onions are soft, golden brown, moist, and sweet.

While the onions cook, peel and core the tomatoes. I use the easy blanching method: cut a cross in the bottom of each tomato, drop them into boiling water for about 2 minutes, then take them out with a slotted spoon, rinse with cold water, and slip off their skins. Working over a bowl, slice out the cores and stems, then chop or puree the tomatoes. You should have about 5 cups, with all their juice.

In a large nonstick pan, sauté the garlic in 1 tablespoon olive oil over medium heat just until it releases its fragrance, about 2 minutes, then add the pureed tomatoes and 1 teaspoon salt. Lower the heat and simmer the tomatoes until they turn a rich, dark red, about 20 minutes.

Meanwhile, arrange all the peppers on a baking sheet, keeping the jalapeños in their own area, and char them in a broiler, turning them with tongs every few minutes until they are blistered all over. (See "A Word About Charring and Peeling Peppers," p. 227, for details.) Blackened areas are fine, as long as it's just the skin. Drop the charred peppers into a paper bag and let them sweat them for a few minutes, then peel off their skins; sometimes this is easier to do under cool running water. Pull out the stems and cores, and scrape or rinse out the seeds.

Chop the peppers roughly, keeping the spicy jalapeños separate from the sweet red peppers. Add all the sweet peppers and their juice to the simmering tomatoes, along with one of the jalapeños (reserving the rest), 3 cups of vegetable broth, and the golden brown onions. Simmer everything together for another 10 minutes, then stir in the cumin seeds and the remaining 1 tablespoon olive oil.

Puree the soup with an immersion blender, adding a little more vegetable broth if the soup seems too thick. Now taste the soup, correct the salt if needed, and start adding more jalapeño, about half a pepper at a time. Puree briefly after each addition and taste, adding as many of the peppers as you need to get a nice, spicy kick. Jalapeños vary tremendously in their heat level these days, so your taste buds are your guide.

Garnish each bowl of soup with a drizzle of extra-virgin olive oil and, if you like, some cilantro or a few garlic croutons.

Serves 8

In a Flexible Menu...
Let's Have a Pie (p. 246): This light soup is an excellent foil for the hearty and flexible Kabocha Squash and Kale Galette.

PARSNIP AND APPLE SOUP

VEGAN OR VEGETARIAN

A little bit savory and a little bit sweet, this is a delightful cold-weather soup and a lovely way to start a winter dinner party, rich but not heavy.

1 large yellow onion (8 oz.), chopped

2 Tbs. extra-virgin olive oil

4 oz. leek (1 medium), white part only, sliced

4 oz. hearts of celery, sliced (about 1 cup)

½ tsp. sea salt, plus more to taste

1½ lbs. parsnips (10 to 12 medium), peeled and sliced

8 oz. Yukon Gold potatoes (2 medium), peeled and diced

1 Fuji apple (5-6 oz.), cored, peeled, and sliced

4-5 cups vegetable broth

¾ tsp. ground ginger

a pinch of cayenne

2 Tbs. cider vinegar

GARNISHES:

additional olive oil

Point Reyes Blue or Roquefort cheese

chopped walnuts

In a large nonstick pan over high heat, sear the chopped onion in the olive oil for 5 minutes, tossing and stirring until it is limp and showing brown spots. Add the sliced leek, celery, and the salt, turn the heat to low, and cover the pan. Cook the vegetables, stirring occasionally, for about 30 minutes, or until tender and golden.

Combine the parsnips, potatoes, and apple in an ample soup pot with 2½ cups water and 4 cups vegetable broth and bring to a boil. Reduce the heat, add the ginger and cayenne, cover the pot, and simmer for at least 20 minutes, until the vegetables are tender. Stir the cider vinegar into the onions, then add the onion mixture to the soup, deglazing the pan with some of the broth if needed. Simmer the soup another 10 minutes, then puree it with an immersion blender or in a standing blender, in batches. If any tough, fibrous bits of parsnip are left, pass the soup through a coarse sieve. Taste, and adjust the seasoning with more sea salt if needed.

Serve the soup steaming hot, and garnish each bowl with a drizzle of olive oil, a few crumbles of blue cheese, and a scattering of walnuts on top. To keep the soup vegan, garnish with olive oil and walnuts only.

Serves 6 to 8

Omnivore Ways . . .
The gently sweet flavor this soup has from parsnips and an apple is complemented by a pungent blue cheese, or by a garnish of Dana's Bacon and Garlic Crisps (p. 372).

In a Festive Mixed Menu . . .
Cocktails on New Year's Eve (p. 32): Whether in bowls or in teacups, this soup is perfect for the heart of winter.

RED LENTIL SOUP WITH JAPANESE YAMS AND CARROTS

VEGAN

Red lentils are quick to cook, love spices, and deliver a payload of protein without seeming to try. This silky puree is easy and dresses up nicely. Creamy coconut milk, dark green cilantro, pale green pistachios—they all look beautiful on that deep gold soup.

2 cups (12 oz.) red lentils

4–5 cups vegetable broth

1 medium Japanese yam or sweet potato (10 oz.), peeled and diced

2 medium carrots (5 oz.), peeled and diced

1½ Tbs. extra-virgin olive oil, plus more for garnish

1 large onion, chopped

3 cloves garlic, chopped

2 tsp. toasted and ground cumin seeds

1 tsp. ground coriander

1 tsp. turmeric

a pinch of cayenne

1 tsp. sea salt, plus more to taste

1 Tbs. fresh lemon or lime juice, plus more to taste

OPTIONAL:

1 cup unsweetened coconut milk

GARNISHES:

chopped pistachio nuts

chopped cilantro

harissa

Rinse the lentils and put them in a soup pot with 1 quart water, 1 quart vegetable broth, the yam, and the carrots. Bring the liquid to a boil, then lower the heat and simmer about 30 minutes. Meanwhile, heat 1 tablespoon olive oil in a nonstick pan and sauté the onion with a dash of salt, stirring over medium-high heat for 3 to 4 minutes. Lower the heat and cook the onion gently for 20 minutes more, stirring occasionally, until it is golden and soft. Push the onion to the sides of the pan, add the remaining ½ tablespoon oil and the chopped garlic in the center, and stir for a minute or two. Add the onion and garlic to the soup, along with the cumin, coriander, turmeric, cayenne, and salt, and simmer everything for about 5 minutes.

Puree the soup with an immersion blender and taste it. Add salt if needed, and more vegetable broth if it seems too thick. Stir in the lemon juice. For a richer soup, stir in the coconut milk, reserving a bit to swirl into the top of the soup when it is served.

Garnish the soup with the coconut milk or a drizzle of olive oil and a scattering of chopped pistachios or a few cilantro leaves. Pass harissa at the table for those who like it hot.

Serves 6 to 8

Everyday Matchmaking . . .
Pair this golden soup with any center-of-the-plate salad for a lovely vegan meal—it's the hit of protein that can make meal planning easy. Try it with Kabocha Squash and Tuscan Kale Salad (p. 122), or a Tabbouleh variation (pp. 116–17), then expand the salad with some roast chicken for your omnivores.

WHITE GAZPACHO
WITH CUCUMBERS AND GRAPES

Here's your secret weapon for a late-summer heat wave. It's hard to explain how utterly refreshing this soup is, lemony and slightly spicy with a hint of sweetness for mystery. Is it really white? No—palest green. Is it really a gazpacho? Who knows and who cares? It's delicious and easy to make.

1½ lbs. Persian cucumbers

4–5 Tbs. fresh lemon juice

2 cloves garlic

1½ tsp. sea salt, plus more to taste

1 tsp. chopped fresh serrano chile

3 Tbs. extra-virgin olive oil, plus more for garnish

1 lb. (2½ cups) seedless green grapes

1 cup Greek-style yogurt

freshly ground black pepper to taste

GARNISHES:

chopped or sliced roasted almonds

sliced green or red grapes

Wash and trim the cucumbers, test the ends for bitterness, and slice them. (These thin-skinned cucumbers don't need to be peeled.) You should have about 4½ cups.

Put the cucumbers, 4 tablespoons lemon juice, the garlic, salt, and serrano chile into a blender and puree. Add the olive oil and the grapes and puree until smooth. Transfer the soup to a bowl and whisk in the yogurt, grind in some black pepper, and taste. Adjust the seasoning with a pinch more salt or a little more lemon juice if needed.

Chill the soup very well. I get it as cold as possible in my refrigerator, then put it in the freezer for about an hour just before serving and whisk it again before pouring it into bowls. Garnish each bowl of soup with a thin drizzle of oil and a scattering of almonds and grapes.

Serves 5 to 6

An Omnivore Way . . .
A seafood garnish could be added on top of this soup—cold cooked shrimp or crab, tossed with some olive oil, lemon, and a pinch of spicy pimentón.

And in a Flexible Summer Menu . . .
A Salad Supper for the Heat Wave (p. 104) is an al fresco supper for a summer evening that starts with this cooling soup, followed by a shredded kale salad dressed up with corn salsa and a few strips of grilled swordfish for those who want it—all so good!

White Gazpacho *with cucumbers and grapes* (p. 178)

PASTA, POLENTA, RISOTTO

PASTA, POLENTA, RISOTTO

My uncle Stefan came to America shortly after World War II and immediately did something to enhance our sprawling Polish family: he married an Italian girl. My aunt Terenia brought beauty, laughter, and an understanding of pasta that was imprinted in her DNA. She was from Bologna, a city justly famous for its food, where pasta in its myriad shapes and saucings is something like a religion; the devout go to church once a week, but they eat pasta every day.

Terenia's deft fingers flew as she wrapped tiny, perfectly shaped tortellini. The Polish family appreciated this skill—she was an instant expert at wrapping our traditonal *uszki* and pierogi. I was a child when our two families lived in the same house for a while, but something stayed with me from those times when I stood on my tiptoes to see over the edge of the kitchen table.

The pasta dishes in this chapter are straight-forward preparations. They begin with that example of brilliant simplicity, Spaghetti with Garlic and Oil. The name of the dish is almost the entire ingredient list, and once the water boils you can have this on the plate in 10 minutes. Chop fresh garlic and handfuls of flat-leaf parsley; heat the olive oil, sizzle the garlic in the pan, and toss a few crushed red chiles in. Drain the pasta, toss it in the pan with the oil and garlic, and mix the parsley in last. Done. Parmigiano optional. It's a great meal, and as a bonus your house smells like an Italian restaurant for hours. I include that simple, assertive dish because it is perfect in its minimalism, and also a perfect starting point for adaptation. Place a few stir-fried garlic prawns on top of those coils of green- and gold-speckled spaghetti, or Dana's Bacon and Garlic Crisps, or sautéed Italian sausage. The simplest pastas are nimble this way.

Most of the dishes here are ready to be the center of a meal and to expand in just that way, by plan or in the moment. A summer pasta with sweet cherry tomatoes can be garnished with flaked dry-smoked salmon. Penne with rapini and breadcrumbs can be paired with diced roast chicken or calamari.

Approachable, familiar, and loved—the easy pasta or polenta dish is your friend. But there are dishes here for special occasions, too. Polenta takes on uptown style as a torta for the Thanksgiving table, enriched with roasted squash, onions, and cheese. And Lemon Risotto with Sautéed Fresh Fava Beans is as elegant as Chanel's black dress.

The combinations are endless and rewarding. I picked something up by peeking over Terenia's kitchen table, and my son Teddy picked something up peeking over mine. He made a *penne arrabiata* his own way, starting with deeply caramelized onions, then adding garlic, hot peppers, and tomatoes. As I was eating it with him, I realized that this was his own intuitive Polish-Italian fusion.

Grazie, Terenia!

SPAGHETTI WITH GARLIC AND OIL

VEGAN

The confident simplicity of this dish is a hallmark of Italian cooking. A few strong flavors, a simple technique, a perfect result. The good cook knows when to stop. Or how to go on—because you can serve this wonderful dish of pasta on its own or make it a flexible starting point for many other dishes. Sauté some bitter greens with the garlic, or spoon blistered cherry tomatoes on top, or add crispy pancetta croutons . . .

10 cloves garlic

4 Tbs. extra-virgin olive oil

sea salt

½ tsp. crushed red chiles, plus more to taste

1 lb. spaghetti

¾ cup chopped fresh flat-leaf parsley

Put a large pot of salted water on to boil. Peel and chop the garlic. Heat half the olive oil in a very large nonstick sauté pan and sizzle the garlic in it over medium-high heat for a few seconds, then immediately turn the heat down and stir the garlic only until it begins to turn golden, perhaps another minute. Remove the pan from the heat and add a pinch of salt and the crushed red chiles.

Cook the spaghetti in the briskly boiling water until it is *al dente*, tender but still firm. Drain the pasta and add it to the garlic and oil in the pan, along with the parsley. Return the pan to medium heat as you toss the pasta with the oil, garlic, and parsley. Add the remaining 2 tablespoons

recipe continues

OPTIONAL:

grated Parmigiano-Reggiano
cheese

olive oil, remove the pasta from the heat, and serve, passing the cheese at the table for those who want it.

Serves 6 as a main dish

Variation . . . Summer Pasta with Garlic and Cherry Tomatoes

Here's a lusty evolution of the garlic-and-oil classic, sweet with summer tomatoes, pungent with olives. Instead of spaghetti, use cavatappi or fusilli, and to the ingredients above, add

4 cups mixed cherry and grape tomatoes, all colors, halved

2/3 cup coarsely chopped Kalamata olives

1/4 cup capers, drained

2 Tbs. chopped fresh marjoram

3 Tbs. extra-virgin olive oil

Sauté the garlic in a very large skillet, and about 5 minutes before the pasta is done, add the tomatoes, olives, and capers to the pan and toss over high heat for about 2 minutes. Drain the pasta when it is just short of *al dente* and add it at once to the pan, along with the parsley, marjoram, and crushed red chiles to taste. Toss together quickly and add a pinch of salt only if it is needed. Finish the pasta with the remaining 3 tablespoons olive oil and serve, passing a bowl of grated Parmigiano at the table.

Omnivore Ways . . .
A few prawns or calamari, quickly sautéed in even more garlic and dropped on top of this pasta, are perfect. Or add thin slices of spicy Italian sausage. For southern Italian flavor, use your grater for *bottarga*, the dried and pressed fish roe popular in Sicily and Sardinia; it's a strong flavor, so add a few shavings and taste before proceeding to shave more.

An Easy, Flexible Meal . . .
Serve a simple salad, and for your antipasto include smoked tuna in olive oil with any marinated bean salad.

TEDDY'S FUSION ARRABIATA

VEGAN

My son Teddy's *arrabiata* varies from the classic. It starts with a generous panful of beautifully caramelized onions. He feels that caramelized onions are the way to start most any dish, an idea he picked up from his Polish mom. It works beautifully here, setting off a generous amount of garlic and crushed red chiles.

5 Tbs. extra-virgin olive oil, plus more for drizzling

1½ lbs. onions (3 large), chopped

sea salt

1 small head garlic, peeled and finely chopped

2 cups Basic Tomato Sauce (p. 86) or a can of good-quality crushed tomatoes

1 cup chopped fresh flat-leaf parsley

⅓ cup slivered or chopped basil (green or opal)

1 Tbs. crushed red chiles, plus more to taste

1 lb. farro penne

OPTIONAL GARNISH:

large, thin shavings of Parmigiano-Reggianno cheese

Bring a big pot of salted water to a boil. Heat 3 tablespoons olive oil in a large sauté pan and add the onions and ½ teaspoon salt. Cover the pan and cook the onions over medium heat, stirring often, until they are browned and beautiful, about 30 minutes. Push the onions to the edges of the pan, add the remaining 2 tablespoons olive oil in the middle, heat it for a moment, and then sear the garlic in it for about a minute. Add the tomato sauce, herbs, and crushed chiles and give it all a stir.

Cook the pasta in the boiling water until it is just short of *al dente*. Drain the pasta, reserving 1 cup of the pasta water. Add the pasta to the sauce in the pan, and lift and mix the penne and sauce for a minute or two. The pasta will finish cooking in the pan, absorbing some great flavor. Add a bit of the reserved pasta water if needed to loosen the sauce. Taste, and adjust the salt and crushed red chile if needed.

Turn off the heat, pour a little more of your best olive oil over the pasta, give it a last quick stir, and serve.

Serves 6 to 8 (but Teddy and I have been known to eat half of it by ourselves)

Omnivore Meals . . .
The vibrant flavors of this dish can take on other strong personalities—sautéed pancetta, garlic shrimp, or spicy sausage are all garnish choices to offer for omnivores—or a side of Mint-Scented Pork and Pine Nut Meatballs (p. 363).

Penne Rigate with Garlic, Rapini, and Sautéed
Breadcrumbs (p. 187)

PENNE RIGATE WITH GARLIC, RAPINI, AND SAUTÉED BREADCRUMBS

VEGAN

Garlicky breadcrumbs sautéed in olive oil to a crunchy golden brown make this rustic pasta dish something special. Tasty, bitter broccoli rabe, sweet tomatoes, and toothsome farro penne are all set off by those breadcrumbs.

FOR THE BREADCRUMBS:

6 oz. chewy whole-grain bread, hard crusts removed

5 Tbs. extra-virgin olive oil

¼ tsp. sea salt, plus more to taste

4 cloves garlic, finely chopped

FOR THE PASTA:

1½ lbs. tender rapini (broccoli rabe)

2 cups Basic Tomato Sauce (p. 86)

1 lb. farro penne rigate

3–4 Tbs. extra-virgin olive oil

8 large cloves garlic, finely chopped

½ tsp. sea salt, plus more to taste

1 tsp. crushed red chiles

2–4 tsp. fresh lemon juice

OPTIONAL GARNISH:

grated Parmigiano-Reggiano cheese

Cut or tear the bread into small cubes and pulse it in a food processor until you have rough breadcrumbs. Heat 3 tablespoons olive oil in a medium nonstick skillet, add the breadcrumbs and a pinch of salt, and immediately toss toss toss. Sauté the crumbs for 3 to 4 minutes, stirring and tossing constantly, then push them to the edges of the pan, add the remaining 2 tablespoons olive oil in the center, and stir the chopped garlic in it for about 30 seconds, or until it shows the first hint of color. Stir-fry everything together another 2 minutes on medium-high heat, until the breadcrumbs are a deeper golden brown. Remove the crumbs to a plate lined with 3 layers of paper towels.

Wash the rapini and trim off any tough-looking stems (the stems of very young plants are tasty and tender). Cut tender stems in ½-inch pieces and leaves in 1-inch strips.

Warm up the tomato sauce. Bring a large pot of well-salted water to a boil. Add the pasta and set the timer for 2 minutes less than the time suggested on the package.

Heat 2 tablespoons olive oil in a large wok or sauté pan, add three-quarters of the chopped garlic, and stir for 30 seconds on high heat. Add the rapini with the moisture clinging to it, toss in the salt, and stir-fry for 5 to 6 minutes. The rapini will reduce drastically. Add the crushed red chiles and a splash of lemon juice, toss again, then taste and add more salt if needed.

As soon as the pasta is on the firm side of *al dente*, drain it, reserving a cup or so of the pasta water. Add the hot pasta to the pan with the rapini, along with the tomato sauce, and toss over medium heat for another minute or two. The pasta will absorb some of the tomato sauce

recipe continues

as it finishes cooking in the pan; it should not look soupy, but if it seems too dry you can add a few spoonfuls of the reserved pasta water. Stir in about ½ cup breadcrumbs, then serve in warm pasta bowls, scattering a spoonful of the remaining breadcrumbs over each serving. Pass the grated cheese at the table if you wish.

Serves 6 as a main dish, up to 10 as a first course

In a Festive Mixed Menu . . .
Italian Style (p. 28): This lively dish follows an antipasto of roasted vegetables, rosemary flatbread with truffle honey, and tuna in olive oil and capers, and leads the way to steamed ling cod on fennel and onions.

And an Easy Omnivore Way . . .
Rinse and pat dry a big handful of trimmed calamari, both tentacles and rings. Shortly before the pasta is ready, sauté the calamari for a few moments in 2 tablespoons olive oil and a chopped garlic clove, then toss the calamari in their hot pan with some of the reserved breadcrumbs and use as a garnish.

WARM NOODLE SALAD WITH GINGER-SESAME SAUCE

VEGAN

Hot, warm, or cold, this salad is so good with the brightness of ginger and the nutty depth of sesame. Matchstick vegetables, barely cooked, bathe in their marinade as you cook the noodles. Then toss everything together. It's that easy.

FOR THE MARINADE:

2 Tbs. minced fresh ginger

1 large clove garlic, minced

5 Tbs. rice vinegar

3 Tbs. soy sauce

1½ Tbs. light sesame oil

1½ Tbs. dark sesame oil

½ tsp. sea salt, plus more to taste

FOR THE SALAD:

1 lb. slender green asparagus

8 oz. yellow zucchini (2 medium)

8 oz. carrots (4 medium)

1 lb. soba noodles, tagliatelle, or spaghettini

1 bunch green onions, white and green parts, thinly sliced

1 cup roughly chopped fresh cilantro

2 Tbs. toasted sesame seeds

¼ cup chopped toasted almonds

Whisk together all the marinade ingredients in a bowl and set them aside. Snap off and discard the tough ends of the asparagus, and slice the stalks thinly on a slant. Cut the zucchini and carrots into thin strips or matchsticks. In a medium saucepan over medium-high heat, steam the carrots for about a minute, then add the asparagus and zucchini and steam for 3 more minutes, or until the vegetables are barely tender. As soon as the vegetables are ready, put them in a large, warm serving bowl and pour the marinade over them.

Cook the noodles in a large pot of boiling salted water just until they are *al dente*. Drain them and add them to the vegetables and marinade. Lift and turn gently until everything is well combined, then add most of the green onions and cilantro, the sesame seeds, and the chopped almonds. Lift and turn again, and scatter the remaining green onions and chopped cilantro over the top. Serve immediately. Or allow the noodles and vegetables to cool, then mix in the cilantro and green onions and chill everything together.

Serves 6 as a light main dish

Omnivore Meals . . .

You can enrich this salad with almost any leftover meat. Shreds of pork, flaked crabmeat, or smoked duck or chicken can be dressed with more of the marinade and stirred in with part of the salad. Or, if you are serving this as a hot dish, place a small piece of steamed or pan-seared cod on top of individual servings for those who eat fish.

FRESH CORN POLENTA

VEGAN

This polenta, made with fresh corn and caramelized onion, feels rich, yet keeps a bright clarity of flavor. Cheese can be added, of course, but try the polenta on its own first. Pair it with a roasted tomato sauce, a mushroom ragout, or roasted vegetables.

See photo on p. 278.

5 ears fresh sweet corn

4 Tbs. extra-virgin olive oil

1 large onion (12 oz.), finely
    chopped

½ tsp. sea salt, plus more to
    taste

2½ cups vegetable broth

1⅓ cups (8 oz.) coarse-ground
    polenta

GARNISH:

½ cup lightly toasted pine nuts

OPTIONAL GARNISH:

crumbled aged cheddar or grated
    Parmigiano-Reggiano cheese

Slice the corn kernels off the cobs; you need at least 3½ cups. Heat 2 tablespoons olive oil in a medium nonstick skillet, add the onions and the salt, and stir over high heat for 5 to 6 minutes, until the onions begin to color. Turn the heat down, cover the pan, and cook, stirring occasionally, for 30 minutes, until the onions are golden brown and soft.

In a soup pot, heat the vegetable broth and 2½ cups water. Whisk in the polenta, whisking until there are no lumps. Adjust the heat to low, cover the pot, and simmer the polenta for 30 minutes, stirring every 5 minutes at first, more frequently as it thickens. Meanwhile, puree 2½ cups of the corn kernels thoroughly in a food processor. Press the puree through a coarse sieve until the pulp is dry; discard the pulp. You should have about 1 cup of creamy corn puree.

Add the corn puree to the polenta as it cooks. When the onions are caramelized, stir them in as well. Five minutes before the polenta is done, stir in the remaining 1 cup whole corn kernels. Taste, and season with salt as needed, then simmer another 3 to 4 minutes to blend the flavors. Before serving, stir in the remaining 2 tablespoons olive oil.

Serve the polenta in wide, shallow bowls, with mushroom ragout or roasted tomatoes spooned along one side. Pass the toasted pine nuts and the crumbled or grated cheese at the table if you wish.

Serves 6 to 7 as a center-of-the-plate dish

In a Mixed Menu...
Sunday Dinner Comfort Food (p. 279) is a meal that welcomes fall:
polenta and mushroom ragout along with roasted tomatoes, with an
option of roast chicken.

Another Way with Polenta...
I love polenta as a one-bowl meal: a wide bowl of fresh, soft polenta,
a spoonful of chunky dark red tomato sauce along one side, pieces of
creamy feta cheese, and a handful of arugula on top. Easy, right? And
beautiful. A scattering of crumbled Italian sausage or chorizo, sautéed
and drained, would make an ideal topping for your carnivore pal.

Polenta Torta with Roasted Squash and
onion marmalade (p. 193)

POLENTA TORTA WITH ROASTED SQUASH

AND ONION MARMALADE

<u>VEGETARIAN OR VEGAN</u>

Here is polenta upgraded to luxury class. Roasted kabocha squash, red onion marmalade, and Manchego cheese add layers of rich flavor to the polenta, which is formed in the shape of a torte and then cut in wedges. Kabocha squash, now commonly available at supermarkets, is essential for the flavor and texture of the polenta.

The torta can be prepared a day in advance and kept in the refrigerator, tightly wrapped, until a few hours before dinner, when it should be returned to room temperature before baking.

2–3 lb. kabocha squash

2½ cups coarse-ground polenta

5 cups vegetable broth

5 oz. grated Manchego or pecorino Granvecchio cheese

2½ lbs. red onions

2 Tbs. extra-virgin olive oil, plus more for the pan

½ tsp. sea salt, plus more to taste

1 dried chile de árbol

1 Tbs. plus 1 tsp. chopped fresh thyme

½ tsp. spicy smoked paprika, such as pimentón de la Vera

2 Tbs. sweet sherry or Marsala

Preheat the oven to 375°. Cut the kabocha squash in half and scrape out the seeds. Put it cut side down in a lightly oiled baking pan and roast it until it is soft, 45 to 50 minutes. Scoop out the flesh and mash it; you should have 2 cups. If it is lumpy, puree it in a food processor. It should be dense, starchy, and sweet. (Careful about substitutions—watery squash won't work here.)

Combine the polenta, 2½ cups water, and the broth in a large heavy-bottomed pot and bring the liquid to a boil, stirring. Lower the heat, cover the pot, and simmer the polenta gently for 40 minutes, stirring often. Stir in 3 ounces of the grated cheese. When the cheese is melted, stir in the 2 cups of mashed roasted squash. Taste, and add salt if needed.

While the polenta cooks, peel and quarter the onions and slice them thinly crosswise. Heat the olive oil in a large nonstick pan and add the onions, sea salt, and chile de árbol. Toss the onions over high heat for 5 to 6 minutes, until they begin to go limp, then stir in the thyme and paprika. Turn the heat very low, cover the pan, and cook the onions slowly for 50 minutes to an hour, stirring occasionally. When the onions are reduced to a third of their original volume and look like jam, uncover the pan, turn up the heat, and add the sherry or Marsala. As soon as it cooks away, remove the pan from the heat. Discard the chile, stir half the onions into the polenta, and reserve the rest.

recipe continues

Oil a medium spring-form pan. Spoon the hot polenta into the prepared pan, spread it evenly, and then run a spoon around the surface in circles to give it some texture. Chill the torta in the refrigerator until it is firm, at least 2 hours. (The polenta can now be covered tightly with foil and kept in the refrigerator for a day. Bring it back to room temperature before continuing.)

When the polenta is firm, preheat the oven to 350°. Remove the rim from the spring-form pan and use long spatulas to transfer the torta carefully onto a large ovenproof ceramic serving platter or shallow gratin dish. Bake it for about 40 minutes, or until hot through (longer if it is cold from the refrigerator). Sprinkle the remaining 2 ounces of grated cheese over the top and the reserved onions over the cheese, then bake the torta for another 8 to 10 minutes, or until the cheese is melted and beginning to color. If you want, you can finish it with a moment under the broiler to toast the cheese.

Serve the torta on its platter or gratin dish, surrounded by sautéed kale or other vegetables. Cut it in wedges like a cake, carefully: the polenta becomes soft when it is hot, but it will hold its shape if you treat it gently.

Serves 10 to 12 as a center-of-the-plate dish

The Vegan Torta . . .

Cheese is the only ingredient in this dish that is not vegan, and it can easily be eliminated. To add a touch of richness to the nondairy torta, I increase the onions to 3 pounds and then add ½ cup lightly toasted pine nuts and a spoonful of miso paste, stirring them into the polenta before ladling it into the pan. The pine nuts can be left whole, or chopped for a polenta with a coarser texture.

In a Thanksgiving Menu . . .

Thanksgiving for Everyone (p. 20) features this polenta torta, surrounded by seasonal vegetables and sharing the stage with a roasted turkey.

A WORD ABOUT RISOTTO

Risotto is, for the most part, a dish you can make with one hand. Relax and hold a glass of wine in the other hand. Risotto is easy.

To make risotto, you need the right rice, a short-grain, starchy kernel. The best Italian varieties are Vialone Nano, Carnaroli, and Arborio, which is the most widely available here. Once you have your rice, these are the steps: cook some finely chopped onion or shallots in olive oil or butter until soft and fragrant, add the rice and stir, add a little wine and then heated broth, a ladleful at a time, and stir stir stir . . . Somewhere in that cooking time, stir in the flavorings. From start to finish, this takes a little over half an hour.

When the rice kernels are tender but firm, the risotto thick yet creamy enough to make a wavelike movement as a spoon is run through it, it's done. Serve at once. But do not think that because risotto needs last-minute attention it is not a good dinner party dish; for informal entertaining it is perfect. Have some antipasti arranged conveniently on the kitchen counter or nearby. Everyone nibbles, sips wine, and catches up with gossip as the risotto is stirred, and often guests take their turn. When the risotto is ready, there is a moment of hurried excitement, an urgency to serve it at its perfect moment, and hands reach out to carry steaming bowls to the table. This adds to the fun.

Risotto is a good family meal, too. When my children were children, they often stirred the risotto while I made a salad. It is an ideal assignment for an eight-year-old who is tall enough to reach or has a stool to stand on. That child will feel helpful and important, will do a good job, and will absorb, along with the perfume of the shallots and herbs, an important idea: that cooking is easy and fun.

WINTER SQUASH RISOTTO WITH SAGE AND PINE NUTS

VEGAN OR VEGETARIAN

Sage-infused, sautéed kabocha squash gives a deep, layered flavor to this golden risotto, and pine nuts add a satisfying bite. It's best to use a light homemade broth for risotto, but if you need to use a canned broth, choose a good one, avoiding anything too strong or acidic, and dilute it to reduce salt.

1 medium kabocha squash (2½–3 lbs.)

4 Tbs. extra-virgin olive oil, plus more to taste

1 tsp. sea salt, plus more to taste

2 tsp. crumbled dried sage leaves or 1 Tbs. finely chopped fresh sage

1 Tbs. sherry vinegar

2 medium yellow onions, chopped

6–7 cups light vegetable broth

1½ cups Arborio rice

¼ cup Marsala or sherry

freshly ground black pepper to taste

¾ cup lightly toasted pine nuts

OPTIONAL GARNISHES:

1 cup coarsely grated or shaved Parmigiano-Reggiano cheese

4 oz. pancetta cut in squares and browned (instructions follow)

Use a sharp knife or cleaver to cut the squash in half, then scrape out the seeds. Cut the squash into thick strips and slice away the peel, pointing the blade of the knife always away from you. Cut the dense yellow flesh into ½-inch dice.

Heat 2 tablespoons olive oil in a large nonstick pan and add the squash and about ½ teaspoon sea salt. Toss and stir the squash over high heat for about 5 minutes, then add the sage, lower the heat to medium-high, and continue cooking, stirring often, for about 10 minutes, or until the squash pieces are tender and flecked with dark brown. Splash on the sherry vinegar and toss the squash with it quickly.

Heat the remaining 2 tablespoons olive oil in a large nonstick sauté pan, add the chopped onions and a pinch of salt, and stir over high heat for 6 to 7 minutes, until the onions are tender and starting to color. Reduce the heat, cover the pan, and cook the onions slowly, with an occasional stir, for 30 minutes, or until they are soft and evenly caramel-colored. Heat the vegetable broth and keep it just below a simmer as you make the risotto.

Add the rice to the onions, raise the heat to medium, and stir for 4 to 5 minutes. Add the Marsala or sherry and stir as it cooks away—just a few seconds. Add a large ladleful of the hot vegetable broth and adjust the heat to a simmer. Stir slowly, and each time the broth is nearly absorbed, add another ladleful. After 10 minutes, stir in the squash and grind in some black pepper.

Continue in the same manner, adding broth and stirring frequently, until the rice is *al dente*, tender but still firm. It will take 20 to 25 minutes in all. When the rice is just tender, stir in half the toasted pine nuts and a last ladle of broth, then immediately spoon the risotto into wide, shallow bowls. Sprinkle a tablespoon of pine nuts over each serving, and pass grated Parmigiano-Reggiano and sautéed pancetta at the table if you like.

Serves 6 as a center-of-the-plate dish

Omnivore Options . . .
Parmesan cheese can be passed at the table and will add its own inimitable dimension. And if you like meat, then you will want to scatter a few crispy-chewy squares of pancetta over the dish. See the instructions for sautéing pancetta below.

To Sauté Pancetta . . .
The pancetta should be sautéed right before you start making the risotto, or at the same time. Cut about 4 ounces pancetta into slices, then cut the slices into pieces about 1 inch square. Heat a nonstick pan for a minute. Add the pancetta pieces, keeping the heat high, and spread them out to get maximum contact with the pan. You should hear them sizzle. When the pancetta begins to render its fat, lower the heat to medium-high and turn the pieces occasionally for about 5 minutes, or until they are crispy and brown but still a little chewy. Drain the pancetta on paper towels.

RISOTTO AS YOU LIKE IT

When winter squashes begin appearing in the farmers' market, I long for the weather to turn so I can start roasting and simmering them. The perfume of sage fills my house, and everything feels right.

This meal is an enduring favorite of mine for the autumn season. The simple version is a weeknight dinner at the kitchen table. Risotto, as we have all by now learned, is an easy dish: spoon in one hand, glass of wine in the other. This risotto can be dressed to suit, scattered over with cheese and pancetta—or not. Cannellini Salad is in the refrigerator, because you made it on the weekend, or you make a quick version from canned beans. Or simply have the risotto with an easy green salad. Dessert can be a bowl of oranges, or some orange sorbet from the freezer.

But if company is coming, dress the meal up by starting with that classic antipasto combination,

cannellini and tuna—only serve them side-by-side, the marinated cannellini in one bowl, the tuna in olive oil and capers in another. And for dessert, bring out the beautiful chilled orange slices in their caramel syrup, with the option of vanilla ice cream. It all moves easily into a dinner party.

But what if it's April? For a springtime version of the flexible risotto menu, make my other favorite—Lemon Risotto with sautéed fresh fava beans. Favas are a rite of spring, excellent green dots of flavor scattered over the golden rice, happy with a garnish of a few sautéed prawns, and equally happy with shavings of Parmigiano. Start with Fennel and Asparagus Ribbon Slaw if it's a dinner party, or keep it simple with a tossed salad of tender lettuce leaves, and finish with fresh local strawberries for dessert—there is nothing better.

A Practical Note . . .

The satisfying vegan meal consists of marinated cannellini with olives and peppers, focaccia or crostini, winter squash risotto served simply, and chilled orange slices in orange caramel syrup for dessert.

WINTER SQUASH RISOTTO MENU

FOR 5 TO 6

Marinated Cannellini with Olives and Roasted Peppers
Tuna in Olive Oil and Capers

focaccia or Crostini

Winter Squash Risotto with Sage and Pine Nuts
with Parmigiano-Reggiano or sautéed pancetta

Chilled Orange Slices in Orange Caramel
vanilla ice cream

Lemon Risotto *with sautéed fresh
fava beans* (p. 201) *and Prawns
Sautéed with Garlic* (p. 349)

LEMON RISOTTO
WITH SAUTÉED FRESH FAVA BEANS

Although the ingredients are simple, I think of this as a luxury dish: fresh fava beans are a seasonal delicacy, and shelling this many rates as an act of culinary devotion. The risotto is aromatic with lemon zest and richly satisfying with the bright green new favas—a bowlful of spring.

5 Tbs. extra-virgin olive oil, plus more for garnish

4 cloves garlic, minced

2 cups peeled fresh green fava beans, from 1 lb. shelled beans (see note)

3 Tbs. fresh lemon juice

sea salt

¾ cup finely chopped shallots

8–9 cups light vegetable broth, diluted if salty

2½ cups Arborio rice

¼ cup dry white wine

1½ Tbs. finely grated lemon zest

½ cup freshly grated Parmigiano-Reggiano cheese, plus more for the table

Heat 2 tablespoons olive oil in a medium sauté pan, add the garlic, and stir for about 30 seconds. Add the peeled fava beans and sauté them over medium-high heat, stirring almost constantly, for 3 to 4 minutes, or until they color lightly. Add 1 tablespoon lemon juice, sprinkle the beans with a *big* pinch of sea salt, give them one more stir, and remove them from the heat. Set them aside as you prepare the rice.

Heat the remaining 3 tablespoons olive oil in a large sauté pan and stir the shallots in it over medium heat, with a dash of salt, until they are soft, 6 or 7 minutes. Bring the vegetable broth to a simmer, cover it, and keep it hot on the lowest flame. Be sure that your vegetable broth is not too strong or salty.

Add the rice to the shallots and stir over medium heat for 2 to 3 minutes. Add the wine and stir as it evaporates. Add 1 cup of the hot vegetable broth, lower the heat to a simmer, and stir as the broth is absorbed into the rice. Continue adding broth, about a cup at a time, stirring almost constantly. As each cup of broth is nearly absorbed, add the next cup and stir again, and so on until the rice is tender but firm and a creamy sauce has formed around it, 20 to 25 minutes.

Stir in the remaining 2 tablespoons lemon juice and the lemon zest, as well as two-thirds of the sautéed fava beans, reserving the rest for a garnish. Stir in the Parmigiano, and then, just before serving, add a final, generous ladleful of broth. Immediately spoon the risotto into shallow bowls and scatter a few reserved fava beans on top of each serving. Pass the olive oil carafe and the additional grated Parmigiano-Reggiano at the table.

Serves 6 to 8 as a center-of-the-plate dish

recipe continues

A Seafood Variation . . .

Lemon risotto can be made with shrimp instead of fava beans, or along with them. Peel and devein about 1 pound of fresh shrimp, wash them, and have them ready as you begin to cook the risotto. When the rice has been cooking about 15 minutes, sauté the shrimp for a moment in some olive oil with a bit of garlic and a splash of white wine. Stir the shrimp into the risotto, or into part of it, just before serving. Or add a few sautéed shrimp on top of individual servings. The large Prawns Sautéed with Garlic (p. 349), which are left unpeeled, also make a good pairing.

About Those Fava Beans . . .

The well-protected fava beans must first be taken out of their large pods; then the beans need to be peeled, one by one. It's a bit of work, but not so much that it should stop you. I timed myself the last time I peeled a pound of shelled favas (about 3 cups beans in their jackets): 20 minutes. Not a tragedy. So bring a pot of water to a boil and drop in the shelled favas. When the water simmers again, give them 2 to 3 minutes, depending on their size. Drain them, rinse briefly with cool water, and then slip off their skins while they are still warm. You'll have a generous 2 cups when the beans are peeled.

SPINACH AND HERB RISOTTO WITH OYSTER MUSHROOMS

This easy risotto makes a tasty—and very green—weeknight supper for any season. Serve it with a Tatsoi and Radicchio Salad (p. 146) and it's a dinner party.

10 oz. oyster mushrooms

4 Tbs. extra-virgin olive oil, plus more for garnish

4 cloves garlic, chopped

sea salt

4 Tbs. mirin (rice wine)

5 cups light vegetable broth

1/2 small red onion, thinly sliced

3/4 cup thinly sliced green onions, white and green parts

1 1/2 cups Arborio rice

2/3 cup dry white wine

2 packed cups chopped or thinly sliced fresh spinach

1/2 cup chopped fresh flat-leaf parsley

a pinch of oregano

1/2 lemon

1/3 cup grated Parmigiano-Reggiano cheese, plus more for the table

freshly ground black pepper

Clean the mushrooms and slice them lengthwise if large, or simply pull apart the clumps if small. Heat 2 tablespoons olive oil in a medium skillet and sizzle half the chopped garlic in it for about 15 seconds. Add the mushrooms and a big pinch of salt and toss the mushrooms over high heat for 4 to 5 minutes. Add the mirin and continue to stir and toss the mushrooms as the liquid cooks away and the mushrooms develop golden edges, 4 to 5 more minutes. Turn off the heat and leave the mushrooms in the warm pan until needed.

Bring the vegetable broth to a simmer and keep it hot in a covered saucepan. Heat the remaining 2 tablespoons olive oil in a large nonstick sauté pan and sauté the red onion, remaining garlic, and green onions over high heat, stirring, until the onions begin to color, about 6 minutes. Add the rice to the onion mixture and stir it over medium heat for 2 to 3 minutes. Add the wine and keep stirring as it cooks away. Add the spinach, parsley, and oregano and gently lift and turn the rice and spinach together for 2 to 3 minutes, until the spinach wilts.

Add a soup ladle of the hot broth to the rice and stir it in, keeping it just at a simmer. When the liquid is nearly absorbed, add another ladleful. Continue this way, adding broth a bit at a time and stirring constantly with a wooden spoon, until most of the broth is used and the rice is *al dente*, 20 to 25 minutes. A slightly creamy sauce will form around the rice kernels, which are no longer crunchy but still firm. Shortly before the risotto is ready, give the mushrooms another stir over medium heat—just a minute or so.

recipe continues

When the rice has achieved the perfect tender-firm texture, squeeze in a few drops of lemon juice, stir in a last ladle of broth and the grated Parmesan cheese, and taste. Correct the seasoning with another drop of lemon or a bit of pepper if needed.

Spoon the risotto into shallow bowls. Drizzle a little olive oil on top of each serving and top with a spoonful of the sautéed mushrooms. Pass additional Parmesan cheese.

Serves 5 to 6 as a center-of-the-plate dish

Variation . . . Spinach and Sorrel Risotto
For a lemony-tasting green risotto, skip the mushrooms and add at least ½ cup chopped sorrel leaves to the spinach. And if you want to turn this version into an omnivore dish, stir in a few quickly sautéed shrimp at the end, or some flaked, cooked fish. Sorrel and seafood are a match made in heaven—or at least made in France, which is close enough to heaven.

The Vegan Way . . .
The Parmesan cheese can be left out of this risotto—it will still have plenty of flavor. However, if you want some of that creamy richness, you can stir in a small amount of a vegan cream cheese, such as Tofutti, or add ½ cup chopped toasted pine nuts.

The Omnivore Way . . .
To make this as a chicken dish, dice some poached or roasted chicken—leftovers are welcome—and warm it gently in a bit of chicken broth, then stir it into individual portions before topping with the oyster mushrooms.

BARLOTTO WITH BRAISED GREENS, CURRANTS, AND PINE NUTS

VEGAN

Barlotto is like a barley risotto. The braised greens in this one are straight out of a rustic Greek kitchen, cooked with plenty of garlic, olive oil, and onions, a handful of dill, and some lemon. You can vary the chard with beet greens, mustard greens, even kale, but there should always be some spinach. And while the greens at first look like a mountain, they cook right down and become a silky green sauce, spiked with plump currants for sweetness and some crushed red chiles for the love of life, then finished with lemon juice and another drizzle of olive oil.

1 cup (7½ oz.) pearl barley

3 cups vegetable broth

1½ tsp. sea salt, plus more to taste

2 large bunches chard (1½ lbs.)

1 large bunch spinach (8 oz.), roughly chopped

3 Tbs. extra-virgin olive oil, plus more for garnish

1½ lbs. onions, yellow or white, halved and sliced

6 large cloves garlic, chopped

½ tsp. crushed red chiles

¼ cup dry white wine

½ cup coarsely chopped fresh dill weed

⅓ cup dried currants

freshly ground black pepper

2–3 Tbs. fresh lemon juice

GARNISH:

toasted pine nuts

OPTIONAL GARNISH:

feta cheese

Rinse the barley and combine it in a soup pot with the vegetable broth, 3 cups water, and ½ teaspoon salt, a pinch more if the broth is not salted. Simmer the barley for 45 to 50 minutes, until it is tender but still firm and chewy. Drain the barley through a fine colander, and reserve the milky liquid that is left. Meanwhile, wash the greens and slice the chard into strips 1 to 2 inches wide. Chard stems do not need to be removed, though you might want to trim away the rough-looking bottom parts.

Heat 2 tablespoons olive oil in a large nonstick sauté pan. Add two-thirds of the onions and ½ teaspoon salt and cook the onions over medium heat, covered, for about 10 minutes, stirring occasionally. Push the onions out to the edges of the pan and add the remaining 1 tablespoon olive oil in the center, heat it a moment, then add the chopped garlic and stir it around in the center of the pan for a minute, just enough to take off the raw edge.

Turn up the heat and start adding the sliced chard to the pan, several handfuls at a time, stir-frying as it wilts down. Add the spinach and another ½ teaspoon salt, and continue stirring occasionally as the greens cook down for about 5 minutes. If the greens are drying out, add a few tablespoons of water. Stir in the crushed red chiles, wine, dill, and currants, grind in some black pepper, and cover the pan. Simmer the greens over low heat for 5 more minutes.

Add the barley to the greens in the pan. The barlotto can be finished to this point an hour or two ahead and kept in the pan, covered, at room temperature. Shortly before serving, stir in as much of the reserved

recipe continues

barley liquid as needed to make a saucy risotto consistency; the dish should be thick but never stiff. Bring it back to a simmer, stirring, then add the lemon juice.

Serve the barlotto in wide, shallow bowls; drizzle some of your best olive oil over each serving, and then scatter a spoonful of pine nuts on top. Pass the feta cheese at the table if you like.

Serves 6 as a center-of-the-plate dish

A Flexible Meal . . .

One warm summer night we started with a cool Watermelon and Cucumber Salad (p. 143), then had this vivid green dish with a simple Pan-Seared Halibut (p. 341) as an accompaniment for the omnivores.

Barlotto with Braised Greens, Currants, and Pine Nuts (p. 205), paired with Pan-Seared Halibut with Sautéed Trumpet Mushrooms (p. 341)

PILAFS, GRAINS, AND STUFFED VEGETABLES

PILAFS, GRAINS, AND STUFFED VEGETABLES

My friend Cindy is not afraid to play favorites. The day she tried Farro and Black Rice Pilaf, she fell in love. And why not? It's simple, chewy, and tasty, and it looks like beautiful tweed. I moved on, playing the field with red quinoa, bulgur, wild rice, and barley. Not Cindy. Open her refrigerator on any given day and you will see a large bowl of that tweedy pilaf. In warm weather she tosses a salad of peppery mustard greens, sliced kumquats, and chunks of creamy avocado and mounds the pilaf in the center. In cooler weather she roasts a few vegetables or a chicken to go with the pilaf. She has begun calling this dish "my farro and black rice thing." House guests call ahead to make sure the pilaf is on the menu.

For years pilafs have been playing second fiddle, but now, with the greater availability of many ancient grains, high in protein and other nutrients, hearty pilafs take the center of the plate with ease. They are rich in taste and texture, and it's easy to plan a meal around them. Red Quinoa and Pumpkin-Seed Pilaf or warm Farro with Lentils and Lavender are dishes layered with earthy flavor. Add a few grilled or braised vegetables and you have a lovely, satisfying meal. But don't hesitate to add a slice of roast chicken or a grilled sausage. That's flexibility. And sometimes pilaf wants to be A Great Big Star. For those times we have the giant pumpkin filled with a fancier version of that farro and black rice pilaf, exuberant with cranberries, nuts, and vegetables. Or stuffed poblano chiles, plump with red quinoa and corn.

The world of grains is large and kaleidoscopically varied, and grains turn up everywhere in this book—in salads, in soups, in appetizers, and even in desserts. In this chapter you will find a sampling of what is possible when pilafs step forward and shine on their own. Grains, after all, are the food that made civilization possible, and when we sit down in friendship to enjoy a meal together, they keep right on doing it.

BASIC FARRO

Farro is one of my favorite grains. It's an emmer wheat, an ancient variety similar to spelt, and has an appealing, wheaty flavor and satisfying chewiness. Most whole farro sold in stores is the semipearled grain: light brown with creamy streaks. It has had some of its rough outer bran buffed off, and cooks to tenderness in less than half an hour.

1 cup (7 oz.) semipearled farro

1³/₄ cups water

¹/₂ tsp. sea salt

Rinse the farro in a sieve. Bring the water to a boil in a medium saucepan, add the farro and salt, lower the heat to a simmer, and cook the grain, covered, for 25 minutes. Turn off the heat and leave the pot covered for 5 minutes. If liquid is left in the bottom of the pot, drain the farro through a sieve, then return it to the pot and fluff it gently with a fork.

Makes about 3 cups

Another Way . . .
Farro can also be cooked in an ample pot of boiling salted water, as you would cook pasta. When it tests done, drain it through a sieve and fluff it up with a fork.

BASIC QUINOA

Quinoa is a tiny, tasty grain that is high in protein, fiber, and minerals. It cooks up in about 15 minutes, and as it cooks the germ springs loose in a tiny white ring, letting you know it's ready. The grain remains slightly crunchy when tender, easy to fluff up for a pilaf or salad.

Note that quinoa must be rinsed. (Most commercially packaged quinoa has been washed, but I always give it another rinse.) The seeds are naturally coated with saponin, which has a somewhat bitter taste. So put that quinoa in a bowl of water, rub it between your fingers for a few seconds, then rinse it through a sieve.

1 cup quinoa

2 cups water

a big pinch of sea salt

Combine the quinoa and water in a medium pot and bring the water to a boil, then lower the heat to a simmer and cover the pot. Simmer the quinoa undisturbed for 12 to 15 minutes, until all the water is absorbed and the germ rings have sprung loose. Remove it from the heat and allow it to sit in its steam, still covered, for another 5 minutes, then fluff it gently with a fork. Add salt to taste, and if you want to use the grain in a salad, spread it on a baking sheet to cool.

Makes about 3¹/₂ cups

Another way . . .
Quinoa can also be cooked in an ample pot of boiling water, like pasta. When it tests done, drain it, salt it, and fluff it up with a fork.

FARRO AND BLACK RICE PILAF

VEGAN

This easy pilaf has become a standby in my kitchen. Serve it with any plate of roasted vegetables for a meal. Mix it into a winter kale salad, or scatter blistered cherry tomatoes over it in the summer. It seems to go with almost anything, takes little more than half an hour to make, and its sturdy texture means it keeps well for days.

1¼ cups semipearled farro

¾ cup forbidden rice or other black rice

1 tsp. sea salt, plus more to taste

2 Tbs. extra-virgin olive oil

1 large or 2 small yellow onions (12 oz.), quartered and sliced

1 dried chile de árbol

1 tsp. fresh thyme leaves or ½ tsp. dried thyme

2 Tbs. port wine or other sweet wine

freshly ground black pepper

Rinse the farro in a sieve and do the same with the rice, keeping them separate. Add the farro to 2¼ cups boiling water and ½ teaspoon salt. In a separate pot, add the rice to 1½ cups boiling water and ¼ teaspoon salt. Lower the heat under both pots, cover them, and simmer for 30 minutes. Turn off the heat and let the pots stand, covered, for 5 more minutes. If any liquid is left in the bottom of either pot, drain the farro or rice through a sieve. (Why cook them separately? For the color; black rice will stain everything a murky purple.) You should have a generous 3 cups cooked farro and about 2 cups rice. Turn the grains out onto a large rimmed baking sheet and spread them so the steam can escape.

Heat 1 tablespoon olive oil in a nonstick pan and add the onions, the remaining ¼ teaspoon salt, the chile, and the thyme. Cook over high heat, stirring often, for 4 to 5 minutes, then cover the pan, lower the heat, and cook the onions another 20 to 30 minutes, until they are soft and a beautiful golden brown. Add the wine and stir the onions as it sizzles away. Cover the pan again and cook the onions over low heat for 10 more minutes, until they are jammy.

In a large bowl, combine both grains with the cooked onions and the remaining 1 tablespoon olive oil and mix well. Taste, and add a pinch more salt if needed, as well as a generous amount of freshly ground black pepper.

Serve the pilaf hot, warm, or cool—it's always good. If you are cooking ahead and want to keep the pilaf for a day or two, allow it to cool before putting it in a covered container in the fridge.

Serves 6 to 8 when accompanied by salad or roasted vegetables

Another Way . . .

For a drier, toastier pilaf, spread the mixture back on the large rimmed baking sheet and toast it in a 375° oven for 20 minutes, stirring occasionally. The grains will have a chewier texture, with a few crunchy bits, and the onions will have crispy edges.

Farro and Spelt . . .

Farro is often confused with spelt, and though both are emmer wheats, they are cousins, not twins. Spelt takes longer to cook. Most farro is semipearled, and cooks in 25 to 30 minutes. Whole spelt needs at least 45 minutes.

In Mixed Menus . . .

This pilaf moves with ease from fancy holiday menus to simple everyday meals. In A Salad Supper for the Heat Wave (p. 104), it is a bed for Summer Chop Salad with Corn and Pepper Salsa and is garnished with optional pan-grilled swordfish slices. And it is also the start of an exuberant concoction that fills The Great Stuffed Pumpkin (p. 228).

RED QUINOA AND PUMPKIN-SEED PILAF

VEGAN

Quinoa, the supergrain from Peru, shows its affinity for other New World foods—potatoes and pumpkin seeds—in a pilaf that is just the sort of high-protein dish we like to put in the center of the plate. It feels almost like showing off to mention how tasty it is. Serve it warm with a platter of roasted root vegetables and a spicy relish—there's dinner. Or let it cool and toss it with spinach leaves and a citrus-spiked vinaigrette for a wonderful grain salad. And see the menu that follows for a splendid omnivore meal.

1½ cups (10 oz.) red quinoa

sea salt

1 medium yellow onion (8 oz.)

1 small red bell pepper (6 oz.)

1 large Yukon Gold potato (8–10 oz.)

1–2 fresh jalapeño peppers

3 Tbs. extra-virgin olive oil

½ cup (2½ oz.) hulled, unsalted pumpkin seeds

1–2 Tbs. fresh lime juice

3 Tbs. vegetable broth or water

1 cup (2 oz.) chopped fresh cilantro

Rinse the quinoa: rub it lightly with your fingers in a bowl of water, then drain it in a sieve and run fresh water through it for a moment. Bring 2½ quarts water to a boil, add 1 teaspoon salt and the rinsed quinoa, and let the grain boil gently over medium heat for 14 to 15 minutes, or until the little white rings are breaking free and the grain is tender but still crunchy. Drain the quinoa and set aside; you should have about 4 cups cooked quinoa.

Quarter the onion and slice it thinly. Trim and seed the bell pepper, cut it in 1-inch-thick strips, then cut the strips crosswise into thin slices. Scrub the potato and cut it into small dice. Finely chop the jalapeño peppers, tasting one for heat. You should have 3 to 4 tablespoons, but jalapeños vary so much in their level of heat that you may have to adjust the quantity up or down a bit.

Heat 2 tablespoons olive oil in a large nonstick skillet, add the onion, potato, and ½ teaspoon sea salt, and toss over high heat for 2 minutes. Add the pumpkin seeds and sauté another 3 to 4 minutes. You will see some brown spots, and the onion will be wilted. Add the bell pepper and jalapeño, another pinch of salt, and 2 tablespoons water. Turn the heat down to medium-low, cover the pan, and cook for 12 to 15 minutes, stirring and turning a couple of times. All the vegetables should be tender.

Add 1 tablespoon fresh lime juice to the vegetables and stir as it cooks away. Add the cooked quinoa and the vegetable broth or water, give everything a stir, and cover the pan for 5 minutes. The quinoa should be steaming hot and moist.

Just before serving, toss the hot pilaf with the chopped cilantro and the remaining 1 tablespoon each lime juice and olive oil.

Serves 6 to 8 as a center-of-the-plate dish

Working Ahead . . .
This quinoa pilaf can be made several hours ahead, up to the point of adding the cooked grain to the vegetables. Cook the quinoa and prepare the vegetables. Just before serving, put them together, heat 5 minutes, and toss with cilantro, lime juice, and olive oil.

Red Quinoa and Pumpkin-Seed Pilaf (p. 214),
Citrus-Glazed Roasted Root Vegetables (p. 271), and
medallions of Pan-Roasted Pork Tenderloin (p. 362)

PILAF AND FRIENDS

MENU - FOR 5 TO 6

Tatsoi and Radicchio Salad *with fresh cranberry vinaigrette*
creamy feta cheese

———

Red Quinoa and Pumpkin-Seed Pilaf

Citrus-Glazed Roasted Root Vegetables

Pan-Roasted Pork Tenderloin medallions in citrus glaze

———

tangerines and walnuts
or
Apple Pecan Crisp with a slice of blue cheese

Meals built around a great pilaf make so much sense. Of course, I'm talking about pilafs that flex their nutritional and flavor muscles with grains like quinoa, bulgur, barley, farro, and black rice. Add nuts, seeds, herbs, and aromatics, and the pilaf demands the center of the plate. A platter of roasted vegetables is the perfect companion, but a pilaf meal easily expands to take on poultry, meat, or seafood.

This pilaf meal celebrates winter flavors—cranberries, root vegetables, dark greens, citrus, walnuts, apples—all circling happily around red quinoa combined with pumpkin seeds and potatoes. The weeknight version is a one-plate meal: pilaf in the middle, roasted vegetables on one side and a salad on the other, dessert from the fruit basket.

If you're having a few friends over, serve a wedge of Maytag Blue cheese with Apple Pecan Crisp for dessert. If you'd like meat, serve the salad as a first course, then have pork loin medallions along with the pilaf and roasted vegetables. Use the same citrus glaze you've whisked up for the vegetables to marinate your pork.

A Practical Note . . .
For vegans the meal begins with tatsoi and radicchio salad, followed by the pilaf and roasted vegetables, with tangerines and nuts for dessert.

Fried Black Rice with Peanuts (p. 219)

FRIED BLACK RICE WITH PEANUTS

VEGAN

Forbidden rice is always beautiful, but this one is especially so, flecked with bright green cilantro leaves and golden peanuts. I love the way this dish elevates an easy stir-fry of vegetables, tofu, or fish to a special meal.

1 Tbs. peanut oil

1 Tbs. dark sesame oil

1³/₄ cups (6 oz.) sliced green onions, white and green parts

¹/₄ tsp. sea salt, plus more to taste

4¹/₂ cups cooked black rice

1¹/₂ Tbs. fresh lemon juice

1 Tbs. agave nectar or simple sugar syrup

1 tsp. finely grated orange zest

1 cup fresh cilantro, whole leaves or coarsely chopped

²/₃ cup (3 oz.) roasted peanuts, coarsely chopped

Heat the two oils in a large nonstick sauté pan, add the green onions and the salt, and stir the onions over medium-high heat for about 4 minutes, until they are softened and beginning to show golden spots. Add the cooked rice and stir-fry for 3 to 4 minutes, until the rice is heated through.

Stir in the lemon juice, agave nectar or simple syrup, and orange zest and turn off the heat. Just before serving, stir in the cilantro, which will wilt in the heat of the pan but remain bright green, and the peanuts. Taste, correct the seasoning with a pinch more salt if needed, and serve the rice hot.

Serves 6 to 8 as a side dish

In a Flexible Stir-Fry Menu . . .
Stir-Fry Is a Verb! (p. 293): Bright green stir-fried asparagus, amber glazed tofu, and steamed ling cod with miso all harmonize with the black rice and peanuts.

Do-Ahead . . .
When serving this rice with stir-fry dishes, you will want to give all your last-minute attention to the wok, so it's good to know that you can have this ready a little ahead of time; it will keep warm for half an hour or so without suffering, and you only need to hold back the cilantro and peanuts to stir in just before serving.

FARRO WITH LENTILS AND LAVENDER

VEGAN

Farro and lentils have virtually identical cooking times, so this is amazingly easy. And it's good hot or cold—I've made delicious salads with it, adding wild arugula, sliced pears, red grapes, walnuts, cherry tomatoes, in whatever combination is in season.

2 Tbs. extra-virgin olive oil

1–2 dried chiles de árbol

3 cloves garlic

1 bay leaf

1½ cups (10 oz.) semipearled farro, rinsed

½ cup (3 oz.) Le Puy lentils, rinsed

2½ cups mild vegetable broth

1 tsp. herbes de Provence

1 tsp. crushed dried lavender

a sprig of fresh thyme

Heat the olive oil in a medium sauté pan. Break the chile pods in half and shake out their seeds. Add the chiles to the pan along with the garlic cloves and bay leaf and stir over medium-high heat for about 3 minutes. Add the rinsed farro to the aromatics and stir for about 5 minutes.

Add the lentils, vegetable broth, 1 cup of water, and the herbs. Bring the liquid to a boil, then lower the heat to a simmer, cover the pan, and cook for 25 minutes. Check the grain and the lentils. If both are tender, turn off the heat; if the pilaf feels a little underdone, give it another 5 minutes. At that time, all or most of the liquid should be absorbed. Turn off the heat and leave the lid on for 5 minutes. If there is any broth left in the bottom of the pan, drain it off through a sieve.

Fluff the pilaf lightly with a fork, discard the chiles and bay leaf, and serve warm with any vegetable or cold in a salad.

Makes 5 to 6 center-of-the-plate servings when paired with a salad or vegetable dish

In a Menu . . .
Vegetables in the Center (p. 265): this fragrant pilaf pairs up with Ratatouille from the Charcoal Grill and optional grilled lamb sausage or lamb chops.

Ingredient Note . . .
Culinary lavender is mild and fragrant and is a component of the herbes de Provence blend; if you don't have lavender, use a bit more of the herb blend.

PEPPERS AND TOMATOES STUFFED WITH RICE AND LENTIL PILAF

VEGAN, VEGETARIAN, OR OMNIVORE

Stuffed vegetables are found in every cuisine. I grew up eating my mom's stuffed cabbage, later devoured more than my share of spicy *chiles rellenos*, and then fell in love with the summer vegetables on every Mediterranean *mezze* table, like these cinnamon-scented, pine nut–studded, olive oil–drenched beauties. Start with a plate of cured olives, then serve these stuffed vegetables with an Armenian Summer Salad (p. 137), and have a plate of ripe figs for dessert.

FOR THE RICE AND LENTIL STUFFING:

1½ lbs. tomatoes

¾ cup (5½ oz.) brown or green lentils

3–4 Tbs. extra-virgin olive oil

1 large yellow onion (9 oz.), finely chopped

1¾ tsp. sea salt, plus more to taste

3 cloves garlic, finely chopped

1¼ cups (9 oz.) short- or medium-grain rice

½ cup (3 oz.) raisins

¾ tsp. ground cinnamon

freshly ground black pepper

¼ cup chopped fresh mint leaves

3 Tbs. chopped fresh parsley

¾ cup pine nuts

1 tsp. lightly toasted cumin seeds

Peel the tomatoes: cut a cross in the bottom of each one with a sharp knife, drop them into boiling water for about 60 seconds, then transfer them with a slotted spoon to a bowl of cold water for a moment. Slip off their skins and cut them into ½-inch dice, reserving all the juice. You should have at least 3 cups of diced tomatoes with plenty of juice. Rinse the lentils and set them aside.

Heat 2 tablespoons olive oil in a large sauté pan, add the chopped onion and ¼ teaspoon salt, and stir over high heat for about 4 minutes to sear. Push the onions to the edges of the pan, add another tablespoon olive oil, drop the garlic in it, and stir another minute. Add the rice and lentils, along with a little more oil if the pan seems dry, and stir over medium heat for 5 minutes.

Add 2 cups water, the chopped tomatoes with their juice, the remaining 1½ teaspoons salt, the raisins, the cinnamon, and plenty of black pepper. Bring the liquid to a boil, cover the pan, then lower the heat and simmer gently for 25 minutes; the liquid should be absorbed. Turn off the heat and leave the pan covered for another 15 minutes, then fluff up the pilaf with a fork, mix in the chopped mint and parsley, pine nuts, and cumin seeds, and taste for seasoning. Add salt if needed.

This makes about 8 cups, enough to stuff a dozen medium bell peppers, or 6 medium tomatoes and 6 peppers.

Select firm tomatoes of even size and firm, well-shaped, medium-sized peppers that can stand up straight. You will need more peppers and tomatoes if you are increasing the amount of filling by adding meat to part of it, as described in the variation below.

recipe continues

TO STUFF THE VEGETABLES:

6–8 medium bell peppers (2–2½ lbs.)

6–8 medium tomatoes (3–4 lbs.)

sea salt

freshly ground black pepper

4–5 Tbs. extra-virgin olive oil, plus more for drizzling

3 Tbs. fresh lemon juice

1 cup vegetable broth, if needed

With a small, sharp knife, cut the tops off the tomatoes; cut around the core with the point of your knife slanting in toward the center of the tomato. Lift out the top and keep it. Use a teaspoon to carefully hollow out the inside of each tomato, leaving a wall about ⅓-inch thick. Reserve all the tomato pulp and juice, and chop up any large pieces.

Slice the tops off of the peppers, cutting straight across, about ½ inch down from the top. As with the tomatoes, keep the tops so you can put them back on like lids after stuffing. Scoop out the seeds and cores and discard them.

Lightly salt and pepper the insides of the hollowed vegetables and drizzle a few drops of olive oil into each one. Fill them with the pilaf, packing it down gently with your fingers and mounding it slightly over the top. Replace the tops of the peppers and tomatoes, which should now be sitting slightly higher on the mounded filling, like little hats.

Preheat the oven to 375°. Fit the stuffed vegetables into medium baking dishes, one for tomatoes and another for peppers, making sure that the vegetables fit together snugly. You need the right size dishes for this. Mix together the reserved tomato pulp and juice, at least 4 tablespoons olive oil, the lemon juice, and ½ teaspoon salt. Pour this liquid evenly over and around the stuffed vegetables, enough to have about ½ inch liquid in the dish. If you need more liquid, use the vegetable broth.

Cover the baking dishes with foil or with their lids and bake, 40 minutes for the tomatoes and an hour or so for the bell peppers. Check the vegetables after 30 minutes to be sure they are moist, and add a few spoonfuls of broth if it's needed.

You can serve the stuffed vegetables hot, warm, or at room temperature, but I think the flavor is best when they are just slightly warm.

Serves 6–8 as a main dish, more as part of a *mezze* table

The Omnivore Way . . .
These stuffed vegetables can easily be prepared and cooked in two versions, one for the vegans and vegetarians, another for the omnivores. Prepare the fragrant rice and lentil stuffing—a big batch—then reserve some to combine with ground lamb and additional herbs. See the lamb stuffing variation that follows.

Another Vegetarian Way . . .
Crumbled feta cheese can be stirred into some or all of this stuffing. Or you can top some of the stuffed vegetables with cheese before putting their "lids" on.

Variation . . . Peppers and Tomatoes Stuffed with Rice, Lentils, and Lamb

By adding lamb to part of this stuffing you will be increasing the total amount a bit, so you will need a few more peppers or tomatoes to fill.

Make the rice and lentil pilaf as above, then take out about 2 cups of it and mix it with sautéed, seasoned lamb, like this:

FOR THE LAMB, RICE AND LENTIL STUFFING:

2 Tbs. extra-virgin olive oil

1 medium yellow onion, chopped

2 large cloves garlic, chopped

1 lb. ground lamb

1/2 tsp. sea salt

freshly ground black pepper

2 Tbs. chopped fresh flat-leaf parsley

2 Tbs. chopped fresh mint leaves

1/2 tsp. crushed red chiles

2 cups Rice and Lentil Stuffing (recipe above)

Heat the olive oil in a medium sauté pan and sauté the onion over high heat for about 5 minutes, stirring often. Add the garlic and stir over high heat for another minute. Add the ground lamb, salt, and some black pepper and sauté the lamb over medium heat, stirring it and breaking it up, until it is cooked through, about 10 minutes. Drain off the excess fat, and stir in the chopped parsley and mint and the crushed red chiles. Taste, and correct the seasoning with more salt or pepper as needed.

Combine the prepared rice and lentil stuffing with the sautéed lamb mixture, mixing it up well, and proceed to stuff peppers and tomatoes as described above.

POBLANO CHILES STUFFED WITH QUINOA AND CORN

VEGAN, VEGETARIAN, OR OMNIVORE

Glossy dark green peppers, pyramids of sweet corn, and tables lined with juice-heavy red tomatoes—that's what I saw at the summer market. My mouth watered, and the idea for this dish was born. I filled my peppers with quinoa, pumpkin seeds, potatoes, cilantro, and sweet, sweet corn—New World flavors. Instead of frying them (no disrespect to the fabulous traditional *chiles rellenos* I have often enjoyed!), I baked them in a pool of simple fresh tomato sauce and served them with hot cornbread.

See photo on p. 226.

1 recipe Red Quinoa and
Pumpkin-Seed Pilaf (p. 214)

2 large ears sweet corn

8–10 large fresh poblano chiles
(3 lbs.)

3 cups Cumin-Scented Tomato
Sauce (p. 86)

extra-virgin olive oil for drizzling

OPTIONAL:

4 oz. creamy fresh goat cheese or
queso fresco

Prepare the pilaf according to the recipe. While the vegetables are cooking, slice the kernels off the ears of sweet corn; you should have 2 cups. Stir the corn into the vegetable mixture when you add the cooked quinoa. You should have at least 7 cups of pilaf with corn, enough to fill 8 to 10 large poblano chiles.

Char the chiles under a broiler or on a grill until they are blistered all over, put them in a covered bowl to sweat for 10 minutes, then peel them. (For detailed instructions, see "A Word About Charring and Peeling Peppers," p. 227.)

Taking one pepper at a time, cut a slit down one side from near the stem to near the tip. Remove the seeds, and leave the stems intact. Spoon enough of the filling into each pepper to plump it up; about 2/3 cup does it for an average poblano, a bit more for a large one. Push the sides of the pepper up so that they almost meet over the filling. If you like, you can dot the top of the filling with some fresh goat cheese or *queso fresco*.

Preheat the oven to 375°. Choose a large gratin dish or baking dish, something that will hold all the peppers in a single layer, or 2 smaller baking dishes. Pour most of the prepared tomato sauce into the dish; there should be a thin layer of tomato sauce covering the bottom. Use a spatula to transfer the peppers, arranging them on top of the tomato sauce, close together but not overcrowded. Drizzle a little olive oil over the peppers and sauce.

Cover the dish with aluminum foil and bake the peppers until they are hot through, 35 to 40 minutes. The peppers can be prepared hours ahead and kept in the refrigerator, but in that case you will have to adjust the oven time up to about 50 minutes.

Serve the stuffed peppers in wide, shallow bowls, like risotto bowls, and spoon some of the tomato sauce around them.

Serves 6 to 8 as a main dish

An Omnivore Variation . . . Poblano Chiles Stuffed with Quinoa, Corn, and Pork

---

This dish can easily be made two ways, keeping half the filling vegan and expanding the other half with pork. Pork loin, diced and quickly sautéed with onion and garlic, is a good match with the savory-and-sweet quinoa and corn filling.

8–9 oz. pork loin

2 Tbs. extra-virgin olive oil

1 small yellow onion (5 oz.), finely chopped

½ tsp. sea salt, plus more to taste

2 cloves garlic, finely chopped

1 Tbs. red wine vinegar

1 Tbs. agave nectar

a pinch of crushed red chiles

½ recipe of quinoa and corn filling for poblano chiles (above)

Trim the fat off the pork and cut the meat into small dice. Heat 1 tablespoon oil in a medium nonstick pan and sauté the onion in it with a pinch of salt for 6 to 7 minutes, until it begins to color, then add the remaining 1 tablespoon oil and the garlic and stir for 1 minute.

Add the diced pork and the remaining salt and stir often over medium heat until the meat is cooked through, probably no more than 4 or 5 minutes. Stir in the wine vinegar, agave nectar, and crushed red chiles, cover the pan, and turn the heat down to a simmer for about 2 minutes as the glaze permeates the pork.

Stir the cooked pork into the quinoa and corn filling and fill half the peppers with this version. Proceed with baking the peppers in tomato sauce as above, using 2 smaller baking dishes so you can keep the two versions distinct.

Poblano Chiles Stuffed with Quinoa
and Corn (p. 224)

A WORD ABOUT CHARRING AND PEELING PEPPERS

The flavor of freshly roasted peppers is wonderful, and an added benefit is the way the house smells. The process is simple and worth the 20 minutes' investment. Basically, you put the peppers under a broiler or on a grill until they are charred all over, then sweat them for a few minutes, and then peel off their thin skins.

For the broiler method, line a baking sheet with aluminum foil and arrange the peppers on it in a single layer. Place the pan on the middle rack of the oven, under a preheated broiler, and check the peppers every few minutes. In 7 or 8 minutes their tops will be speckled with blisters and charred spots. Use tongs to turn them over, and start checking them every couple of minutes, turning as needed until the peppers are blistered all over. This usually takes 12 to 15 minutes.

For the grill method, place the peppers directly on a hot grill, watch them carefully, and use tongs to turn them occasionally until they are blistered and lightly charred all over. The time will vary with the heat of the grill.

Put the charred peppers in a paper bag or a covered bowl. After a few minutes they will have cooled slightly, and you should be able to pull off their cellophane-like skins easily. If the skins are sticking, a few seconds under a gentle stream of cool running water can help. If your recipe calls for *rajas*, which are strips of roasted peppers, or for diced peppers, you can be casual about all this; a little extra charring won't hurt.

But for stuffed peppers . . .

If you want to make stuffed peppers, however, you need to watch your peppers more closely, because you don't want them to come apart when you're peeling them—and that means *don't overchar them*. Browned and blistered skin is good enough. If you let them get black all over, the peppers will be overcooked and likely to tear. Handle the peppers gently, and all will be well; you will have beautiful whole peppers to fill and bake.

THE GREAT STUFFED PUMPKIN

VEGAN

This is a festive and playful dish. It's fun to bring it out on a platter, to lift off its hat and release that fragrant cloud of steam, and then to slice thick wedges and watch them fall away as the pumpkin opens like a giant orange chrysanthemum, with savory stuffing spilling from the center. *See photo on p. 23.*

1 large pumpkin (7–8 lbs.)

2 Tbs. extra-virgin olive oil, plus more for the pumpkin

2 cups diced red onion

2 cups diced fennel bulb

1 tsp. sea salt, plus more to taste

2 cups diced celery

1 tsp. herbes de Provence

½ tsp. crumbled dried sage

a pinch of crushed red chiles

2 cups diced, peeled apples (from about 2 large apples)

⅔ cup raisins or dried cranberries

2 cups roughly chopped mustard greens

3 Tbs. chopped fresh flat-leaf parsley

1 recipe Farro and Black Rice Pilaf (p. 212)

2 Tbs. red miso or other miso

2 Tbs. mirin (rice wine)

1 cup (4 oz.) chopped walnuts or pecans

freshly ground black pepper to taste

Preheat the oven to 375°. Wash the pumpkin well and dry it. Pierce the skin with the point of a sharp knife in at least one place along the line where you will cut out the cap. Place the pumpkin in a baking pan and roast it for about 45 minutes, until it gives just a little when pressed with your thumb or a wooden spoon. It should still be firm, but this prebaking makes it easier to cut and clean the pumpkin and reduces the roasting time when it is stuffed. Allow the pumpkin to cool enough so that you can easily handle it.

Cut a circle out of the top of the pumpkin, at least 6 inches across, slanting your sharp knife toward the center of the pumpkin. Lift the lid and scrape out all the seeds and strings. If there is a lot of juice in the pumpkin, pour it off into a bowl and reserve it. Use a small, sharp knife to slice away a bit of the flesh from the thickest part of the lid and the sides, but don't overdo it. Dice this up and save it to add to the stuffing.

Heat the olive oil in a large sauté pan. Add the onions and fennel with ½ teaspoon salt and sauté them over high heat for 7 to 8 minutes, stirring often. Add the celery, herbes de Provence, sage, and crushed red chiles, lower the heat, cover the pan, and cook another 20 minutes, stirring often. The vegetables should be tender and golden brown. Add the apples, raisins or cranberries, mustard greens, and parsley and cook another 10 minutes. Stir in 4½ cups of the farro and black rice pilaf and 1½ cups of the diced pumpkin.

In a small bowl, whisk together the miso and mirin. Add the nuts to the pilaf mixture, drizzle in half of the miso mixture, mix well, and taste. Add as much more of the miso mixture as you like, but take care not to oversalt; miso adds a lovely depth of flavor, but it is salty.

Preheat the oven to 375°. Oil the inside of the hollow pumpkin and sprinkle it lightly with salt and pepper. Fill the pumpkin with the pilaf mixture, replace the top, and place the pumpkin in a large, shallow gratin dish. The dish should be deep enough to catch the juices that may drip out and attractive enough to use as a serving dish. Remember, the pumpkin needs some room to open up when you slice it, so make sure the baking dish is large enough, with several inches of clearance all around.

Roast the stuffed pumpkin for 1½ hours, or longer for a larger, denser pumpkin. Cooking time will depend on the size and type of pumpkin and the temperature of your stuffing going in. It is done when the pumpkin gives with a gentle push from a wooden spoon, juices are flowing into the baking pan, and a cloud of steam is released when you lift the lid. If in doubt, open the pumpkin, test the inside of the filling for heat, and cut out a tiny piece from the inside wall of the pumpkin itself to check for tenderness. When roasting a big pumpkin, it's best to allow plenty of time, and nothing will be harmed if the pumpkin has to wait on the counter, covered in a foil tent, for half an hour or so. It will not cool off quickly, don't worry.

To serve, bring the roasted pumpkin to the table on its ample gratin dish. Lift the pumpkin's cap and cut the pumpkin into fat wedges, slicing through the skin, which is now soft. The wedges will fall away as the pumpkin blooms like a flower, and pilaf will spill out from the center. Place a wedge of pumpkin on each plate and spoon pilaf over it.

Serves 8 to 10 as a center-of-the-plate extravaganza

Choosing Your Great Pumpkin . . .
You will want a large pumpkin, 7 to 8 pounds, and, most important, tasty. The French market pumpkin is a good one; it has wide, plump ridges, a pale apricot-colored skin, and a pleasantly vegetal flavor. Blue Hubbards are also excellent, and slightly sweeter. I love the superb flavor of kabocha squash, but it may be difficult to find one large enough, and kabocha is also denser than the others, so you might have to add some broth to the filling. And remember, different pumpkins are available in different areas, so ask at the local farmers' market. To be really sure what you are getting, buy a smaller pumpkin the week before and test it: roasting even a few wedges will tell you what you need to know.

In a Flexible Thanksgiving Menu . . .
This dish was improvised one Thanksgiving day, and The Great Pumpkin (p. 22) is the relaxed holiday menu built around it. It is accompanied by roast turkey breast, persimmon and cranberry relish, and a brilliantly refreshing chicory and kale salad.

PIZZA AND OTHER
SAVORY PIES

PIZZA AND OTHER SAVORY PIES

There are few food cultures that do not include some form of bread wrapped around a savory filling. It is the portable meal. In some cases it has become a cultural icon, and a survival mechanism. Where would we be without pizza? Thousands of college students would simply perish instead of graduating and going on to lead productive lives.

And who does not love a savory deep-dish pie? A generous, overfilled pastry, layers of vegetables, cheeses, or meats wrapped in the warm embrace of freshly baked bread . . . A big tart or cobbler, so splendid on the table . . . The meal plan is easy. Pair a wedge or a fat slice with a fresh salad in warm weather, with a steaming soup on a chilly day, and there you are.

I love pizza, and I love big galettes made with olive oil dough, with the plump golden crown of the crust surrounding the savory filling. Savory galettes are pizza with the edges folded up so they can hold more filling. They are excellent hot from the oven, just as tasty at room temperature, so they can be made well ahead. And a galette made with olive oil dough is sturdy enough to travel to a picnic or potluck. By the slice, it's a brown bag star.

With both pizzas and galettes, you can make a large batch of dough, then divide it to make smaller pies with varied ingredients, some for the vegans, some for the omnivores. One of my favorites is the Onion Agrodolce: red onions cooked to a tangy sweet-sour marmalade and piled on top of roasted tomatoes and garlic. But a few slices of prosciutto or some crisp, spicy Italian sausage could be layered on top of those onions, and so could a soft white cheese. Other galettes in these pages can be adapted in similar ways.

And for the coldest winter day, treat yourself to an Eight-Vegetable Cobbler just out of the oven. Again, so easy to divide this homey comfort food into two smaller cobblers and make one of them a chicken pot pie.

A final word: impressive as these pastries appear on the table, there is nothing mysterious about the techniques involved in making them. Some involve more prep time than others because there are more vegetables to chop or sauté, but in the end . . . easy as pie.

Tomato and Tomato Pizza
with garlic slices (p. 234),
part with fresh mozzarella

TOMATO AND TOMATO PIZZA
WITH GARLIC SLICES

VEGAN, VEGETARIAN, OR OMNIVORE

Not everyone has special pizza pans, stones, and peels. But almost everyone with an oven has a couple of large rectangular baking sheets, and with that you're in business. You can have mouthwatering homemade thin-crusted pizza.

The addition of thin raw tomato slices on top of the sauce is not redundant—it's a spike of bright, acidic flavor that is delightful. Customize this one with slices of fresh mozzarella or slivers of cured ham for the omnivores in your crowd.

FOR THE PIZZA DOUGH:

1²/₃ cups lukewarm water

1 Tbs. active dry yeast

1 tsp. sugar

3¼ cups white bread flour (15 oz.), plus more for rolling out

1 cup whole wheat flour (5 oz.)

1¼ tsp. salt

olive oil for the bowl and the pans

FOR THE EASY PIZZA SAUCE:

one 28 oz. can San Marzano tomatoes, with juice (about 3 cups)

3 cloves garlic

2 Tbs. extra-virgin olive oil

1 tsp. red or white wine vinegar

a pinch of sea salt

a pinch of crushed red chiles

¼ cup sliced basil leaves

Make the dough: Whisk together the water, yeast, and sugar and wait 3 or 4 minutes until a little foam begins to form on top, showing you that the yeast is alive. If you are confident that your yeast is fresh, skip the wait.

In a large mixing bowl, whisk together the flours and the salt and stir in the liquid. Work the mixture gently with your hands only until a sticky dough forms, less than a minute. Turn the dough into an oiled bowl, cover it loosely with plastic wrap, and leave it in a warm area until the dough has at least doubled in size, 1½ to 2½ hours. The time will vary with the warmth of the room and the temperature of the liquid.

Turn the dough out onto a large, floured board and cut it into 2 pieces for large pizzas or 4 for smaller ones. Form each piece into a ball, cover the balls with a slightly damp kitchen towel, and leave to rise again for 30 minutes. At this point the dough is ready to be pressed into a pan or rolled out.

If you are not ready to make pizza yet, wrap the balls of dough well in plastic wrap or in a freezer bag and put them in the refrigerator for up to a day, or freeze for a month. Allow the dough to return to room temperature before proceeding.

Make the sauce: Combine the San Marzano tomatoes and their juice, the garlic, olive oil, vinegar, salt, and chiles in the container of a blender and puree. Pour the sauce into a bowl—it should be soupy but not runny—and stir in the basil leaves. Taste, and add a pinch more salt or crushed chiles if you like. This makes about 3¼ cups sauce, a bit more than you need for 2 large pizzas, but it keeps well in the refrigerator for at least a week.

FOR THE TOPPING:

6 medium tomatoes, any color, very thinly sliced

12 large cloves garlic, very thinly sliced

extra-virgin olive oil

sea salt

freshly ground black pepper

OPTIONAL:

1 lb. water-packed mozzarella, drained and cut in cherry-sized pieces, or 6 oz. prosciutto, cut in strips

Shaping and baking: Preheat your oven to 550° and smear your baking pans liberally with olive oil. Use 2 large rectangular pans or 4 smaller ones—and while it's easier to get a true circle on a round pan, you can make round pizzas on a cookie sheet if you like.

For a large pizza, take half the dough and press it into a thick oval. Place the oval in the middle of an oiled pan and use your hands to gently push and stretch the dough over the pan until it reaches the edges and the thickness feels even. Repeat with the other half of the dough and the second pan.

If you've cut your dough into 4 pieces for smaller, round pizzas, flatten a ball of dough, then roll it out from the center until it is about 8 inches across. Lay the circle of dough over the back of one hand and turn and stretch until you have a 13-inch circle. Lay the circle on an oiled pan. Repeat with the remaining balls of dough.

Spoon about a cup of the tomato sauce over a large pizza and spread it evenly. (If you are making smaller pizzas, use ½ cup per pizza.) Lay the thin slices—and I mean thin—of fresh tomato over the sauce and sprinkle them lightly with salt. Mix the garlic slices with 1 teaspoon of olive oil and a pinch of salt and place them here and there over the tomatoes and sauce. Grind on some black pepper. If you like, dot the pizza with pieces of fresh mozzarella or strips of prosciutto.

Bake the pizza for 12 to 16 minutes, until the edges are browning and crisp and beginning to pull up from the pan. If you slide a spatula under the pizza, it should lift up easily and show you a golden, crusty bottom. Exact time will vary with the true heat of the oven, the thickness of the crust, and the moisture in the toppings, so keep an eye on the pizza during the last few minutes. When the pizza is done, let it rest on the counter for 4 or 5 minutes before slicing.

Makes 2 large thin-crusted pizzas, which can be made in 13-by-18-inch baking pans, or 4 smaller ones, such as 13-inch rounds. Enough for 6 to 8 pizza lovers

---

The Vegan, Vegetarian, Omnivore Way . . .
Everyone loves pizza, so make several smaller pizzas and let everyone into the action, choosing the toppings, adding cheeses, vegetables, sautéed Italian sausage, pepperoni, or whatever appeals. See the variations for more of my favorite toppings.

---

recipe continues

Variation . . . Sweet Onion Pizza

Onions are cooked down to golden sweetness before being slathered over the tomato sauce on the pizza. This comes out of the oven like a bit of heaven.

TO TOP ONE LARGE PIZZA:

3 Tbs. extra-virgin olive oil

3 large yellow onions (about 2 lbs.), quartered and sliced

½ tsp. sea salt, plus more to taste

1 tsp. fresh thyme leaves

2 Tbs. balsamic vinegar, plus more to taste

6–7 Kalamata olives, cut in thin slivers

1 cup Easy Pizza Sauce, plus more to taste

OPTIONAL:

Parmigiano-Reggiano cheese to taste

Preheat the oven to 550° and prepare the dough as instructed above. Heat 3 tablespoons olive oil in a large sauté pan and add the onions, salt, and thyme. Toss the onions on high heat for 7 to 8 minutes, until they are limp and showing brown spots. Add the balsamic vinegar and toss another few seconds, then turn the heat low, cover the pan, and cook the onions gently in their steam another 12 to 15 minutes. Stir in the olives.

Spread the tomato sauce on the unbaked pizza, then scatter the onions over it. If you like, grate some Parmesan over the onions, covering them with a fine dusting. Bake the pizza for 12 to 16 minutes, until done, and leave it to rest for a couple of minutes before slicing.

Variation . . . Potato and Mushroom Pizza

This is the robust comfort-food topping, thick with sautéed mushrooms, potatoes, and onions. It can be topped with provolone cheese for an even heartier meal.

TO TOP ONE LARGE PIZZA:

3 Tbs. extra-virgin olive oil

5–6 cloves garlic, chopped

1 lb. cremini mushrooms, cleaned and sliced

½ tsp. sea salt, plus more to taste

2–3 Tbs. vermouth

1 large onion (8 oz.), quartered and sliced

3 medium yellow potatoes (12 oz.)

a large pinch of crushed or chopped fresh marjoram leaves

½ tsp. chopped fresh thyme leaves

1 cup Easy Pizza Sauce, plus more to taste

OPTIONAL:

3 oz. grated provolone cheese

1 oz. grated Parmigiano-Reggiano cheese

Preheat the oven to 550° and shape the pizza dough as instructed above. Heat 1½ tablespoons olive oil in a large sauté pan and sizzle the garlic in it for 30 seconds, then add the mushrooms and a big pinch of salt and toss them over high heat for 6 or 7 minutes, until they release their water and it cooks away. Add a splash of vermouth, stir as it cooks away, and remove the mushrooms to a bowl.

Give the pan a wipe, add the remaining 1½ tablespoons olive oil, and sauté the onion with a pinch of salt over high heat for about 5 minutes. Meanwhile, scrub the potatoes, quarter them, and thinly slice them. Add the potatoes and herbs to the onions with ¼ teaspoon salt, and continue cooking over medium heat, stirring and turning often, only until the potatoes are tender, 15 to 20 minutes. Stir the mushrooms into the potato mixture.

Spread a cup of pizza sauce over your unbaked pizza, then distribute the mushroom and potato mixture evenly over that. If you like, sprinkle the grated cheeses over the vegetables. Bake the pizza for 12 to 16 minutes, until done, and leave it to rest for a couple of minutes before slicing.

PI DAY PIE
ONION, RED PEPPER, AND SPINACH GALETTE WITH THREE CHEESES

VEGETARIAN

The country block where I live is 3.14 miles around. That's a good morning walk, and also a famous number, the mathematical constant called pi. So when my friend Holly learned that there was an official Pi Day (March 14, of course), she thought we should celebrate with a block party. We decided on a walk around the block followed by a pie potluck. Pi and Pie Day has become a happy neighborhood event.

Here is the robust savory galette I made for the inaugural Pi and Pie Walk. It's large, meant to be shared.

1 large batch whole-wheat Olive Oil Bread Dough (p. 245)

3 lbs. onions, quartered and sliced

3 Tbs. extra-virgin olive oil, plus more for brushing

1 tsp. sea salt, plus more to taste

2–3 Tbs. chopped garlic

1 lb. spinach, washed and chopped

1 or 2 roasted red peppers, seeded and sliced

a few basil leaves, chopped

a big pinch of crushed red chiles

8 oz. *queso fresco*, crumbled

2–3 Tbs. grated Pecorino Romano cheese

3–4 oz. fresh white goat cheese

Make the filling while your dough rises. In your largest sauté pan, sear the onions in 2 tablespoons olive oil, with the sea salt, tossing and stirring over high heat for about 5 minutes, until they show brown spots. Lower the heat, cover the pan, and stir the onions occasionally for 20 to 25 minutes. They should be soft, moist, and golden.

Heat the remaining 1 tablespoon olive oil in a nonstick pan, stir the garlic in it for a minute, then add the spinach and a pinch of salt. Cook the spinach over high heat until it is wilted and excess moisture cooks away, 5 to 6 minutes. Stir the spinach into the onions, along with the sliced red peppers, basil leaves, and crushed red chiles. Remove from the heat. Stir the *queso fresco* and Pecorino Romano into the vegetables.

On a large, well-floured board, roll out the dough to a large circle, or an oval about 20 inches long. Transfer it carefully to an oiled baking sheet, letting it overhang the pan. Spoon the filling evenly over the dough, leaving a 2-inch border all around. Break up the goat cheese into bits and scatter them over the filling. Now pull the border of dough up and over the edges of the filling, folding it into loose pleats.

Leave the pastry to rest for about 20 minutes as you preheat the oven to 400°, then bake the galette for 30 to 40 minutes. Check it after 20 minutes, and if the crust is browning quickly, lay a piece of foil loosely over the top. It is done when the crust is nicely browned and sounds hollow when tapped and the filling bubbles a little.

Brush the top of the pastry generously with olive oil, and let the galette cool slightly before slicing into wedges to serve. Eat it hot, warm, or at room temperature.

Serves 8 to 10 as a center-of-the-plate slice, more as an appetizer

Omnivore Toppings . . .

With the Mediterranean flavors of this big pie, prosciutto or *jamón serrano* is an easy match. Mix strips of ham with the goat cheese on top, a method that allows you to make a half-and-half pie, one side with ham and the other side vegetarian. Another interesting garnish for meat-eaters is Mint-Scented Pork and Pine Nut Meatballs (p. 363); cut them in half and place them cut side down between the chunks of soft cheese.

A Vegan Filling . . . Green Galette *with spinach, potatoes, and basil*

Use this zesty green filling for a pie made without cheese.

3½ Tbs. extra-virgin olive oil, plus more for brushing

2 medium yellow onions (12 oz.), coarsely chopped

1½ tsp. sea salt, plus more to taste

3 medium Yukon Gold potatoes (12 oz.), scrubbed and cut into ½-inch dice

freshly ground black pepper

4–5 cloves garlic, chopped

1½ lbs. spinach, chopped

⅔ cup (1 oz.) coarsely chopped basil leaves

2 tsp. fresh lemon juice

⅓ cup pine nuts

1 large batch Olive Oil Bread Dough (p. 245)

Heat 1½ tablespoons of the olive oil in a large nonstick pan and sear the onions with ½ teaspoon salt over high heat, stirring often, for 4–5 minutes. Add the potatoes and a big pinch of salt and toss over medium-high heat for 5 minutes, then lower the heat, add a tiny bit of water for steam, and cover the pan. Stir once or twice for the next 15 minutes. The potatoes should be very tender. Add a few grinds of black pepper.

Sauté the chopped garlic in 2 tablespoons olive oil for a minute or two, add the chopped spinach and ½ teaspoon salt, and cook over medium heat, stirring now and then, until the spinach is wilted and all the excess liquid is gone, about 10 minutes. Add the basil and lemon juice and toss over medium heat another minute or two. Stir the potatoes and onions and the pine nuts into the spinach mixture. Proceed to roll out and fill the dough, and bake the galette as described in the recipe above.

ONION *AGRODOLCE* GALETTE

VEGAN OR VEGETARIAN

The red onions in this galette are the *agrodolce*—a little sweet and a little sour—and they are piled on top of roasted plum tomatoes and garlic. The result is pungent, rich, deeply satisfying. You can add a fresh white cheese or not; either way, it's a wealth of flavor.

1 regular batch Olive Oil Bread Dough (p. 245)

3 lbs. fresh plum tomatoes, peeled, or 2 large cans peeled plum tomatoes

4 Tbs. extra-virgin olive oil, plus more for brushing

½ head garlic, separated into cloves, not peeled

1 tsp. sea salt, plus more to taste

1½ lbs. red onions, quartered and sliced

1 tsp. chopped fresh thyme

¼ cup raisins

1 Tbs. red wine vinegar

OPTIONAL:

4 oz. crumbled white goat cheese or other fresh cheese

Prepare the dough according to the recipe, and while it is rising, prepare the filling. (If your dough is ready in the fridge, let it come to room temperature.)

Preheat the oven to 375°. Cut the tomatoes in half lengthwise and drain them briefly in a colander, reserving the juice. Mix the tomatoes with 2 tablespoons olive oil, the unpeeled garlic cloves, and ½ teaspoon salt and spread them in a single layer on a large rimmed baking sheet. (If using canned tomatoes, drain them well, reserving the juice, then proceed the same way but skip the salt.) Roast the tomatoes for 1 to 1½ hours, until they are soft and showing brown spots on the bottom.

Heat 2 tablespoons olive oil in a large sauté pan and sauté the onions in it with the remaining ½ teaspoon salt, tossing over high heat for about 5 minutes. Lower the heat, cover the pan, and cook the onions gently for 30 to 35 minutes, stirring now and then, until they are soft and sweet. Stir in the thyme, raisins, and vinegar. Taste, and add salt if more is needed.

Pull the garlic cloves out of the roasted tomatoes, squeeze out the soft garlic, and discard the peels. Mash the garlic slightly with a fork and mix it back into the tomatoes. Add enough of the tomato juice to make a thick sauce. You should have about 2 cups.

Roll out the dough on a lightly floured board, making a circle 15 to 16 inches across. Transfer the dough carefully to an oiled baking sheet, letting the edges hang over, and brush it lightly with olive oil. Spread the thick roasted tomato sauce evenly over the dough, leaving a 2-inch border all the way around. Spread the onion mixture on top of the tomatoes. If you are adding cheese, scatter crumbles over the onions.

Fold the border of the dough up over the edge of the filling in loose pleats.

Leave the galette to rest for about 20 minutes as you preheat the oven to 400°, then bake it for 30 to 35 minutes. The folded-over pastry should be puffed up and golden brown, the filling in the center bubbling hot.

Brush the pastry border with olive oil, and allow the galette to cool slightly before cutting it in wedges to serve. It is delicious hot, warm, or at room temperature.

Serves 6 as a center-of-the-plate dish, more if served as an appetizer

---

An Omnivore Meal . . .
Make a meal for everyone by pairing this savory pastry with fennel-scented Italian sausages for the omnivores, quickly grilled or sautéed—they're a fine flavor match for the agrodolce. And for everyone at the table, add a salad of dandelion greens or wild arugula and a bowl of olives.

In a Festive Menu, with something for everyone . . .
Cocktails on New Year's Eve (p. 32): Taste your way into a new year with this galette and a dozen other flavors, including pumpkin-seed pesto, mint-scented pork, mojo verde, farro with dandelions and dried cherries, smoked trout . . .

Kabocha Squash and Kale Galette (p. 243)

KABOCHA SQUASH AND KALE GALETTE

VEGAN OR VEGETARIAN

Kale and kabocha, that handsome, tasty winter pair, step out together in a hearty pie that looks as fabulous as it tastes. I've made galettes with every winter squash I love. Kabocha wins—delicious, widely available, and it does not have to be peeled.

1 medium-small kabocha squash (about 2 lbs.)

3 Tbs. extra-virgin olive oil, plus more for brushing

1¼ tsp. sea salt, plus more to taste

1 lb. yellow onions (2 medium), quartered and sliced

2 large cloves garlic, finely chopped

½ lb. Tuscan kale, stemmed and cut into thin strips (8 cups)

3-4 Tbs. golden flame raisins or tart dried cherries

3-4 Tbs. pine nuts

¼ cup vegan cream cheese or ¾ cup crumbled *queso fresco*

1 regular batch Olive Oil Bread Dough (recipe follows)

Preheat the oven to 400°. Scrub the squash—you're not peeling, remember?—cut it in half, scrape out the seeds, and then cut it up into fairly thin wedges, about ½ inch at the rind. Toss the squash wedges in a large bowl with 1 tablespoon olive oil and ½ teaspoon salt, rubbing them lightly with your hands until all of them are coated. Spread the squash on a baking sheet in one layer and roast it for 35 to 40 minutes, turning the wedges over once halfway through. The squash will be tender and browned.

Meanwhile, heat 1 tablespoon of olive oil in a large nonstick pan, toss the onions in it with ½ teaspoon salt, and cook over high heat for 5 minutes. Lower the heat, cover the pan, and cook the onions slowly for 30 to 35 minutes, stirring occasionally, until they are soft and golden brown.

Push the onions out to the edges of the pan, add the remaining 1 tablespoon of olive oil in the center, then add the chopped garlic and stir it for a minute or two. Add the kale and the remaining ¼ teaspoon salt and toss everything together for a few minutes, until the kale has wilted. Add a couple of tablespoons of water to the pan, cover it, and leave the kale to cook in its steam for about 15 minutes, checking once or twice to make sure it is moist. Remove the kale from the heat and stir in the raisins, pine nuts, and vegan cream cheese or *queso fresco*.

When the squash is ready, put aside 6 or 8 of the best-looking wedges and cut the rest into ½-inch pieces; you'll have about 2 cups. Stir the squash cubes gently into the onion and kale mixture. Use your hands for this, as you don't want the pieces of squash to break up completely.

recipe continues

On a large, floured board, roll out the dough into a thin round about 15 or 16 inches across. Transfer it to an oiled baking sheet and spoon the filling into the center of the dough, spreading it evenly and leaving a 2-inch border all around. Fold the edges of the dough up over the filling in loose pleats. Arrange the reserved squash wedges randomly in the exposed center of the galette.

Preheat the oven to 400°. Bake the galette for 30 to 35 minutes. Check it after 10 minutes, and if it is beginning to brown quickly, cover it loosely with a piece of foil. The galette is done when the pastry is lightly browned and sounds hollow when tapped. Remove it from the oven and brush the pastry generously with olive oil. Serve the galette hot, warm, or at room temperature.

Serves 6 to 8 as a center-of-the-plate slice, more if cut into small wedges for appetizers

Add Cheese . . .

This galette can be a vegan dish—that was the first way I made it—but an excellent version can also be made with *queso fresco* or cream cheese. If you are using *queso fresco*, go a little lighter on the salt and adjust the seasoning to taste when everything is stirred together. An omnivore's pie can be made as well, with slices of sautéed smoked sausage layered in between the squash wedges that decorate the top.

Matchmaking . . .

Any savory galette can be paired with a bowl of soup for a fast lunch or easy supper, an elevated version of the soup-and-sandwich tradition. And see the Menu on p. 246.

OLIVE OIL BREAD DOUGH,
REGULAR AND LARGE BATCH

VEGAN

Use any proportion you like of white and whole-wheat flour; I usually do a fifty-fifty mix, which makes a dough that is easy to work with yet full of nutty whole-wheat flavor. Whole-grain flour is heavier than refined flour, so if you use only whole-wheat flour, the rising time will be a bit longer, and you'll get a denser pastry.

FOR A REGULAR BATCH, A GALETTE TO SERVE 6:

1 tsp. active dry yeast

2 tsp. sugar

1 cup lukewarm water

2¼ cups flour (12 oz.), plus more for the board

1 tsp. sea salt

2 Tbs. extra-virgin olive oil, more for the baking sheet

FOR A LARGE BATCH, 1 VERY LARGE GALETTE OR 2 SMALLER ONES:

1⅓ tsp. active dry yeast

2 tsp. sugar

1⅓ cups lukewarm water

3½ cups flour (1 lb.), plus more for the board

1⅓ tsp. sea salt

3 Tbs. extra-virgin olive oil, plus more for the baking sheet

Dissolve the yeast and sugar in the warm water and set it aside for a few minutes, until it begins to foam up. In a mixing bowl, mix the measured flour with the salt.

Whisk the measured olive oil into the yeast mixture. Pour the liquid into the flour and mix with a wooden spoon until a dough forms; it should be quite soft. Turn the dough out onto a lightly floured board and knead it for 3 to 4 minutes, until it is smooth and pliant, springing back when pushed down. Add sprinkles of flour only as you need them to keep the dough from sticking, but don't let it get stiff and dry.

Form the dough into a ball and put it into an oiled bowl, turning it once. Cover the bowl with a towel or with plastic wrap and leave the dough in a warm, draft-free place to rise for about an hour, or until roughly double in size. Rising time can vary depending on air temperature. When the dough has doubled in volume, punch it down. It is now ready to roll out, fill, and shape according to the recipe.

Working Ahead . . .
You can wrap this dough well (freezer bags are good) and put it away in the refrigerator for a day or two. Even in the refrigerator it will want to keep rising, though very slowly. Don't worry—just punch it down again when ready to use it. This dough can also be frozen. Allow it to thaw completely and come to room temperature before proceeding with a recipe.

LET'S HAVE A PIE

This galette is a deep-dish beauty, with layers of savory goodness under that pleated rim of olive oil dough. It's piled with sautéed onions and greens and topped with burnished roasted squash wedges. What could be better on a fall day? And it's adaptable: add *queso fresco* to the vegetable mix for a richer pie, or layer in some thinly sliced smoked sausage if you're going the omnivore way. My galettes are all about adding more. If you want galettes for a mixed crowd, nothing is easier than dividing a big batch of dough and baking two smaller galettes, with customized fillings.

Because the galette is so big and bready and chewy, I like to keep the rest of the menu light. I love the slightly crunchy, intensely green parsley salad with its sting of radish. It's one of the best salads I know for the cold season. And the Roasted Red Pepper Soup is a warm, sweet and spicy counterpoint to all the green; it elevates this to a substantial meal.

Of course, for an everyday lunch or supper, simply pair a fat wedge of galette with either the soup or the salad, and have an apple for dessert. The same kind of easy pairing can be done to make a meal of any one of these savory pies. I match the Green Galette with spinach, potatoes, and basil with a tomato salad in the summer, and with any radicchio salad in winter. Eight Vegetable Cobbler can be made in two versions, one of them a chicken pot pie, and needs nothing more than a salad with some spicy bite to it, like Watercress and Chicory with pumpkin seeds, to be a satisfying meal on a chilly night. Are you ready to spend just a bit of time in the kitchen? Let's have a pie.

A Practical Note . . .

The soup and the salad are both vegan, and so is the apple compote if served without ice cream. The kabocha squash and kale galette can be made in a vegan, vegetarian, or omnivore version.

THE SAVORY PIE MENU

FOR 6 TO 8

Roasted Red Pepper Soup with Tomatoes

———

Kabocha Squash and Kale Galette
with cheese or with smoked sausage

Parsley and Radish Salad

———

Basil-Scented Apple Compote
vanilla ice cream

Chicken and Vegetable Cobbler (p. 250)

EIGHT-VEGETABLE COBBLER

VEGETARIAN OR OMNIVORE

An array of winter vegetables, roots and dark greens, come together in this generous, old-fashioned cobbler topped with buttermilk biscuits. Comfort food. Serve this with a bright-flavored salad, maybe watercress, or a slaw with some fresh citrus.

4 Tbs. extra-virgin olive oil, plus more to taste

1¼ lbs. red onions (2 large), coarsely chopped

2½ tsp. sea salt, plus more to taste

2 cloves garlic, chopped

8 oz. cremini mushrooms, cleaned and sliced

1–2 tsp. chopped fresh thyme

2 dried *chiles de árbol*

12 oz. young carrots (1 bunch), peeled and sliced

2 medium potatoes (10–12 oz.), peeled and cut into ¾-inch dice

12 oz. yams, peeled and cut into ¾-inch dice

1 large celery root (12 oz.), peeled and cut into ¾-inch dice

8–10 oz. Tuscan or curly kale (1 bunch), sliced or cut into bite-sized pieces

Heat 1½ tablespoons olive oil in a nonstick pan and sauté the chopped onions with a big pinch of salt for 5 minutes over high heat, stirring, then lower the heat, cover the pan, and cook them gently for 40 minutes, until they are golden brown and jamlike.

Meanwhile, in a large sauté pan, heat the remaining 2½ tablespoons olive oil and sizzle the garlic in it until it barely colors, then add the mushrooms, a pinch of salt, the thyme, and the chile de árbol. Toss the mushrooms over high heat until they release their moisture, then lower the heat to medium and stir for a few minutes, until they take on a golden color. Add the carrots, potatoes, yams, celery root, and 1 teaspoon salt and stir occasionally over medium heat for 10 minutes. Add the kale and the vegetable broth, lower the heat, cover the pan, and let the vegetables simmer and steam for another 5 to 6 minutes.

Stir in the peas, milk, chopped parsley, several grinds of black pepper, and the well-caramelized onions. Stir together for a minute or two, then turn off the heat. The mixture should be a robust vegetable stew, with the potatoes falling apart just a little to thicken the liquid. If it seems too thick—no actual sauce around the vegetables—add a bit more vegetable broth. Taste, correct the seasoning with more salt if needed, and spoon the vegetable stew into a large gratin dish.

Preheat the oven to 400°. Combine the flour, baking soda, baking powder, the remaining 1 teaspoon salt, and a few grinds of black pepper in a food processor. Add the butter, cut in pieces, and pulse briefly, until the mixture looks like cornmeal. Transfer the mixture to a bowl, stir in

recipe continues

1½ cups vegetable broth, plus more as needed

1½ cups green peas (frozen peas are okay)

1½ cups whole milk

3 Tbs. chopped fresh flat-leaf parsley

freshly ground black pepper

2 cups (9 oz.) unbleached white flour

1 tsp. baking soda

2 tsp. baking powder

3½ Tbs. butter, cold

2 oz. sharp cheddar cheese, grated

1⅓ cups buttermilk

the grated cheese, then stir in most or all of the buttermilk, just until a dough forms—don't overmix. Spoon the biscuit dough evenly over the vegetable stew. Bake the cobbler for 30 to 35 minutes. The biscuit topping should be puffed up and golden brown.

Serves 8 as a hearty meal

An Omnivore Variation . . . Chicken and Vegetable Cobbler
Turning part of this cobbler into a biscuit-topped chicken pot pie is the work of a moment. When the vegetable filling is ready, divide it into two portions, one a bit larger than the other. To the smaller portion, add ½ pound of roasted chicken, skinned and cut into medium dice. That's about 2 cups. Then, instead of using your biggest gratin dish, spoon the two fillings into 2 large deep-dish pie pans. Make the biscuit topping as above, spoon it over the two mixtures, dividing it equally, and proceed to bake the cobblers.

CHRISTMAS EVE PIEROGI
WITH POTATO FILLING
OR CABBAGE FILLING

VEGETARIAN OR VEGAN

Delicate, rich, melt-in-your-mouth morsels . . . and plenty of Polish soul-food flavor. These bite-sized pastries are labor-intensive, but somehow, every year as Christmas approaches, we decide again that they are worth the effort. The rolling and filling becomes a communal task. We make a couple hundred, which means 3 or 4 batches of dough and both fillings. And I now make at least one batch with the vegan pastry dough (p. 255).

CREAM CHEESE PASTRY
FOR PIEROGI

VEGETARIAN

2¾ cups (12½ oz.) unbleached all-purpose flour

1 tsp. sea salt

8 oz. butter, cold, cut into pieces

8 oz. cream cheese, cold, pulled into pieces

3–4 Tbs. cold milk or cream, as needed

Put the flour and salt into the container of a food processor, add the butter and cream cheese, and process briefly, until you have an even, mealy texture with no big lumps. Add a bit of chilled milk or cream and pulse again, just until the dough holds together. Remove the dough and form it into a disk about 1-inch thick. Wrap it in plastic wrap and put it in the refrigerator to chill for at least 30 minutes, longer if possible.

This is enough for 45 to 50 pierogi, a few more if you reroll the dough scraps

recipe continues

POTATO FILLING
FOR PIEROGI

VEGAN

---

2 lbs. Yukon Gold potatoes or other creamy potatoes

1 tsp. sea salt, plus more for the pot

2 Tbs. extra-virgin olive oil

2 medium yellow onions (1 lb.), very finely chopped

freshly ground black pepper

OPTIONAL:

2–3 Tbs. vegan cream cheese (I use Tofutti)

Cook the potatoes gently over medium heat in boiling salted water until they are just tender enough to pierce with a fork, 20 to 35 minutes, depending on their size. Remove them and let them cool until you can handle them, but don't let them get cold. Pull off their skins, cut them into thick slices, then put them through the fine blade of a food mill or through a ricer.

Heat the olive oil in a large nonstick pan and add the chopped onions and ½ teaspoon salt. Stir frequently over high heat for 7 to 8 minutes, until the onions are limp and show flecks of golden brown, then turn the heat to low, cover the pan, and stir occasionally for the next 45 minutes to an hour, until the onions are golden brown and jammy.

Add the riced potatoes to the caramelized onions in the pan, along with the remaining ½ teaspoon salt, plenty of freshly ground black pepper, and 2 tablespoons vegan cream cheese, if you are using it. Mash everything together with a potato masher and continue to cook, stirring frequently, as the mixture reduces to a fairly thick paste, probably 7 to 8 minutes, but the time depends on moisture content. Taste, and add more salt and pepper if needed. Put the filling in a covered container and chill it; it will stiffen and be much easier to handle.

You'll have about 3 cups of potato filling, enough for 60 to 70 pierogi

CABBAGE FILLING
FOR PIEROGI

VEGAN

1½ lbs. trimmed green cabbage

2 Tbs. extra-virgin olive oil

2 medium onions (about 1 lb.),
very finely chopped

1½ tsp. sea salt, plus more to
taste

1 Tbs. vegan butter, such as Earth
Balance

1 Tbs. cider vinegar

4 Tbs. finely chopped fresh dill

1 small Yukon Gold potato (4 oz.),
cooked and mashed or riced

Shred or chop the cabbage very finely, using a food processor. You should have about 4 cups of packed shredded cabbage. (You won't believe this when you start, but you will have about 2 cups of filling at the end.)

Heat 1 tablespoon olive oil in a large nonstick pan and add the finely chopped onions and ½ teaspoon salt. Stir frequently over high heat for 7 to 8 minutes, until the onions are limp and show flecks of golden brown, then lower the heat, cover the pan, and stir occasionally for the next 45 minutes to an hour, until the onions are deep brown and jammy-sweet. Don't eat them. You need them for this recipe.

Meanwhile, heat the remaining 1 tablespoon olive oil and the vegan butter in another large nonstick pan and add the shredded cabbage and a scant teaspoon of salt. Stir over high heat for 5 minutes, then turn the heat to low, cover the pan, and cook the cabbage slowly, stirring now and then. If the cabbage appears to be drying out and in danger of scorching, add a spoonful of water.

When the cabbage is golden and dramatically reduced, stir in the cider vinegar. Combine the onions and cabbage in one pan, add the dill and the potato, and mash it all together with a potato masher. Continue cooking over low heat, stirring as the mixture reduces, until you have a thick paste. Depending on the moisture content, this could take from 10 to 20 minutes. Taste, and add a pinch more salt if needed. Chill this before using, as it will become stiffer and easier to handle.

You should have about 2 cups of dense, savory brown filling, enough for 45 to 50 pierogi

recipe continues

ROLLING, SHAPING, AND BAKING PIEROGI

additional unbleached all-purpose flour, for rolling out

1–2 egg yolks per batch of dough

Have your filling ready; I like to shape little nuggets of filling, the size of large cherries or small walnuts, and line them up on a tray.

Sprinkle flour on a large board and roll out half the dough, working carefully and adding flour as needed to keep the dough from sticking, until you have an even sheet of pastry about ⅛-inch thick—very thin! Run your hand over it lightly to feel for thicker or thinner spots and try to make it as uniform as possible. Cut the dough in 3-inch rounds, using a cookie cutter. Lift away the scraps and cover them with plastic wrap. Now give each circle of dough a quick roll to expand its size slightly; this takes only seconds.

Whisk the egg yolk(s) with 2 tablespoons water. Brush the edges of the pastry rounds with the egg yolk wash, and place a nugget of filling in the center of each one. Fold each pastry circle over its filling and press the moistened edges together gently but firmly to seal them. Then press the sealed borders of each pastry all around with the tines of a fork to secure the seal and crimp the border. Finally, pierce the top of each pastry with a fork to let air escape; I make different patterns with the fork to mark cabbage or potato. Repeat this process with the remaining dough. You can press together all the scraps and roll them out for another batch, but I don't recommend rerolling more than once.

Preheat the oven to 400°. Make more egg yolk wash and brush the pastries lightly, then bake the pierogi for 20 to 24 minutes, until they are golden brown and nearly firm. Serve hot, warm, or at room temperature.

Working Ahead . . . Unbaked pierogi can be frozen and held up to several months. Arrange them in a single layer on a parchment-lined baking sheet, freeze them, then transfer them to a container or a sealed freezer bag for storage. To defrost, arrange them once again in a single layer on parchment-lined baking sheets.

It seemed like a crazy idea: to make cream cheese pastry without the cream cheese. But Christmas has its own rules. My son Teddy, newly vegan, was willing to skip all the buttery Polish foods—he didn't want to be a bother. But I knew he loved these pierogi, so I decided to crack the code on a vegan version. I tweaked the proportions, tried different products, and settled on Earth Balance, with Tofutti playing the part of cream cheese. A batch or two later, I had a pastry that rolled out and handled like a champ.

2¾ cups (12½ oz.) unbleached all-purpose flour, plus more for rolling out

1 tsp. sea salt

5½ oz. (10 Tbs.) vegan butter, such as Earth Balance, very cold

7 oz. vegan cream cheese, cold

3–4 Tbs. plain soy milk, as needed

½ tsp. tamari or soy sauce

Put the flour and salt into the container of a food processor. Cut the butter into slices, and divide the cream cheese into a few pieces. Add the butter and cream cheese to the flour and pulse briefly, stopping to push the dough down from the sides. If the pastry does not hold together and remains very crumbly, add a teaspoon of water or soy milk and pulse again. Repeat with another teaspoon if needed, but be cautious—you don't want too much moisture. I generally do not need to add liquid unless the weather is unusually dry. As soon as the pastry begins to hold together, remove it from the processor and form it into a disk about 1-inch thick. Wrap it in wax paper or plastic wrap and put it in the refrigerator to chill for at least 30 minutes, longer if possible.

Shape the filling into nuggets, and roll and cut the dough as described above. Whisk 3 tablespoons plain soy milk with 1 tablespoon of flour, and use this mixture to brush the edges of the pastry rounds. Fill, fold, and crimp the pierogi as described above, and pierce each one with the fork.

Preheat the oven to 400°. Take the remaining soy milk and flour mixture and stir the tamari or soy sauce into it. Brush the pierogi lightly with this mixture, and bake them for 20 to 24 minutes, until nicely browned and nearly firm.

In My Christmas Menu . . .
My Christmas Eve (p. 25) is the meal where these pierogi are stars, with porcini soup, Dennis's smoked salmon, and vegetable salad from a family heirloom recipe.

VEGETABLES

VEGETABLE LUCK

I live in a place where there is an abundance of fresh produce all year, and I like to cook, so I get to eat all the vegetables I want—plenty! It is one of the joyful moments of my week to wake on a Sunday morning and head to our local farmers' market. I feel lucky.

Sometimes I make elaborate dishes of vegetables. I love a beautiful risotto studded with golden pieces of kabocha squash, or a big galette with the crust folded over layers of spinach, red peppers, onions, and mushrooms. I've roasted a giant pumpkin stuffed with such a cornucopia of other vegetables that I grunt at the weight when I lift it out of the oven. You will find those and other vegetable extravaganzas in their various chapters—*vegetables are everywhere in this book.*

In this chapter you'll find vegetables on their own. There are substantial dishes, like the charcoal-grilled ratatouille I make in July, when gleaming purple eggplants and juice-heavy tomatoes call to me from the farm stand, or the roasted root vegetables glazed with citrus, burnished in the oven, ready to be eaten by a cozy fire on a winter night.

But here is my favorite way with vegetables: whatever is in season, prepared with a minimum of fuss. The perfect vegetable in its perfect simplicity.

Crisp green asparagus in spring—I snap off the ends, shave it into ribbons, add a drop of lemon and olive oil, and there's a salad.

Broccolini, cut in generous pieces and tossed in the hot wok with slices of garlic, a touch of sea salt, a drop of rice vinegar.

Giant, shiny leaves of rainbow chard, cut up with stems and all, braised with onions, raisins, and pine nuts, just a few minutes in the hot olive oil and a few more in the moisture that is captured under a lid.

Little green Padrón peppers, blistered in a pan with nothing more than olive oil and a sprinkle of coarse salt as they are served, and watch out for the hot ones.

String beans, tossed with oil and sea salt and roasted on a cookie sheet until they are half green and half golden brown, crispy at the ends—like potato chips, only so much better.

Or zucchini (that maligned vegetable!) from the grill, the charred spears mixed with lemon and mint.

A meal composed of a couple of minimalist vegetable dishes like these and a chewy grain or a quick omelet—is there any better argument for home cooking? When I eat this way, I taste the field, the sun, the rain—it's fresh and real, there on my plate. I feel lucky.

CENTER-OF-THE-PLATE VEGETABLES

Ratatouille from the Charcoal Grill (p. 263)

RATATOUILLE FROM THE CHARCOAL GRILL

VEGAN

Ratatouille, the great vegetable dish of Provence, is the pure expression of those sunny fields and gardens. This is a twist on the traditional. The fresh summer vegetables that go into a classic ratatouille are given a smoky upgrade: marinated in a garlicky vinaigrette, and then cooked over hot coals instead of in a pan.

1½ lbs. firm young eggplants

1 lb. green and yellow zucchini

1½ lbs. red and green bell peppers

2 large onions (1¼ lb.)

1½ lbs. ripe red tomatoes

FOR THE MARINADE:

½ cup extra-virgin olive oil, plus more for garnish

2 Tbs. red wine vinegar

2 Tbs. balsamic vinegar, plus more to taste

1½ tsp. sea salt, plus more to taste

freshly ground black pepper to taste

4–6 cloves garlic, minced

1 Tbs. chopped fresh thyme

½ tsp. fennel seeds, lightly pounded

½ cup chopped fresh flat-leaf parsley

Cut all the vegetables in large pieces for the grill. Slice large eggplants about ½-inch thick and thin ones in half lengthwise. Slice the zucchini lengthwise a little thinner than the eggplant. Cut the bell peppers lengthwise in thirds and trim out the cores and seeds. Thickly slice the onions crosswise. Cut the tomatoes in half.

Whisk together all the marinade ingredients, or pulse them briefly in a blender.

Layer the vegetables in a large glass or ceramic dish, brushing them generously on both sides with the marinade as you put them in and leaving the tomatoes for last. Drizzle the remaining marinade over the vegetables in the dish and place the tomatoes cut side down on top of them. Leave the vegetables to marinate for at least an hour, longer if you have plenty of time.

Fire up the coals! When they are ready, grill the vegetables until they are charred and blistered just the way you like them, and tender enough to be flexible but not mushy. The exact time is impossible to call, as it varies with the heat of the coals and the distance between the grate and the coals, but probably 3 to 4 minutes on a side if the coals are nice and hot. I start with the peppers, and then amuse myself by pulling off their charred skins as I grill the eggplants, zucchini, and onions. Grill the tomatoes last, giving them a minute or two on the cut side, then turning them and leaving them on the coals, on their skins, until they are completely soft, up to 7 minutes.

Let the vegetables cool until you can handle them, then scoop the tomatoes out of their skins into a bowl and discard the skins. Drizzle the marinade left in the dish over the tomatoes and crush them with your hands, breaking them up. That's the sauce.

recipe continues

Cut all the other vegetables into generous bite-sized strips and mix them with the tomatoes. Taste, and add more salt, pepper, and balsamic vinegar if needed to get the proper level of zinginess. Serve hot, with a pilaf or rice or orzo, and drizzle a little olive oil on top of each serving.

Serves 6 as a center-of-the-plate dish

Many Easy Ways . . .
Pair ratatouille with a chewy farro pilaf, grilled polenta wedges, or rice. And ratatouille is just as good cold; it loves to go to a picnic, makes a fine filling for wraps or a topping for crostini, maybe with a bit of creamy goat cheese under it.

In a Flexible Dinner Party Menu . . .
A large platter of glistening, freshly made ratatouille is a beautiful centerpiece for a summer meal. See the menu that follows, Vegetables in the Center.

VEGETABLES IN THE CENTER

MENU - FOR 6 TO 8

Farmers' Market Tomato Salad
fresh goat cheese, duck pâté

———

Ratatouille from the Charcoal Grill

Farro with Lentils and Lavender

grilled lamb sausage or Garlic-and-Herb-Rubbed Lamb Chops

———

grilled peaches, or a plate of figs
vanilla ice cream

It's a celebration of summer. The meal starts with a salad of sun-ripened tomatoes and goes on with the gift from Provence, ratatouille—but this is ratatouille from the grill, charred, smoky, juicy, and so good with warm farro scented with herbs from those same Provençal hills. If you like grilling, this is for you. In its simplest form it's a family dinner: a plate of sliced tomatoes sprinkled with herbs, an easy pilaf, and ratatouille. Summer fruit for dessert. But it wants to be a dinner party. So add goat cheese and a pâté with the salad, and elaborate your epic ratatouille with grilled lamb sausage or chops for the omnivores.

If you have pilaf and ratatouille left over, mix them together for one of my favorite grain salads. Add salad greens, or pine nuts, or sliced cured olives. A splash of olive oil and lemon juice. Best lunch ever.

A Practical Note . . .
A beautiful vegan meal starts with the tomato salad, goes on to ratatouille with farro and lentils, and ends sweetly with grilled peaches or figs.

BRAISED WINTER VEGETABLES

VEGAN

Simple root vegetables combined with aromatic fennel, onions, and garlic, seared in a hot pan and then simmered to melting tenderness—this is a deep-flavored dish for fall or winter, not heavy but so satisfying when served with a substantial pilaf or a polenta.

1 lb. carrots

12 oz. parsnips

12 oz. fennel (1 large bulb)

12 oz. celery root (1 large)

12 oz. turnips

8 oz. small yellow or redskin potatoes

6 oz. curly kale (½ bunch)

3 Tbs. extra-virgin olive oil, plus more for garnish

2 dried chiles de árbol

2 bay leaves

½ head garlic, peeled and sliced

2 medium yellow onions (1 lb.), cut in thin wedges

1½ tsp. sea salt, plus more to taste

1½ tsp. chopped fresh thyme

freshly ground black pepper

¼ cup sherry

2 cups diluted vegetable broth

1 Tbs. sherry vinegar

Clean and peel all the root vegetables. Cut the carrots and parsnips in thick slices on a slant. Trim the fennel bulb, quarter it lengthwise, and slice it thickly. Cut the celery root, turnips, and potatoes into pieces of a similar size to the other vegetables. Strip the kale off its stems and tear it into manageable pieces.

Preheat the oven to 375°. Heat the olive oil in a large ovenproof sauté pan, add the chile pods and bay leaves, and stir over high heat for 30 seconds. Add the garlic, onions, fennel, and ½ teaspoon salt and sauté over high heat for 8 to 9 minutes, stirring almost constantly. Add all the root vegetables, the remaining 1 teaspoon salt, the thyme, and plenty of black pepper and sauté for 10 minutes more, stirring often. Lower the heat to medium only if the vegetables are in danger of scorching, but don't be afraid to let them brown; those dark, crusty edges are a good thing.

Add the sherry and toss quickly as it cooks away, then add the vegetable broth, cover the pan, and put it into the hot oven for 15 minutes. Take the pan out and add the torn kale, lifting and turning gently to mix it into the simmering roots, then replace the lid and put the pan back into the oven for another 10 minutes. Check the vegetables: they should be perfectly tender, though still holding their shape. If they are not fully tender, give them a few more minutes in the oven. Just before serving, stir in the tablespoon of sherry vinegar.

Serve the braised vegetables hot and drizzle olive oil on each serving.

Serves 6 generously

Flexible Omnivore Meals . . .

Warm Farro with Lentils and Lavender (p. 220) is my favorite match with this vegetable stew. The farro and green lentils combine for a protein punch; the vegetables bring their savory flavors and juicy textures. For an omnivore meal, add pulled pork or a plump steamed sausage: vegetables on one side of the pilaf, pork on the other, and your favorite spicy relish passed at the table.

This is also an ideal dish for the days after Thanksgiving, when everyone is tired of heavier food. Serve the vegetables over polenta, and heat up slices of leftover turkey for a garnish on the side. Add Parsley and Radish Salad (p. 149), and it's a company meal.

RAJAS CON HONGOS
POBLANO PEPPERS WITH PORTOBELLO MUSHROOMS IN A SKILLET

Rajas are torn strips of charred green chiles—the word literally means "rags"—and they are so delicious with mushrooms, bringing the warmth of peppers to the woodsy, umami depth of fungi.

1 lb. fresh green poblano or pasilla chiles

1 lb. portobello mushrooms

4 Tbs. extra-virgin olive oil

6 cloves garlic, finely chopped

3/4 tsp. sea salt, plus more to taste

a big pinch of crushed red chiles or cayenne

2 tsp. dried epazote, lightly crumbled, or 2 Tbs. chopped fresh epazote

1 lb. red onions, halved and sliced

1 Tbs. balsamic vinegar

2 tsp. chopped fresh oregano or 1 tsp. dried oregano

freshly ground black pepper

1/2 cup coarsely chopped fresh cilantro

GARNISH:

Guajillo Chile Salsa with Tomatillos (p. 73) or other medium-hot table salsa

Char the chiles under a broiler, then pull out their stems and seeds and peel them. (For details, see "A Word About Charring and Peeling Peppers," p. 227.) Tear the clean peppers into roughly 1/2-inch strips. Brush or quickly rinse the mushrooms to clean them, then remove or trim the stems. Cut the large caps in half and slice them crosswise about 1/2-inch thick.

Heat 2 tablespoons olive oil in a large nonstick pan and sizzle the chopped garlic in it for a minute, until it begins to color. Add the sliced mushrooms, 1/2 teaspoon sea salt, a pinch of crushed red chiles or cayenne, and the epazote and sauté over high heat for 12 to 15 minutes, stirring frequently as the mushrooms cook down to a dark, gleaming half of their former volume. Taste, add more salt if needed, and remove the mushrooms from the pan.

Give the pan a wipe and heat the remaining 2 tablespoons olive oil. Sauté the sliced onions with the remaining 1/4 teaspoon salt over medium-high heat for 15 to 20 minutes, stirring until the onions are limp and speckled with dark brown spots. Add the vinegar and toss the onions as it cooks away, then lower the heat. Add the mushrooms and chiles to the onions, along with the oregano and plenty of freshly ground black pepper. Simmer everything together for a few minutes on low, stirring occasionally, to marry the flavors, and add the cilantro just before serving.

recipe continues

Serve the peppers and mushrooms hot, either as a taco filling or wrapped in a larger tortilla for a burrito, or straight up on a plate with a savory rice pilaf and a salad, and pass the salsa at the table.

Serves 6

In an Easy Make-Your-Own Meal . . .
Wrap this flavorful stew in a fresh tortilla, with black beans, queso fresco, and a garnish of shredded cabbage. See Taco Night at Home (p. 312) for more suggestions about the meal where we all make our own, adding shreds of chicken, salsa, vegetables . . .

CITRUS-GLAZED ROASTED ROOT VEGETABLES

VEGAN

Hot out of the oven, these earthy vegetables are tossed in a light glaze that has the irresistible tang of lemon juice and orange zest. So good! And sunchokes (Jerusalem artichokes) lift this above the usual winter combination. Look for them—their nutty taste, reminiscent of sunflower seeds, is worth the trouble.

1 lb. sunchokes (Jerusalem artichokes)

1 lb. carrots

1 lb. celery root

1 lb. purple or white turnips

1 lb. sweet potatoes

2 Tbs. extra-virgin olive oil

1½ tsp. sea salt

freshly ground black pepper to taste

2 tsp. chopped fresh rosemary or 1 tsp. dried rosemary

2 tsp. chopped fresh thyme or 1 tsp. dried thyme

2 tsp. chopped fresh sage or 1 tsp. dried sage

3–4 Tbs. Citrus Glaze (p. 92)

Submerge the sunchokes in a bowl of cool water and scrub them with a vegetable brush. Cut or snap off any knobs that are creating pockets to trap grit, and give them a final rinse under running water. Bring 5 cups salted water to a boil and cook the sunchokes in it for 7 to 8 minutes, or until you can pierce the thick part of one with a fork; you don't want them soft, just not rock-hard. Cut the sunchokes into thick slices or 1-inch pieces, trimming away any discolored bits.

Peel and trim the carrots, celery root, and turnips. Cut the carrots in thick, angled slices and the celery root and turnips in similar-sized pieces. Parboil the celery root over high heat in a pot of salted water for 3 minutes, then drain. Peel the sweet potatoes and cut them into pieces similar in size to the other vegetables. Combine all the vegetables in a large bowl, drizzle them with the olive oil, sprinkle with sea salt, pepper, and the chopped herbs, and toss until everything is thoroughly combined.

Preheat the oven to 400°. Spread the vegetables on 2 baking pans and roast for about an hour, stirring and turning them two or three times, until they are tender and turning golden brown in spots.

Transfer the vegetables to a large, shallow bowl, and just before serving pour about 3 tablespoons of the glaze over them and toss them gently until they are evenly glistening. Add more of the glaze to taste, or pass it at the table.

Serves 6

In a Mixed Menu for Winter . . .
Pilaf and Friends (p. 217) is a meal that pairs these tasty vegetables with scarlet quinoa and pork tenderloin medallions marinated in the same citrus glaze.

ROASTED WINTER VEGETABLE ANTIPASTO
WITH ROSEMARY AND GARLIC

VEGAN

Roasted vegetables are arrayed on a platter in their individual burnished beauty: whole baby carrots and fingerling potatoes, florets of cauliflower, fat wedges of onion and fennel. I love to have this platter at the start of a festive dinner. The vegetables can be a finger food to serve with an aperitif or fork-and-knife food, mingling with other antipasti. And they are perfect at room temperature, so they can be prepared ahead.

The platter described here is made of winter vegetables, but the same idea can be applied in any season, with the vegetables that are best at that moment.

See photo on p. 30.

½ cup extra-virgin olive oil, plus
 more to taste

4 cloves garlic, minced

1 lb. slender carrots

1 lb. slender parsnips

1 lb. fingerling potatoes, any color

1 medium purple or white
 cauliflower (about 1½ lbs.)

3 medium red onions

2 medium fennel bulbs

sea salt

freshly ground black pepper

2–3 Tbs. minced fresh rosemary

OPTIONAL GARNISH:

sprigs of fresh rosemary

Mix the olive oil with the minced garlic and set it aside.

Prepare the vegetables, keeping them separate. Scrub or peel the carrots, leaving ½ inch of the green stems at the end. If some carrots are fatter than others, cut them in half lengthwise, aiming for similar thickness. Do the same with the parsnips. Scrub the fingerling potatoes and trim away any blemishes. Trim the cauliflower and break it into florets roughly the size of a small egg. Peel the onions and cut them in wedges, leaving a bit of the root end on each wedge so they don't fall apart into slices. Trim and wash the fennel bulbs and cut them into wedges the same way, leaving a bit of the core to hold them.

Preheat the oven to 400°.

Stir up the olive oil and garlic. Put the carrots in a wide, shallow bowl and drizzle 1½ to 2 tablespoons of the oil over them. Add ½ teaspoon sea salt, some freshly ground black pepper, and a teaspoon or two of the minced rosemary and mix the carrots up until each one is coated. Spread the carrots in a single layer on a baking sheet.

Put the fingerling potatoes in the same oily bowl and repeat the process: add oil and garlic, and a bit more salt and rosemary this time, then mix well. Spread the potatoes on a baking sheet or in a large pie pan. Do the same for the cauliflower and then the parsnips, omitting the rosemary for these vegetables. Continue with the fennel and red onions, mixing them together.

Each vegetable should be spread in its own pan, large enough to hold the pieces in a single layer, so that each can stay in the oven as long as it needs to reach its tender, caramelized ideal. If any vegetables look dry, add an extra drizzle of olive oil.

Roast the vegetables, from time to time moving them around on their pans and switching pan positions from upper to lower racks. Most of these vegetables need at least 45 minutes, maybe a bit more, to become tender, with browned, caramelized edges. The potatoes will have wrinkly skins. The fennel and onions will be soft.

Arrange the vegetables attractively on a large platter, in their individual groups, and garnish the platter with branches of rosemary if you have some to spare.

Serves 8 to 12 generously, in an antipasto with other dishes

In a Festive Mixed Menu . . .
Italian Style (p. 28) is an exuberant feast that begins with this platter of vegetables on an antipasto table. The celebration goes on with pasta and a steamed fish before arriving at the dessert table. It's Christmas Eve, or New Year's. But on some other, quieter winter evening, the vegetable array itself would make an attractive meal, maybe with a wedge of polenta or a crusty loaf of bread.

ROASTED WILD MUSHROOMS

VEGAN

I love the woodsy perfume of mushrooms, intensified by roasting and set off by garlic, herbs, and wine. This is a simple dish, but made extravagant by the addition of porcini, with their incomparable taste and texture.

If you cannot get fresh or frozen porcini, increase the amounts of other mushrooms and add 3 ounces top-quality dried porcini, rehydrated and rinsed. Save the soaking liquid, strain it through a filter, and use it to moisten the mushrooms as they roast.

2 lbs. mixed mushrooms, such as shiitakes, portobellos, and trumpet mushrooms

1 lb. porcini, fresh or flash-frozen

2 large onions

3 Tbs. extra-virgin olive oil

¼ cup Marsala, plus more if needed

3–4 cloves garlic, minced

1 Tbs. chopped fresh thyme

sea salt to taste

freshly ground black pepper to taste

vegetable broth as needed

Clean all the mushrooms, brushing off the sand and grit and giving them a quick rinse if necessary. Trim stem bottoms if they are woody, but use as much as possible of the thick porcini stems. Leave small mushrooms whole, and cut larger ones into halves or quarters. Large porcini look wonderful when sliced in half lengthwise, to show off their unique shape. Cut portobellos and large shiitakes in ¼-inch slices.

Preheat the oven to 375°. Cut the onions in half and slice them thickly. Combine all the ingredients except the broth in a large bowl and mix gently with your hands, lifting and dropping until all the mushrooms are coated, then spread the mushrooms and onions in a large baking pan and cover tightly with foil.

Roast for 45 minutes, then remove the foil, stir the mushrooms, and roast uncovered for 20 to 30 minutes more. You might have to add a spoonful of vegetable broth or a bit more Marsala if the mushrooms are drying out. There should not be much liquid left in the pan, just enough to glaze the mushrooms and keep them moist.

Serves 8 as a center-of-the-plate dish with polenta, pilaf, or rice

Omnivore Meals on the Wild Side . . .
Serve these deluxe roasted mushrooms with the simplest accompaniment: a bowl of polenta or a pilaf and a crisp salad—perfect. But for your omnivores, you can elaborate the meal with a game meat if any is available; venison and wild mushrooms are a great match, or boar sausage along with that polenta.

SHERRY-GLAZED ROASTED BRUSSELS SPROUTS
WITH FENNEL, RED ONIONS, AND PARSNIPS

VEGAN

A favorite Thanksgiving dish. Brussels sprouts have such character when they are roasted, developing a warm, nutty flavor, and the other vegetables bring their natural sweetness to the mix in the sherry glaze. At the holiday table this robust dish is one of many, but it becomes a vegan meal when paired with lentil and farro pilaf, a bowl of brown rice and a relish, or a simple bulgur dish.

2 lbs. Brussels sprouts (I start with about 2¼ lbs. to allow for trimming)

1½ lbs. red onions

1 lb. fennel bulbs, trimmed

1½ lbs. parsnips, peeled and thickly sliced

1 lb. carrots, orange or pink, peeled and thickly sliced

FOR THE MARINADE:

7½ Tbs. extra-virgin olive oil

6 Tbs. sherry vinegar

2½ tsp. sea salt, plus more to taste

4 Tbs. sherry

1½ Tbs. agave nectar

a pinch of cayenne

1 Tbs. chopped fresh thyme

Trim the Brussels sprouts, pull off damaged leaves, and wash them. Cut larger ones in half lengthwise, aiming for the size of a walnut. Peel the onions and cut them into thin wedges, about ½-inch thick at the outside. Quarter the fennel bulbs lengthwise and cut into ¼-inch slices. Combine all the vegetables in a large bowl. Whisk together all the ingredients for the marinade in another bowl, add two-thirds of it to the vegetables, and mix gently but thoroughly.

Preheat the oven to 400°. Spread the vegetables on 2 large rimmed baking sheets, and roast them for 45 minutes, switching the positions of the pans halfway through and stirring all the vegetables to insure even roasting. After 45 minutes, check them every 5 minutes, stirring each time, until they are tender and golden brown in places. Some of the outer leaves of the sprouts will curl away into crisp brown edges. (The vegetables can be held for several hours at this point, at room temperature, covered with foil.)

Combine the roasted vegetables on one of the sheets—they are reduced now and will fit—and toss them with the remaining marinade. Return the vegetables to the oven, uncovered, for 5 to 10 minutes more, depending on how caramelized you like them. If you have allowed the vegetables to cool, rewarm them in the oven for about 10 minutes, still covered, then toss them with the marinade and return them to the oven, uncovered, for the last 5 or 10 minutes. They should be glossy, moist, and tender.

Serves 10 to 12 as a side dish at Thanksgiving, or 6 to 8 as a substantial dish with a hearty pilaf

FARMHOUSE MUSHROOM RAGOUT

It's a straightforward, homey dish, but with the right mushrooms it's fabulous. Use three or four different varieties for a complex and interesting flavor. I often combine shiitakes with small portobellos and king trumpets. And wild mushrooms—the ones you buy from a knowledgeable source, not the ones on your lawn—will add a lot of depth to this dish.

See photo on p. 278.

about 2 lbs. fresh mushrooms (several kinds)

1 oz. best-quality dried porcini

1 lb. large shallots

6 Tbs. extra-virgin olive oil

1 tsp. sea salt, plus more to taste

4 cloves garlic, chopped

1 tsp. chopped fresh thyme

a pinch of cayenne

freshly ground black pepper to taste

½ cup fortified wine, such as sherry or Marsala

½–1 cup vegetable broth

1½ Tbs. white rice flour

3–4 Tbs. chopped parsley

Clean and trim all the mushrooms, using a mushroom brush or giving them a quick rinse in cool water as you rub off any grit or dirt.

Put the dried porcini in a bowl, pour boiling water over them just to cover, and soak them for 30 minutes or until completely pliable. Remove the porcini, reserving the liquid, and rinse them quickly if you feel any grit, then slice or chop them. Strain the reserved liquid through a coffee filter to take out any dirt.

Slice all the mushrooms into fairly large pieces. Portobellos should be cut in half and then sliced thinly crosswise. Cremini, or Italian browns, just need to be trimmed at the stems and cut in quarters. Trumpets look nice when cut lengthwise up the fat stem and through the cap, into halves, quarters, or fat slices, depending on size. Shiitakes are best cut in thicker slices.

Peel and slice the shallots. Heat 2 tablespoons olive oil in a large sauté pan and sauté the shallots with ½ teaspoon salt over medium-high heat, stirring often, for 12 to 14 minutes. They should be soft and beginning to brown. Remove the shallots from the pan.

Heat 2 more tablespoons olive oil in the same pan and sauté the garlic for about a minute, stirring, then add all the sliced mushrooms, including the porcini, and the thyme, cayenne, black pepper, and remaining ½ teaspoon salt. Toss and stir the mushrooms over high heat until they give up their excess water and it cooks away, then turn the heat down to medium and give them another 5 minutes to develop a golden-brown color. Add the wine and stir for a minute as it steams off.

Pour the filtered mushroom water into a measuring cup and add enough vegetable broth to make 2 full cups. Heat it to a simmer. In a small saucepan, heat the remaining 2 tablespoons olive oil and stir the rice flour into it. Let the oil and flour bubble for about 3 minutes, stirring often. Add the heated broth mixture in a steady stream, whisking it into the roux, and keep whisking until there are no tiny lumps left. Raise the heat and let the sauce boil gently for 5 minutes, whisking occasionally. Add the sauce to the mushrooms, heat everything together for a few minutes, and stir in the parsley.

Serve with rice, with a farro pilaf, or, best of all, with a soft polenta.

Serves 6 when paired with any grain

In a Flexible Menu...
Sunday Dinner Comfort Food (p. 279) pairs this earthy ragout with a fresh corn polenta, along with an easy roast chicken with lemons for the omnivores.

Farmhouse Mushroom Ragout (p. 276)
over Fresh Corn Polenta (p. 190)

SUNDAY DINNER COMFORT FOOD

MENU - FOR 5 TO 6

Pumpkin-Seed Pesto with crackers

———

salad of spicy greens

———

Fresh Corn Polenta
with
Farmhouse Mushroom Ragout

roasted summer tomatoes

Easiest Roast Chicken *stuffed with lemons*

———

Pear and Rosemary Sorbet

This meal says, *Enjoy the last days of summer, fall is on the way.* Sweet late-summer corn turns polenta into something special—a rustic dish with an upgrade. The deep, foresty flavor of a mushroom ragout is the ideal match, and evokes the cooler season to come. Farmhouse Mushroom Ragout is a sauté and a simmer, and can be made with whatever mushrooms are available. Serve polenta and ragout simply, with a spicy salad, for a fine light meal. But if it's Sunday dinner with the family and some are omnivores, a roast chicken fits in with all the flavors. And in late summer, drizzle ripe tomatoes with olive oil and roast them while the chicken is roasting.

A Practical Note . . .
The vegans at your table will dine well—every dish in this menu save the roast chicken is deliciously vegan.

POTATOES AND POBLANOS IN A SKILLET

VEGETARIAN

I'm sentimental about this old-fashioned skillet dish; I learned it long ago from my father-in-law, Rudy, and I used to make it for a late breakfast on Sundays when my kids were small. Rudy's version was made with Ortega chiles, from a can. It's a good, quick dish that way, but I like to use fresh poblanos, which are blessedly plentiful where I live. The fresh green chiles are so bright and full of flavor—a real upgrade.

4 large fresh poblano chiles (about 1 lb.)

2½ lbs. Yukon Gold or redskin potatoes

3 Tbs. extra-virgin olive oil

1 large onion (10 oz.), coarsely chopped

sea salt to taste

2 cloves garlic, chopped

freshly ground black pepper to taste

a handful of chopped fresh cilantro

5 oz. Monterey Jack or cheddar cheese, grated

Char the peppers in a broiler, pull out their stems and seeds, and peel them. (For details on charring peppers, see p. 227.) Cut them into strips or 1-inch pieces. You should have about 1 cup. Boil the potatoes in their jackets in well-salted water until they are barely tender; the time will depend on the size of the spuds. Drain them, let them cool, peel them, and cut them in 1-inch pieces.

Heat 2 tablespoons olive oil in a large nonstick sauté pan, add the onion and a big pinch of salt, and stir over medium-high heat for 6 to 7 minutes, until the onion colors. Make a space in the middle of the pan, add the remaining 1 tablespoon olive oil, and a few seconds later the chopped garlic. Stir the garlic for a minute or so, then stir it into the onion.

Add the cut-up potatoes, at least 1 teaspoon salt, and pepper to taste and sauté everything over medium heat, turning gently but frequently, until the potatoes have brown, crisp edges, 8 to 10 minutes. Stir in the charred poblano peppers and the cilantro, and stir over medium-high heat for another couple of minutes.

Give the pan a shake to spread everything out evenly, then sprinkle the grated cheese over the top, cover, and turn off the heat. Wait 2 minutes—without touching that lid! When you do lift it, the cheese will have melted into the potatoes and chiles in a mouth-wateringly attractive way. Serve at once.

Serves 5 to 6

Potatoes and Poblanos for Tacos . . .
For a divine taco filling to pair with black beans, sauté the potatoes and peppers as described, but skip the cheese at the end. See the menu Taco Night at Home (p. 312) for more matchmaking.

GRATIN OF POTATOES, LEEKS, AND CABBAGE

VEGETARIAN

It was born from a memory of bubble and squeak, a humble Irish dish of potatoes and cabbage, but by the time I added fennel, leeks, and cream, this version had a personality all its own. The vegetables are slowly baked in their rich amalgam of cream, cheese, and vegetable juices until they are tender inside and golden-crusted on top.

1 small head cabbage (about 1½ lbs.)

1 large leek, light green and white parts

1 onion, quartered and sliced

1 Tbs. extra-virgin olive oil

1 Tbs. butter, plus more for the dish

2 large fennel bulbs, quartered and sliced

2 tsp. sea salt, plus more to taste

freshly ground black pepper

½ tsp. dried thyme

1¼ lbs. Yukon Gold potatoes, scrubbed

3 oz. sharp cheddar cheese, grated

1½ cups whole milk

¾ cup heavy cream

Core the cabbage and cut it into 2-inch pieces. Scald the cabbage in boiling water for a minute, then drain. Cut the leek in half lengthwise, wash it thoroughly, then slice it.

In a large nonstick pan, sauté the onion and leek in the olive oil and butter over high heat for 5 to 6 minutes, until soft. Add the fennel and the blanched cabbage, 1 teaspoon salt, plenty of black pepper, and the thyme. Cook over medium heat, stirring often, for 15 minutes, or until the vegetables are tender and have given up some moisture. Meanwhile, cut the potatoes into 1-inch pieces, boil them in salted water over medium-high heat until barely tender, about 10 minutes, and drain.

Preheat the oven to 375°. Gently mix the potatoes into the cabbage mixture, taste, and add salt and pepper if needed. Butter a large gratin dish and spread the vegetables in it. Sprinkle the grated cheese over them evenly. Pour in the milk, and finish by pouring the cream over the top.

Bake the gratin for about an hour, or until it is bubbling at the edges and has formed a golden-brown crust. Serve hot from the oven, with a salad on the side.

Serves 6

Make It an Omnivore Meal . . .
Like most casseroles, this gratin can easily be made two ways. Cabbage, potatoes, cheese—the flavors are a natural with ham. Divide the mixture in half, mix a cup of diced ham into one part, then make two smaller gratins. Or garnish any part of the gratin with crisply sautéed cubes of pancetta.

VEGETABLE SMALL PLATES AND SIDE DISHES

CHAMPIÑONES AL AJILLO
MUSHROOMS IN GARLIC AND PARSLEY

VEGAN

In this familiar bar tapa, the mushrooms are sautéed in a blizzard of garlic and parsley; feel free to use twice as much garlic and a bigger handful of parsley.

1 lb. cremini or button mushrooms

2–3 Tbs. extra-virgin olive oil

5–6 cloves garlic, chopped, or more to taste

½ tsp. sea salt

¼ cup chopped fresh flat-leaf parsley, or more to taste

freshly ground black pepper

a big pinch of crushed red chiles

¾ cup dry white wine

GARNISH:

pieces of crusty, chewy bread

Wash the mushrooms quickly and cut larger ones in halves or quarters.

Heat the olive oil in a medium pan and sauté the garlic in it for 30 seconds or so. Add the mushrooms and salt and stir over high heat until the mushrooms release their juice and it cooks away, 10 to 12 minutes. When the mushrooms sizzle in the hot pan and start turning golden brown, add the parsley, black pepper to taste, the crushed red chiles, and the white wine. Stir as about half the wine cooks away.

Serve on small plates, spooning the mushrooms over chunks of bread to soak up the juices.

Serves 6 to 8 as part of a tapa assortment. This recipe can easily be doubled.

In Flexible Menus . . .
Champiñones fit into any spread of tapas or *mezze*. Serve them with *jamón serrano*, garlicky prawns, Roasted Potato Wedges with Mojo Verde (p. 302), Manchego cheese . . .

BLISTERED CHERRY TOMATOES

VEGAN

You can make these the perfectionist way, with every little tomato blistered yet holding its shape, or you can do my version, where they hang together in a mess of garlicky oil and vinegar mixed with their own sweet juices. Best thing I ever tasted! Spoon them onto crostini or grilled fish. Or toss them with cooked capellini for an easy summer pasta.

2 Tbs. extra-virgin olive oil

4–6 cloves garlic, chopped

2 cups small cherry tomatoes

sea salt

3 Tbs. balsamic vinegar

Heat the olive oil in a medium nonstick pan. When the oil is hot, add the garlic and a few seconds later slide in the tomatoes. Stand back! Add a big pinch of sea salt and move the tomatoes around in the pan, turning them over as they spit and sizzle.

When the tomatoes begin to blister and char and collapse, about 3 minutes, add the balsamic vinegar and swirl it around as it bubbles down to a syrup. Turn off the heat. Your tomatoes are ready to use now, and will also be fine later at room temperature.

Makes about 2 cups

Blistered Cherry Tomatoes (p. 284)

BRAISED CHARD WITH RAISINS AND PINE NUTS

VEGAN

Really easy. I made this on the spur of the moment one evening to go with a frittata when a friend dropped by. It was the hit of our *al fresco* supper. And even though we both had seconds, I had some left for lunch the next day and found it just as good cold.

1¼ lbs. rainbow chard (2 bunches)

3 Tbs. extra-virgin olive oil, plus more to taste

3 large cloves garlic, chopped

a big pinch of sea salt, plus more to taste

2–3 Tbs. fresh orange juice

1 Tbs. rice vinegar or fresh lemon juice, plus more to taste

¼ cup raisins

¼ cup pine nuts, raw or lightly toasted

OPTIONAL:

crushed red chiles

Wash the chard, including the stems. Slice the stems in ½-inch pieces. Cut the leaves lengthwise in half, then crosswise in 1- or 2-inch strips, including the ribs.

Heat 2 tablespoons olive oil in a large wok or sauté pan and sizzle the garlic in it for about 45 seconds, until it barely colors. Add the chard and the salt and stir-fry over high heat for 3 or 4 minutes, until the chard wilts.

Add the orange juice, rice vinegar or lemon juice, and the raisins, toss to mix, then lower the heat to medium and cover the pan. Let the chard steam for about 3 minutes. Lift the lid, toss again over medium-high heat for another 2 or 3 minutes, until the excess liquid is cooked away, and taste. Correct the seasoning with another pinch of salt or a little more rice vinegar or lemon juice. Add the pine nuts, and the crushed red chiles if you like it spicy.

Pile the chard onto a serving platter and give it a finishing drizzle of olive oil.

Serves 4 to 6 as a side dish

Even Easier . . .
Here is the stripped-down version, chard with lemon juice: fast, and excellent hot or warm. Drop the orange juice, rice vinegar, raisins, and pine nuts. Instead, when the chard has wilted and it's time to add acid, splash in 2 or 3 tablespoons of fresh lemon juice, give it a quick toss, and cover the pan. Steam for 5 minutes, then taste for salt, and add a pinch of crushed red chiles. Done and delicious.

SAUTÉED KALE WITH GARLIC

VEGAN

Easy as can be, and always appealing—greens with garlic, my favorite vegetable.

2 lbs. kale (Tuscan, Russian, curly—any kind you like)

2 Tbs. extra-virgin olive oil

4–6 cloves garlic, finely chopped

1/2 tsp. sea salt, plus more to taste

2 Tbs. fresh lemon juice

Wash the kale thoroughly and tear it off its stems. Cut the greens into bite-sized pieces.

Steam the kale over high heat for 3 to 4 minutes, until it is tender but still holds its shape. Shortly before serving, heat the olive oil in a large sauté pan or wok and sizzle the chopped garlic in it for a minute. Add the kale and the salt and toss over high heat for 3 to 4 minutes. Sprinkle on the lemon juice, add more salt if needed, and serve.

Serves 8 as a side dish

Other Greens, Other Easy Ways . . .
More delicate greens, such as spinach, beet greens, chard, and broccolini greens, can be sautéed without the initial steaming to tenderize them.

CHARRED ZUCCHINI WITH LEMON AND MINT

VEGAN

Zucchini mysteriously transforms into something smoky and seductive as it chars over coals or under a broiler, loses moisture, cooks down. This can be a cool, lemony zucchini salad or a warm vegetable dish. It begins with well-charred zucchini spears and lemon, but you can vary it—add a dab of thick Greek-style yogurt or a pinch of oregano.

See photo of Charred Zucchini without yogurt on p. 120.

4 lbs. small or medium zucchini

3 Tbs. extra-virgin olive oil

1 tsp. sea salt, plus more to taste

3-4 Tbs. fresh lemon juice

2 Tbs. finely chopped fresh mint leaves

freshly ground black pepper

OPTIONAL:

½ cup Greek-style yogurt

Wash and trim the zucchini and cut them lengthwise in quarters to make spears, then cut the spears into 3-inch lengths. Toss the zucchini with 1½ tablespoons olive oil and the salt and spread it out on a large baking sheet or two smaller ones.

Grill the zucchini over coals or roast it in a 400° oven or under a hot broiler, turning the spears once or twice, until they are tender and golden brown with charred spots here and there. This can take 30 to 45 minutes, depending on the heat of the coals or broiler.

Let the zucchini cool slightly, then transfer the spears to a large bowl, drizzle with the remaining 1½ tablespoons olive oil and 3 tablespoons lemon juice, add the chopped mint and as much freshly ground black pepper as you'd like, and mix gently. Some of the zucchini might break into smaller pieces, which is fine. Taste and add more salt or lemon as needed.

If you want to add yogurt, stir it in gently at the end, to all or part of this.

Serves 6 to 8 as an appetizer or part of a *mezze* table.

In a Mixed Menu . . .
No One Eats *Mezze* Alone (p. 118) is an easy party menu where this zucchini salad keeps company with Roasted Eggplant and Poblano Chile Spread, Tabbouleh with Chickpeas and Preserved Lemon, Baked Kibbeh Wedges, and other Middle Eastern plates.

Charred Zucchini with
Lemon and Mint (p. 288)
with Greek-style yogurt

A WORD ABOUT STIR-FRY

Remember that *stir-fry* is a verb before it is a noun. Once you understand the verb—the action part—the noun will turn out to be delicious!

Stir-frying is all about being intently present in your task for those few moments. It doesn't take long. It's about seeing, smelling, and feeling, and, of course, tasting.

It is impossible for me to tell you exactly how long it will take for your stir-fry to be ready. Because: How big are the pieces? How much is in the wok? How hot is your flame? How much moisture clings to the leaves of your tatsoi or bok choy or broccoli? So stop worrying about time and give yourself to the experience.

Oil, *hot* oil, then garlic, and a pinch of salt rubbed between your fingers—sizzle! The aroma hits your nose. In go the slivers of onion, toss toss toss, then the broccoli or the Napa cabbage or tatsoi—it's all cut up, ready and waiting, just toss it in. High heat. Sizzle! Toss toss, watch it shrink, and the green color suddenly brightens.

You are at 2 or 3 minutes. A dash of rice vinegar or a few drops of tamari, toss toss, a few spoonfuls of broth or mirin, cover the wok—*whoosh!* Watch the cloud of steam fill it. A minute later, open and taste . . .

And that is the most important part, and all you really need to know. Does it taste good? Tender but still crunchy? Done! Or is it too raw? Then toss toss, and give it another minute or two. The same with the seasoning. Taste. A few crushed red chiles? A drop more vinegar? Here's the wonderful thing: you will *know*.

And you will easily, happily eat good fresh vegetables.

STIR-FRIED ASPARAGUS AND MUSHROOMS

VEGAN

This delicate springtime stir-fry makes good use of cremini mushrooms—Italian browns—or oyster mushrooms, both widely available. However, if you can get morels in their season, don't hesitate. And look for fat asparagus stalks, not the pencil-thin ones.

See the mixed menu that follows.

See photo on p. 292.

2 lbs. asparagus, trimmed

10 oz. cremini or oyster mushrooms

3 Tbs. peanut oil or golden sesame oil

4 large cloves garlic, finely chopped

1/2 tsp. sea salt, plus more to taste

1/4 cup mirin (rice wine)

2 Tbs. tamari or soy sauce

2 Tbs. fresh lemon juice

1 tsp. finely grated lemon zest

2 Tbs. black sesame seeds

As with all stir-fry dishes, have your ingredients measured and lined up by the stove before you fire up your wok. The actual cooking time is 9 to 10 minutes, and the stir-fry is best served as soon as it's done.

Wash the asparagus and snap off the tough bottoms of the stalks. Slice the trimmed asparagus on a deep slant into pieces about 2 inches long. Clean the mushrooms, remove tough stems, and slice them thickly.

Heat the peanut or sesame oil in a large wok, add the chopped garlic, sizzle it for about a minute, then add the mushrooms and the salt. Stir-fry the mushrooms over high heat for about 4 minutes. They should give up their excess liquid and become tender.

Add the sliced asparagus and stir-fry for a minute, then add the mirin, cover the wok to capture moisture, lower the heat slightly, and let the vegetables steam for 3 to 4 minutes, just until the asparagus is tender-crisp. Add the tamari or soy sauce and lemon juice, and stir-fry over high heat again in an open wok for a minute or two to reduce any remaining liquid to a sauce, then stir in the lemon zest and the sesame seeds. Taste, and add salt if needed.

Serves 6 in a combination with other dishes

Stir-Fried Asparagus and Mushrooms (p. 291)

STIR-FRY IS A VERB!

MENU - FOR 5 TO 6

Fried Black Rice with Peanuts

Stir-Fried Asparagus and Mushrooms

Amber-Glazed Tofu

Steamed Cod with Miso and Bok Choy

Lemon Sorbet and an almond cookie

A stir-fry meal expands easily. It can be something simple for the family or a theatrical piece of fun for company—just add another stir-fry. Two woks are better than one, and anyone can learn to toss those vegetables.

These dishes are easy and lovely: bright green asparagus against inky black rice, and golden glazed tofu. The flavors are full, with mirin, tamari, sesame oil, and garlic providing savory depth, brightened with green onions, cilantro, and citrus. Have plain steamed black rice and a mandarin orange from the fruit bowl for dessert. For a dinner party with friends, add a more unusual stir-fry, like Japanese turnips and carrots, or an appetizer, like Spinach with Sesame Dressing (p. 295).

The beauty of stir-fry, of course, is that it is quick—and freshness is essential, so the wok action must happen at the last minute. But you can work ahead! The rice can be held warm for 20 to 25 minutes with no loss of flavor; just mix in the cilantro at the last moment to keep its bright green color. The glazed tofu can also be done several hours ahead of time and reheated in its glaze for a few moments before serving. Only the stir-fried vegetables need your attention in the final minutes, so have all the ingredients lined up, ready to go into the wok. Serve the asparagus first, with the tofu, then serve the cod, which is steamed in the wok on top of its stir-fried greens.

And the Vegan Way . . .
With the exception of steamed cod with miso, every dish in this menu is vegan, as are the additional dishes suggested above—stir-fried Japanese turnips and carrots, and spinach with sesame dressing.

STIR-FRIED JAPANESE TURNIPS AND CARROTS WITH GINGER

VEGAN

Japanese turnips are small and white, about the size of plums. Thin-skinned and delicate, they stir-fry to perfection in just a few minutes. The sweetness of carrots and the snap of ginger set them off beautifully.

12 oz. sweet young carrots

1 lb. Japanese turnips

1 bunch very slender green onions

2½ Tbs. peanut oil

½ tsp. sea salt, plus more to taste

2 Tbs. freshly grated ginger (use a microplane or other fine grater)

3 Tbs. mirin (rice wine)

1–2 Tbs. fresh lemon juice, plus more to taste

2 tsp. slivered preserved ginger (the pickled, salty kind)

Trim and thoroughly scrub the carrots and turnips; there is no need to peel either. Slice the carrots thinly on a slant. Slice the turnips ¼-inch thick; if very large, cut them in half first. Trim and wash the green onions and cut off most of the green part, leaving the white or red bulb with about 2 inches of green. Line up all your prepared and measured ingredients next to the stove.

Heat the peanut oil in a wok or large sauté pan until it is just beginning to smoke and a piece of carrot dropped in the pan sizzles. Add the sliced carrots and the salt. Stir and toss over high heat for about 4 minutes. Add the turnips and the grated ginger and toss toss toss for another 3 minutes.

Add the mirin, give the pan a shake, immediately cover the pan to capture the steam, and lower the heat slightly. After about 2 minutes, add the onions and a spoonful of lemon juice. Toss and stir again in an open wok as the onions go limp. Taste, and add more salt or lemon juice if needed, then quickly stir in the preserved ginger.

Serves 6 when served with rice and other vegetable dishes

Other Vegetable Combinations . . .
Once you feel easy with stir-frying, you will find many tasty combinations and fling them into the wok with zest. Try broccolini with garlic, or kale with trumpet mushrooms. Stir-fry can become a wonderful habit.

SPINACH WITH SESAME DRESSING

VEGAN

I've often enjoyed this simple preparation in Japanese restaurants—slightly salty, slightly sweet, bright green spinach, with a fortune of sesame seeds scattered through the leaves. Served at room temperature as an appetizer, it may be my favorite part of the meal.

1½ lbs. spinach

2½ tsp. tamari or soy sauce

6 Tbs. golden sesame seeds, plus more for garnish

2 Tbs. agave nectar

2 Tbs. mirin (rice wine)

½ tsp. dark sesame oil

sea salt if needed

Trim off the thickest spinach stems and wash the spinach thoroughly. In a large pan or wok, steam the spinach over medium heat in the water that clings to the leaves for about 3 minutes, long enough to wilt it completely. Plunge the wilted spinach into cold water, then immediately drain it and press down on it in the colander to squeeze out excess moisture. Slice the spinach leaves a few times if they are large, but don't chop them. Sprinkle the spinach with ½ teaspoon tamari or soy sauce and toss gently.

Toast the sesame seeds lightly in a dry skillet over medium heat, shaking and stirring until they begin to pop and give off a toasty aroma, just a few minutes.

Whisk together the agave nectar, mirin, sesame oil, and measured toasted sesame seeds. Pour the dressing over the spinach and mix, lifting and turning gently until all the spinach leaves are coated. Taste, and add a pinch of salt if desired. Chill if you like, though this is not necessary.

Arrange the spinach on a serving dish or in small individual bowls and sprinkle with additional sesame seeds.

Serves 6 as an appetizer

STEAMED GREEN BEANS AND CARROTS IN CHARMOULA SAUCE

VEGAN

The snappy, refreshing charmoula sauce can be made a day in advance and kept in a tightly covered container in the refrigerator. Toss the green beans and carrots with the sauce just before serving. But don't think of charmoula as a one-dish wonder—use it with other vegetables, spread it on a sandwich, or use it as a salad dressing.

2 lbs. slender green beans

1 lb. carrots

FOR THE SAUCE:

2 large cloves garlic

1 cup (3 oz.) chopped fresh flat-leaf parsley,

½ cup (1 oz.) chopped fresh cilantro

6 Tbs. extra-virgin olive oil

3 Tbs. fresh lemon juice

¾ tsp. sea salt, plus more to taste

½ tsp. pimentón de la Vera or other spicy smoked paprika

½ tsp. toasted and ground cumin seeds

Wash and trim the green beans and cut them in half if very long. Peel the carrots and cut them into spears about 4 inches long and about as thick as the green beans.

In a food processor, briefly spin the garlic to chop it up, then add all the remaining sauce ingredients and pulse several times. Scrape down the sides of the container with a spatula and pulse again, just until you have a rough pesto consistency. Taste, and adjust the salt if needed. You should have about 1 cup of sauce.

Shortly before serving, steam the green beans over high heat for about 4 to 5 minutes, enough to be tender-crisp, and do the same for the carrots. Steaming the two vegetables separately is preferable, as you can adjust the timing to fit the size and density of each, but if you have cut your carrot spears to mimic the beans in size, you can get away with putting them into the steamer or into boiling salted water all together.

When the beans and carrots are ready, drain them and shake them in a colander briefly to get rid of excess moisture, then toss them with about three-quarters of the charmoula sauce. Add more sauce to your taste and enjoy. This dish is good hot, warm, or at room temperature.

Serves 10 as a side dish

In a Festive Mixed Menu . . .
In Thanksgiving for Everyone (p. 20) the spicy, raw green sauce on these beans and carrots adds zip to the lineup of traditional holiday flavors.

CALABACITAS

WARM SALAD OF STEWED SQUASH, CORN, AND PEPPERS

VEGAN

Calabacitas are any little squashes, and this traditional Mexican dish is a summer essential—a tasty and simple way to bring the abundance of the garden to the table. Serve it as a warm salad, a taco filling, or alongside whatever you might put on the grill.

2 large fresh poblano chiles

1 lb. zucchini (any kind)

4 ears sweet yellow corn

4–5 bell peppers (½ lb.) , red, yellow, or mixed

3 Tbs. extra-virgin olive oil

1 lb. yellow or white onions, coarsely chopped

1½ tsp. sea salt, plus more to taste

1 Tbs. wine vinegar

2 cloves garlic, chopped

1 cup chopped fresh cilantro

2–3 Tbs. fresh lemon juice

OPTIONAL:

1 fresh jalapeño pepper, finely chopped

Char the poblanos under a broiler, pull out their stems and seeds, and peel off the skins. (For details on charring and peeling peppers, see p. 227.) Tear the chiles into strips and cut the strips into 1-inch pieces. Trim the zucchini and cut them into ¾-inch dice. Slice the corn kernels off the cobs. Trim the bell peppers and cut them into ¾-inch dice.

Heat 1½ tablespoons olive oil in a large nonstick skillet and sear the chopped onions in it with ½ teaspoon salt, stirring them over high heat for 5 to 6 minutes or until they show golden brown spots. Lower the heat and cook the onions, covered, for another 4 to 5 minutes, then deglaze the pan with the vinegar and remove the onions from the pan.

In the same pan, heat the remaining 1½ tablespoons oil and sizzle the chopped garlic in it for a minute, then add the zucchini, bell peppers, and the remaining 1 teaspoon of salt. Toss over medium heat for a few moments, add 2 tablespoons water, and cover the pan. Cook the vegetables just until they are tender, 5 to 6 minutes. Add the corn and the poblano strips and cook another 4 to 5 minutes, then stir in the cilantro and 2 tablespoons lemon juice. Taste, and add salt or lemon if needed.

If you want spicy *calabacitas*, stir in the chopped jalapeño chile, a little at a time.

Serves 4 to 6

Another Way . . .
Calabacitas are a natural with black beans. Add 2 or 3 cups of cooked black beans to the vegetables, along with another tablespoon of olive oil and about 1½ tablespoons fresh lemon juice. Now you have a robust squash and bean salad that can argue for its place in the center of the plate. And it is good warm or cold.

HARVEST BREAD STUFFING IN A CASSEROLE

VEGETARIAN OR VEGAN

So many vegetables and fruits—but it turns out to be just the right amount. Baked in its gratin dish, this stuffing forms a buttery crust and stays moist and chewy inside, with the crunchy counterpoint of walnuts. The vegetarians at your table will enjoy it as it is, and turkey-eaters may want to drizzle some Madeira sauce over it. Delicious either way.

1½ lbs. chewy whole-grain bread (about 15 cups cubed)

5 Tbs. extra-virgin olive oil

6 Tbs. butter, plus more for the pan

1 lb. onions, chopped (2½ cups)

12 oz. celery, chopped (2 cups)

1 medium leek, white part only, sliced

1–2 tsp. sea salt

freshly ground black pepper to taste

2 Tbs. cider vinegar

2 cloves garlic, finely chopped

8 oz. brown mushrooms, thinly sliced

1 lb. crisp, tart apples, peeled and diced

1½ cups (5½ oz.) chopped walnuts

¾ cup (4 oz.) dried tart cherries

Cut the bread into pieces ½ to ¾ inch in size and put it in your gigantic mixing bowl.

Heat 4 tablespoons olive oil and 4 tablespoons butter in a very large sauté pan and add the chopped onions, celery, sliced leek, 1 teaspoon of salt, and plenty of freshly ground black pepper. Sauté the vegetables over high heat for about 15 minutes, stirring often, then turn the heat down, cover the pan, and cook, stirring occasionally, for 15 minutes as they soften and color. Stir in the cider vinegar and transfer the vegetables to the bowl with the bread.

Add the remaining 1 tablespoon olive oil to the pan, heat it, stir the garlic in it for a minute, then add the sliced mushrooms and a big pinch of salt. Sauté the mushrooms over high heat, stirring often, until they are golden brown, 9 to 10 minutes. Add the mushrooms to the bread mix, along with the diced apples, chopped walnuts, dried cherries, prunes, and all the herbs. Use your hands to toss everything together gently but thoroughly.

Pour 2 cups of the vegetable broth over the mixture and mix again. Add more vegetable broth as needed; how much depends on how dry your bread was. You want a mixture that is soft and moist throughout but not soggy or soupy. When the consistency feels right to you, taste and correct the seasoning with more salt and pepper if needed.

Preheat the oven to 350°. Pile the mixture into a well-buttered gratin dish; spread it evenly but don't pack it down. Bake for 30 minutes, or 45 minutes if the stuffing was in the refrigerator, then take it out and

3/4 cup (4 oz.) pitted prunes, diced

3/4 cup chopped fresh flat-leaf parsley

1 Tbs. chopped fresh thyme

2 Tbs. crumbled dried sage

2 tsp. crumbled dried marjoram

2–4 cups vegetable broth

check to make sure it is hot through. Dot the top of the stuffing with the remaining 2 tablespoons butter and put it back into the oven for 5 to 10 minutes, depending how crisp and crunchy you like that top.

Serves 10 to 12 as a side dish

Working Ahead . . .
The stuffing can be prepared up to 2 days ahead and kept in a tightly covered container in the refrigerator, then brought to room temperature and baked.

The Vegan Way . . .
The only ingredient that is not vegan is the butter, and you can replace that with a top-quality vegan margarine, such as Earth Balance, to have a fine vegan stuffing.

In a Thanksgiving Menu . . .
Thanksgiving for Everyone (p. 20) features this delectable stuffing, along with an array of traditional vegetables and relishes and, yes, a roasted turkey.

CURRIED ROASTED CAULIFLOWER

Cauliflower is an underappreciated vegetable. It is wonderful when roasted very simply, in nothing more than a touch of olive oil and some salt and pepper. But this is cauliflower dressed to impress in a spicy golden coat. It can be served hot or warm, or you can allow it to cool and use it in a marvelous salad.

2 large heads cauliflower (about 3½ lbs.)

4 Tbs. extra-virgin olive oil

2 Tbs. fresh lemon juice or orange juice

3 Tbs. minced fresh ginger

1½ tsp. sea salt

2½ Tbs. curry powder

1 tsp. toasted and ground cumin seed

½ tsp. ground coriander

¼ tsp. dry mustard

a pinch of cayenne

Preheat the oven to 400°. Scrub and trim the cauliflower and break it into small florets, the size of large walnuts. You'll have about 3½ quarts of florets, but they will shrink dramatically as they roast.

Whisk together the remaining ingredients in a large bowl, add the cauliflower, and mix together thoroughly. Take your time, making sure that the curry paste is evenly distributed over all the florets.

Spread the cauliflower out on a large baking pan, or 2 smaller ones, and roast for 35 to 45 minutes, giving it a stir every 10 minutes or so. The cauliflower is done when it's tender but still firm and showing dark brown spots here and there.

Serves 6 to 8 as a side dish

Variation . . . Curried Cauliflower Salad
When the cauliflower is cool, add thinly sliced red bell pepper, slivered snap peas, a tiny bit of thinly sliced red onion, some cilantro, pine nuts or almonds . . . and maybe a few raisins or chopped dried apricots. For a spicy salad, add slivers of fresh jalapeño. Toss all this with a lemon vinaigrette and serve it on its own or over leafy greens.

Curried Roasted
Cauliflower (p. 300)

ROASTED POTATO WEDGES WITH MOJO VERDE

VEGAN

Crisp potato wedges served with bright, spicy *mojo* are a favorite tapa of mine, and they beat everything in an appetizer smackdown. You need potatoes with a creamy, dense texture, such as Yukon Gold or Yellow Finn. And the recipe can be reduced or multiplied easily: the formula is 1 pound of potatoes to 1 tablespoon of olive oil.

See photo on p. 35.

3 lbs. Yukon Gold or Yellow Finn potatoes

3 Tbs. extra-virgin olive oil

1 tsp. sea salt, plus more to taste

1 recipe Mojo Verde with Mint (p. 60)

Preheat the oven to 400°. Scrub the potatoes and trim away rough or discolored parts, but do not peel them. Cut the potatoes into wedges, about ¾ inch at the widest part, and toss them with the olive oil and sea salt until they are evenly coated. Spread the potatoes on 2 large baking sheets and roast them for at least 45 minutes, longer if needed, stirring and turning them a few times. They will be tender before that time is up, but you are looking for a beautiful golden brown, crisp finish, and that takes longer.

When the potato wedges have that burnished look, slide them onto a large platter and taste one. Needs salt? Sprinkle or grind on a bit more. Then serve the potatoes hot or warm, with a bowl of *mojo verde* for dipping.

Serves 10 to 12 as an appetizer or in a tapas spread

Variation . . . Roasted Spring Potatoes with Green Garlic
For a springtime treat, scrub 2½ pounds of tiny round or fingerling potatoes, then mix them well with 3 tablespoons olive oil and 2 tablespoons each of finely chopped rosemary and finely chopped green garlic—the first springtime shoots—as well as at least 1 teaspoon sea salt and plenty of freshly ground black pepper. Roast in a hot oven for 30 to 45 minutes.

In a Festive Mixed Menu . . .
These *patatas con mojo* are so good you will want to start the new year with them. See Cocktails on New Year's Eve (p. 32) .

CASSEROLE OF ROASTED YAMS WITH GREEN CHILES

VEGETARIAN OR VEGAN

My friend Larry dreamed this up: a casserole of twice-baked yams with two kinds of chiles, fresh poblanos and smoky chipotles. They're the best yams I've ever had. But unless you are a chile-head, add the chipotles a bit at a time, tasting for the kick of heat.

3 lbs. yams

3 Tbs. extra-virgin olive oil, plus more for oiling the dish

1½ tsp. sea salt, plus more to taste

2 medium fresh poblano chiles (8 oz.)

2 large onions, coarsely chopped

3–4 Tbs. maple syrup

2 Tbs. fresh lime juice, plus more if needed

1 or 2 small chipotle chiles in *adobo*, minced

OPTIONAL:

2 Tbs. butter or vegan margarine

Preheat the oven to 400°. Scrub the yams, slice them in thick rounds, and mix them with 2 tablespoons olive oil and 1¼ teaspoons sea salt. Arrange them in a pan and bake them for 45 minutes, or until they are tender and slightly caramelized. Allow the yams to cool, and peel them.

Char the poblano chiles under a broiler, pull out their stems and seeds, peel them, and cut them into 1-inch pieces. (For details on charring and peeling peppers, see p. 227.) Sear the chopped onions with a sprinkle of sea salt in the remaining 1 tablespoon of olive oil, tossing over high heat for 5 minutes. Lower the heat, cover the pan, and cook the onions gently for 20 minutes, stirring occasionally.

Whisk together the maple syrup, lime juice, and 1 minced chipotle with the *adobo* sauce clinging to it. When the onions are soft and golden, pour the maple syrup mixture over them and raise the heat for a minute or 2 as the glaze bubbles and thickens.

If you turned off the oven, preheat it to 400° again. Mash the yams or, for a rustic gratin, break them up into pieces with your fingers. Combine the yams with the poblano chiles, and the onions in their glaze. Mix everything together, taste, and correct the seasoning with a pinch more salt if needed and more minced chipotle chile if you like. Spoon the yam mixture into an oiled gratin dish and dot the top with butter or margarine if you like. Bake the yams for 30 minutes, or until hot through and browning on top.

Serves 6 as a robust side dish

In a Festive and Flexible Menu . . .
It doesn't have to be Thanksgiving for you to enjoy Larry's yams. But Thanksgiving is better with them! See Thanksgiving for Everyone (p. 20).

CRISP ROASTED GREEN BEANS

VEGAN

Toasty green beans roasted in a hot oven until they are turning golden brown and the thin ones are crisp are one of my favorite finger foods. They taste like potato chips, only better. Put out a large platter of these with the aperitifs and watch them vanish.

3 lbs. tender thin green beans

3–4 cloves garlic, thinly sliced

2 Tbs. extra-virgin olive oil

1 tsp. sea salt, plus more to taste

Preheat the oven to 400°. Wash and trim the green beans. Combine them in a large bowl with the garlic slices, olive oil, and salt and mix with your hands until every bean is glistening. Spread the beans out on 2 large baking sheets. Roast the beans for 35 to 45 minutes, turning them once or twice during the cooking time. The exact time will depend on the thickness of the beans, but they are ready when they are blistered with golden brown spots and the thinnest ones are crisp. Taste: if you like it, it's done. Add salt if it's needed.

Slide the hot roasted beans out onto a platter and serve. The beans are good when hot, warm, or at room temperature, but I like them best fresh from the oven.

Serves 8 to 9 as an appetizer or side dish

Variation . . . Roasted Asparagus with Garlic Slivers
The same toasty-crispy magic can be worked with asparagus. Choose asparagus stalks of medium thickness, as uniform as possible for even roasting. Snap off the tough bottoms of the stalks, then oil them as described above and roast for 25 to 30 minutes, or until they are turning golden brown and their tips are crisping up.

ROASTED CIPOLLINI AND GREEN BEANS

VEGAN

Red pearl onions roasted to a soft sweetness are a beautiful partner to toasty green beans. This has been a great favorite at my Thanksgiving table.

1½ lbs. red pearl onions

½ lb. tender thin green beans

2 Tbs. extra-virgin olive oil

1 tsp. sea salt, plus more to taste

Preheat the oven to 375°. Scald the onions in a pot of boiling water for 2 minutes, then drain. Let the onions cool slightly, then peel them, trimming them at the stem and slipping off their skins. Wash and trim the green beans.

Toss the onions with 1½ tablespoons of the olive oil and ¾ teaspoon of the salt and spread them in a shallow baking pan or on a rimmed baking sheet. Toss the green beans with the remaining olive oil and salt, and spread them on another baking sheet.

Roast the beans and onions for about 45 minutes, stirring them several times. The onions should be soft and well browned in spots. When both the onions and the greens beans have reached their perfect moment, mix them together. Taste, and add a tiny sprinkle of sea salt if needed.

Serves 8 to 10 as a side dish

In a Festive Menu . . .
These caramelized cipollini are part of the vegetable spread in Thanksgiving for Everyone (p. 20)

See Also . . .

BEANS AND LEGUMES

BEANS AND LEGUMES

Give them some respect.

Beans don't get the respect they deserve, and alas, it is precisely because of some of their great qualities that this is so. Beans are cheap, plentiful, and easy to cook—and they are among the best, healthiest sources of protein on the planet. Perhaps if they were rare, costly, and confoundingly difficult to prepare, we might show them more love and have fancy restaurants dedicated to them.

But we keep eating them, because they are also just damn delicious. Think about that almost sweet, purpley black bean soup or dusky chili with the snowy white cheese and the salsa on top; or that cannellini salad on the antipasto table, creamy white beans glistening with olive oil and tangled up with strips of red pepper; or chickpeas and lemon and garlic tasting as if they were born together. And the spicy refried beans in your burrito, the fragrant Indian dal . . .

My bean pantry is a colorful place, with cranberry beans, yellow eye beans, black turtle beans, red lentils, green split peas, beluga lentils, Swedish brown beans, fat white lima beans, green Le Puy lentils . . . Yes, I love beans. Why, then, in a book that is tilting vegan, is this chapter not voluminous? Because beans, in their variety and usefulness, cannot be contained in one chapter. Beans are everywhere in this book.

They are in my favorite Smoky Split Pea Soup and in Old-Fashioned Winter Minestrone. They are in the mint-spiked Fresh Fava Bean Puree and other dips and spread, in Farro with Lentils and Lavender, and in stuffed vegetables. They get around. So this chapter is simply a little collection of power-packed dishes in which the beans and lentils want to be the center of attention.

And if they were twice the price, they'd be worth every penny.

A WORD ABOUT COOKING BEANS

Let's celebrate these tasty little miracles of nutrition by taking the slight care required to bring out their best. Beans that you have cooked yourself are so much better than beans from a can that there is little reason to open that can. Okay, spontaneity might be that reason; you do have to think ahead to cook beans. But if you can plan in advance, invest the 60 seconds it takes to rinse some beans and put them in a pot. It's worth it.

And start with good, fresh beans. Yes, dried beans need to be fresh for best results. Ideally, that means beans harvested within the past year, and no more than two years ago. And since you can't tell their age by looking at them, it's best to buy beans from a store that does a brisk business in beans and has good turnover, or to order beans online from a reliable source. (I have ordered excellent heirloom beans from Rancho Gordo.) It makes a difference, because the age of beans affects their cooking time. Older beans will take longer to cook, and really old beans will never achieve the soft creaminess we are looking for. So don't keep those beans sitting around in the back of the pantry. Cook them.

Here's the method: Rinse your beans and put them in a pot with enough water to cover by about 2 inches. Do not add salt. Do add a few peeled cloves of garlic and a few sage leaves if you are cooking cannellini, or garlic and a few epazote leaves if you are cooking black beans or pinto beans. A chile de árbol won't hurt.

Simmer the beans for an hour or longer, until you test one and it is tender. Add a couple teaspoons salt to the pot and simmer another 20 minutes. Now, wasn't that easy?

And for Pete's sake, don't throw out that liquid. It's the savory broth for your next soup.

About Soaking . . .

It's allowed, but it isn't required. If you soak your dried beans in cool water overnight, or even for a few hours, the cooking time will be reduced. I only soak the largest of dried beans, such as Fasolia Gigante or giant limas, and sometimes garbanzo beans. But for the most part I'm in the no-soak camp.

RED LENTIL DAL WITH TOMATOES AND WHOLE SPICES

<u>VEGAN</u>

If you love lentils as I do, you might sometimes crave a spicy dal, savory, complex, and hot enough to be exciting. This is the one. It's based on a traditional Bengali dal but is less fiery. Add more green and red chiles if you have asbestos lips.

1½ cups (10 oz.) red lentils

1½ tsp. sea salt, plus more to taste

1 fresh green serrano chile, stemmed and chopped

½ tsp. turmeric

3 medium tomatoes (12 oz.)

3 Tbs. peanut oil

1 medium white or yellow onion, chopped

1 Tbs. finely grated fresh ginger

½ tsp. cumin seeds

½ tsp. fennel seeds

½ tsp. mustard seeds

1–2 bay leaves

a pinch of crushed red chiles

4 cloves garlic, finely chopped

Rinse the lentils and combine them in a pot with 1 quart water, the salt, the chopped green chile, and the turmeric. Simmer the lentils and spices, covered, for 25 minutes.

Peel the tomatoes and dice them, saving all the juice, and add them to the lentils. Heat 2 tablespoons peanut oil and sauté the onions in it with a pinch of salt, tossing over high heat until the onions are golden brown and some bits are crispy, about 12 minutes. Add the ginger to the onions, stir for a minute, then add the onion mixture to the lentils and simmer them another 20 minutes. They should be very soft.

Heat the remaining 1 tablespoon oil in a small pan and add the cumin seeds, fennel seeds, mustard seeds, bay leaves, crushed red chiles, and chopped garlic. Stir for about 20 seconds as the mustard seeds pop, then remove the pan from the heat and keep stirring the spices around in the hot oil as the garlic loses its raw edge. Pour the spices and oil into the dal, give it one quick stir, and serve.

Serves 6 as a substantial dish, with rice and any vegetable

A Simple Meal That Starts with Dal . . .
A bowl of spicy dal, a bowl of rice, and any fresh chutney—that's already a meal. Now add any steamed or sautéed vegetable, spicy or utterly plain. Add more than one. Add a piece of stewed chicken. Add a yogurt raita with cucumbers. You can elaborate as you like around the idea of the essential lentils and rice. You will always be right.

SPICY BLACK BEANS

VEGAN

This is my good, basic pot of beans, useful in so many ways. Wrap them in a tortilla with salsa and potatoes for a brilliant taco, make a soup by adding broth, have them with *huevos rancheros,* or add a spoonful of savory beans to a salad.

See the easy mixed menu that follows, Taco Night at Home. *See photo on p. 314.*

1 lb. dried black beans

2 Tbs. dried, loosely crumbled epazote or 5–6 fresh epazote leaves

9 garlic cloves

2 tsp. sea salt, plus more to taste

2 Tbs. extra-virgin olive oil

2 large onions, chopped

2–3 chipotle chiles in *adobo*

1 Tbs. toasted and ground cumin seeds

1 cup chopped fresh cilantro

Rinse the beans and combine them in a large pot with the epazote, 6 garlic cloves, and 2½ quarts water. Bring the water to a boil, lower the heat, cover, and simmer the beans until they are tender, an hour or more, depending on the age of the beans. Add the salt and simmer gently 10 more minutes. Allow the beans to cool in their broth.

Chop the remaining 3 garlic cloves. Heat the olive oil in a large nonstick pan and add the chopped onions with a pinch of salt. Toss the onions over high heat for 6 to 7 minutes, until they begin to wilt and show brown edges, then add the garlic and keep stirring for another 2 to 3 minutes. Lower the heat, cover the pan, and cook the onions slowly for about 20 minutes, stirring occasionally. They should be soft and golden brown.

Meanwhile, take the chiles out of their *adobo* sauce and pull out any stems. Chop the chiles finely. You should have 2 to 3 tablespoons.

Drain the beans, saving the broth, and add them to the onions and garlic. Add the chopped chiles, cumin, cilantro, and a cup of the bean broth and simmer everything together, stirring occasionally, for about 10 minutes. If you want a thicker sauce around your beans, you can mash a few of the beans with a wooden spoon or a potato masher. If the beans look dry, add more of their broth. (Save the remaining broth so you can add moisture when reheating leftover beans.)

Serves 6 to 8 as a substantial player in tacos, salads, or soups

---

Variation . . . Refried Black Beans
Go easy on the chipotle, and simmer the beans with the onions longer, until they are mushy soft, at least 20 minutes. Then add a splash of olive oil and mash them in the pan with a potato masher—a little or a lot, to taste. Adjust the salt, and stir in a spoonful of salsa if you like.

TACO NIGHT AT HOME

Taco night at home is where the recipe and the menu blur and become one. This great tradition is a perfect idea for flexible eating: everyone designs his or her perfect meal. You line up the components: fresh corn tortillas, warmed in a skillet and swaddled in a cloth napkin; then two or three tasty things to put inside them, for mixing and matching. It might be almost anything—if you can eat it, someone has probably wrapped it in a tortilla. But essential: A couple of wake-up-delicious chile salsas! One raw and one cooked . . . And chopped cilantro, shredded cabbage, slices of picked jalapeño pepper . . . Now pour the beer and let the assembly begin.

Make a traditional mushroom taco: Rajas con Hongos (p. 269) is a beloved dish from rural Mexico with deep, woodsy flavor, and it makes a superb filling for that fresh tortilla. Pair the *rajas* with beans and *salsa roja*, and lots of chopped cilantro. For the omnivore crowd, serve a bowl of roasted or stewed chicken torn into strips.

For another old favorite, spoon slightly spicy black beans and sautéed potatoes with green chiles into a tortilla, and top that with fresh raw pico de gallo and a slice of avocado—*sabroso!* Add some soft white ranchero cheese, or crumbly, yeasty *cotija*, a snowy scattering over black beans.

Or start your taco with carnitas, traditional slow-cooked pork, then add some brick-red guajillo salsa, and maybe beans and potatoes on top of that. You might have to double up the tortillas for that one, taco truck style. And pile shredded cabbage and chopped cilantro on everything! Don't forget that. And lean over your plate when you eat.

Another Taco Night Idea . . . Kimchee Tacos

This is genuine downtown L.A. style, Koreatown bumping up against Latino East L.A., and what a good idea—tangy, fermented kimchee with teriyaki tofu, chile salsa, shredded cabbage, and cilantro, all packed in those little tortillas. Kimchee is also a perfect match for grilled fish, so it's easy to go two ways and make fish tacos with a Korean spin.

A Practical Note . . .

The taco night menu is wide open to personal style, and most of it is food everyone eats. In this lineup, only the *queso* and the carnitas are not vegan. In the variations, kimchee tacos are vegan when made with teriyaki tofu, and *tacos con hongos* are vegan until you add chicken.

TACO NIGHT MENU

FOR 5 TO 6

corn tortillas

Rajas con Hongos: *Poblano Peppers with Portobello Mushrooms in a Skillet*
or
Potatoes and Poblanos *in a Skillet*

Spicy Black Beans or Refried Black Beans

queso ranchero or *cotija*

Carnitas

Guajillo Chile Salsa with Tomatillos
Pico de Gallo

shredded cabbage, chopped cilantro
sliced avocados

fresh papaya, melon, pineapple

Taco Night at Home (clockwise from top left):
Salsa Verde (p. 78), Spicy Black Beans
(p. 311), Guajillo Chile Salsa with Tomatillos
(p. 73), tortillas, shredded cabbage, limes,
Rajas con Hongos (p. 269), shredded chicken

BLACK BEAN CHILI
TWO WAYS, ONE WITH TURKEY

VEGAN OR OMNIVORE

Black bean chili is immensely popular for a reason: it's just so good. Mine begins with a puree of ancho and chipotle chiles and toasted cumin seeds. The flavor is rich and complex: fruity and spicy from the chiles, sweet from slow-cooked onions, and kicked up by a drop of vinegar—a great chili, whether you have the vegan version or the one with turkey. See the easy variation notes below.

1 lb. dried black beans

8–10 fresh epazote leaves or 2 Tbs. crumbled dry epazote

12 cloves garlic

3 tsp. sea salt, plus more to taste

1½ lbs. yellow onions, coarsely chopped

4 Tbs. extra-virgin olive oil

6–7 ancho or pasilla chiles (3 oz.)

3–4 dried chipotle chiles (¾ oz.)

1½ Tbs. cumin seeds

1 Tbs. dried oregano or 2 Tbs. chopped fresh oregano

1 Tbs. red wine vinegar

15 oz. chopped, peeled tomatoes (canned are okay)

4–5 Tbs. chopped roasted green chiles (Ortega canned chiles are okay)

GARNISHES:

chopped cilantro

crumbled *cotija* cheese

your favorite hot chile salsa

diced avocado

Put the beans in a large soup pot with 2½ quarts water, the epazote, and 6 cloves garlic and simmer until tender, 1 to 2 hours. Add 1½ teaspoons salt and simmer for 10 more minutes, longer if you like your beans very soft.

Meanwhile, sauté the chopped onions with ½ teaspoon salt in 3 tablespoons olive oil, stirring over high heat for 5 minutes. Lower the heat, cover the pan, and stir occasionally until the onions are soft, sweet, and golden brown, about another 40 minutes.

Rinse the chile pods and tear out their stems. Put the chiles in a stainless steel pot with enough boiling water to submerge them and simmer for 10 minutes, covered. Push the softened chiles down to release any air bubbles and let them soak for 45 minutes. When the chiles are cool enough to handle, drain them, shake out their seeds, and pull off any translucent skins that are peeling away. Put the chiles in the food processor with about ½ cup of the soaking liquid and puree. Strain the puree through a medium-coarse sieve, then discard the pulp of remaining seeds and skins. Transfer the puree to a measuring cup and add enough of the soaking liquid to make about 2½ cups.

Wash your hands. They are lethal weapons now. Rub them with vegetable oil, then scrub with soap and water and rinse well.

Toast the cumin seeds briefly over medium heat in a dry pan and grind them in a mortar or a spice grinder. Add the cumin, oregano, vinegar, and the remaining 1 teaspoon salt to the chile puree. Drain the cooked beans, reserving the broth and discarding the epazote leaves, and stir the chile puree into the beans with 1 cup of the reserved broth and the browned onions.

Chop the remaining 6 cloves garlic and sauté the garlic in the remaining 1 tablespoon of olive oil for a minute, just until it turns golden, then add it to the chili, along with the tomatoes and the chopped green chiles. (If you plan to make two versions of this chili, divide it now into batches, half and half or whatever proportion works for you.) Simmer the chili gently for at least 30 minutes. Add more of the bean broth as desired to make a thinner stew. (Save the rest for a soup.) Taste the chili, and correct the seasoning with a little more salt if needed.

Serve the chili with the garnishes of your choice and with hot cornbread or tortillas.

Serves 6 to 8 as a substantial meal

A Note About Chiles and Epazote...
Ancho chiles are mild, and they give my chili a lot of savory, fruity chile flavor. Chipotle chiles should be hot, though they can vary. If you are a chile-head, increase the number of chipotles, or replace one or two ancho chiles with guajillo chiles.

Epazote is an herb often used with beans; it is available both fresh and dried in markets that stock Mexican foods. The raw leaves have an astringent, almost medicinal scent but become gentle and fragrant with cooking.

Variation... Black Bean and Turkey Chili

1 lb. turkey, thigh meat if possible, diced fairly small

additional olive oil

additional chopped garlic

chili powder or spicy smoked paprika

Turkey is a good match for the black beans and red chiles in this dish, although you could do the same thing with pork. For the turkey chili version, sauté the diced (not ground) turkey in olive oil with salt and pepper, garlic, and a little chili powder or spicy paprika until it is browned. Add it to half the black bean chili, along with a bit more of the reserved cooking liquid from the beans, and simmer this batch gently, covered, for about 45 minutes.

White Bean Chili
two ways, one with
chicken (p. 319)

WHITE BEAN CHILI
TWO WAYS, ONE WITH CHICKEN

<u>VEGAN OR OMNIVORE</u>

The creamy richness of slow-cooked white beans with the lively flavor of fresh green chiles—heavenly with diced avocados and a scattering of cilantro on top. And this robust vegan dish is also easy to prepare two ways at once; see the variation, White Bean Chili with Chicken.

1 lb. dried cannellini beans

2 fresh sage leaves

6–8 fresh epazote leaves or 1½ Tbs. crumbled dried epazote

10 cloves garlic

2 dried chiles de árbol

sea salt

1¼ lbs. fresh green poblano or pasilla chiles

about 8 fresh green serrano chiles (3 oz.)

4 Tbs. extra-virgin olive oil

2 large yellow onions (1½ lbs.), chopped

1 lb. Yukon Gold potatoes, scrubbed and diced

2½ cups vegetable broth

2 tsp. toasted and ground cumin seeds

2 tsp. chopped fresh oregano or 1 tsp. dried oregano

Put the beans in a pot with water to cover by about 3 inches. Add the sage leaves, the epazote leaves, 6 garlic cloves, and the chile de árbol pods. Bring the water to a boil, then lower the heat and simmer for an hour or more, until the beans are tender. Add 2 teaspoons salt and simmer for another 10 minutes, then taste. More salt? Add a little at a time, and wait a moment to taste.

Char the fresh chiles under the broiler until they blister, core them, and peel them. (For details on charring and peeling peppers, see p. 227.) Cut the poblanos or pasillas into 1-inch dice (you'll have about 1½ cups), and finely chop the serranos. Chop the remaining 4 cloves garlic.

Heat 3 tablespoons olive oil in a large sauté pan and sauté the chopped onions with a pinch of salt over high heat, stirring, for about 5 minutes. Lower the heat to medium and toss the onions now and then for another 10 minutes, until they are soft and speckled with brown. Push the onions to the sides of the pan, add the remaining 1 tablespoon olive oil in the center, and sizzle the chopped garlic in it for a minute or two, until it begins to turn golden. Add the diced and chopped chiles, diced potatoes, vegetable broth, cumin, and oregano. Cover the pan, lower the heat, and let the mixture simmer for about 15 minutes.

Drain the beans, reserving the broth and discarding the sage, epazote, garlic, and *chiles de árbol*. Add the beans and 3½ cups of the broth to the chile and onion mixture and simmer for 10 minutes. If you like

recipe continues

OPTIONAL:

4 Tbs. cornmeal or *maseca* and 1
    cup vegetable broth

crushed red chiles

GARNISH:

chopped fresh cilantro

diced avocados

OPTIONAL GARNISH:

crumbled *queso fresco*

a thicker chili, stir the dry cornmeal or *maseca* into the cup of hot vegetable broth and whisk it over low heat for 5 minutes, then stir it into the chili mixture along with the beans. Taste the chili and add salt if needed. And finally, if you really like it hot, adjust the seasoning with some crushed red chiles.

Serve the chili hot, and garnish as you like with chopped cilantro, diced avocados, and perhaps some crumbled *queso fresco*.

Serves 6 to 8 as a hearty meal

The Omnivore Variation . . . White Bean Chili with Chicken
Trim a couple of boneless chicken breasts or thighs (about 1 pound), taking off the skin and fat. Cut the chicken into cubes and toss it in a bowl with 1 teaspoon salt, plenty of freshly ground black pepper, and some sweet paprika. Heat 2 or 3 tablespoons olive oil in a nonstick pan and add the seasoned chicken. Using tongs or two large spoons, turn and move the chicken in the pan as it cooks, over medium heat, until every piece is opaque and breaks apart easily when pressed with the edge of a spoon. Divide the prepared white bean chili between two smaller pots and stir the chicken into one of them.

WESTERN-STYLE BEAN AND POTATO STEW

VEGAN

I first made this rustic stew with Sangre de Toro beans, an heirloom variety from Rancho Gordo. Those small red beans were very tasty. Later I made the stew with pinto beans. Still tasty. Another time I used cranberry beans: yes, tasty. You can use any small brown or reddish bean. Beans cooked with epazote, garlic, potatoes, green chiles, and cumin are going to taste good. They will be delicious! Use fresh chiles if you can, but if fresh Anaheim or poblano peppers are not available, you can substitute Ortega chiles and increase the amount; use at least 2 cans.

1 cup dried **Sangre de Toro beans** (or pinto beans, or cranberry beans)

5–6 fresh **epazote leaves** or 1 Tbs. crumbled dried epazote

3 large cloves **garlic**

1 tsp. **sea salt**, plus more to taste

2–3 fresh **Anaheim or poblano chiles** (8 oz.)

2 Tbs. **extra-virgin olive oil**

1 large **onion** (10–12 oz.), quartered and sliced

1 large **Yukon Gold potato** (8 oz.)

1 medium **sweet potato** (8 oz.)

2 **carrots** (4 oz.), peeled and sliced

2 cups **vegetable broth**, plus more if needed

1 medium **red bell pepper** (5 oz.), cored and diced

4 oz. **chard or spinach**, chopped (2½ cups)

Put the rinsed beans in a soup pot with 2 quarts water, the epazote, and the garlic cloves and simmer them until they are tender; an hour or more, depending on the variety and age of the beans. Add the salt and simmer gently for another 10 minutes. The beans should be creamy and soft, and you should have about 4 cups broth in the pot.

Char the fresh chiles under a broiler until they blister, pull out their stems, and peel them. (For details on charring and peeling peppers, see p. 227.) Cut the peppers in small dice; you should have about 1 cup.

Heat the olive oil in a sauté pan and sear the onion with a pinch of salt, tossing it over high heat for about 5 minutes, until it shows brown spots. Lower the heat, cover the pan, and cook the onion gently for 15 to 20 minutes, stirring often.

Scrub the potato, peel the sweet potato, and cut both into 1-inch dice. In a large pot, combine the potatoes and carrots with the vegetable broth and simmer them for 10 minutes. Add the diced red bell pepper and chopped chard along with the cooked onions, diced chiles, and cumin.

When the beans are perfectly tender, add them to the vegetables, with all their cooking broth. If you have less than 4 cups broth from the beans, add some vegetable broth. Simmer the stew another 20 minutes, then add the cilantro, simmer 5 more minutes, and taste. Correct the seasoning with a touch more salt, or some crushed red chiles if you want more heat.

recipe continues

1½ tsp. toasted and ground
   cumin seeds

⅔ cup coarsely chopped cilantro

½ tsp. crushed red chiles, if
   needed

Serves 6 to 8 for a meal

Omnivore Ways . . .

This is a sort of Southwest-cowboy hybrid dish, so you can add leftover roast beef or steak, diced up and simmered with a portion of the stew, for the beef-eaters in your crowd; figure 2 ounces per portion. Or, for a crispy garnish, crumbled bacon—and for bacon with an upgrade, try Dana's Bacon and Garlic Crisps (p. 372).

An Easy Meal for Everyone . . .

A big bowl of these cowboy-style beans, served either the vegan way or with the omnivore flourish, needs only a green salad and a big wedge of hot, fresh cornbread.

AMBER-GLAZED TOFU

Here's one of those good things that is so easy it feels like cheating. Slices of tofu are gently sautéed until they are golden, then simmered in a glaze of mirin and tamari until they take on a deep amber color and a gleaming, lacquered finish. Beautiful. The flavor is deeply savory and slightly sweet, perfect with black rice and stir-fried vegetables.

1½ lbs. extra-firm tofu
   (2 packages)

¼ cup mirin (rice wine)

¼ cup tamari or soy sauce

2 Tbs. agave nectar

1 Tbs. peanut or sesame oil

Cut each block of tofu into 6 or 7 thick slices and press out the excess water: Arrange the slices in a glass dish lined with paper towels, layer a couple more towels over them, and press down on them gently with your hands. If the towels are soaking wet, switch them for dry ones and repeat. The tofu slices will feel solid and quite dry. If you like, you can cut each rectangle into two long triangles—purely an aesthetic choice.

Mix together the mirin, tamari or soy sauce, and agave nectar.

Heat the oil in a large nonstick skillet and sauté the tofu slices over medium heat for 4 to 5 minutes on a side. When they are a pale golden color, pour the mirin mixture over them evenly and simmer the tofu in the liquid, over medium-low heat, for another 7 to 9 minutes. Turn the slices once during that time. The liquid will be reduced to a syrupy sauce, and the tofu will be gleaming in its golden brown glaze.

Serve the tofu slices or triangles over rice or alongside it, and drizzle any glaze that is left in the pan over them.

Serves 6 in combination with rice and any vegetable stir-fry

In a Mixed Stir-Fry Menu . . .
Stir-Fry Is a Verb! (p. 293) is a simple but elegant meal that can be done in a smaller or more elaborate version. This amber tofu accompanies a stir-fry of asparagus and mushrooms, followed by an optional steamed cod with miso and bok choy.

TERIYAKI GRILLED TOFU

VEGAN

This simplest way with tofu is ideal for kimchee tacos, and makes an excellent piece of tofu to cut up for a salad or serve with rice and any vegetable stir-fry.

12 oz. firm or extra-firm tofu (1 block)

1 Tbs. peanut oil

2–3 Tbs. teriyaki sauce

Slice the block of tofu into 6 or 7 thick slices and press out the excess water as described in the previous recipe, p. 323. Arrange the slices on a baking sheet, brush them lightly with oil, then brush generously on both sides with teriyaki sauce. Let them rest in the sauce for about 20 minutes.

Put the marinated tofu slices under a hot broiler or charcoal grill for about 5 minutes on one side and 2 or 3 minutes on the other. Exact time will depend on the heat of your broiler or grill, so keep an eye on them. They should be golden brown all over, with some much darker spots.

Serves 3 in tacos or with a stir-fry—and this is easy to double.

In a Mixed Menu . . .
Taco Night at Home (p. 312) features many chile-spiked combinations, and kimchee tacos are right there with this teriyaki tofu in a meal that expands to include fish tacos.

SPICY TOFU SALAD
ON COLD SOBA NOODLES WITH ORANGE-GINGER GLAZE

VEGAN

This intensely flavored little salad is tasty when first made and gets even better as the tofu absorbs the flavors of the sesame, soy, and *chile sambal*. Serve the spicy tofu over cold soba noodles in orange-ginger glaze for a beautiful lunch, or serve it with plain steamed rice or a mixed salad.

1 lb. extra-firm tofu, cut in thick slices

1½ tsp. dark sesame oil

1 Tbs. sambal oelek or other hot red chile paste

1 Tbs. tamari or soy sauce

½ cup chopped fresh cilantro

⅓ cup thinly sliced scallions or spring onions

Cold Soba Noodles with Orange-Ginger Glaze (recipe follows)

Drain the tofu and press the excess moisture out: Arrange the tofu slices on a plate lined with a triple layer of paper towels. Cover them with additional paper towels, place a small cutting board on top of them, and weigh it down with a pot, or anything for a few pounds of weight. After a few minutes, change the paper towels and repeat until the towels are damp, not soaking wet. You can also simply press tofu slices by hand, squeezing them between your palms over the sink, but do this carefully, so as not to crumble the tofu. Cut the pressed tofu into ¾-inch cubes.

In a mixing bowl, whisk together the sesame oil, sambal oelek, and tamari or soy sauce. Add the tofu cubes and mix gently. Add the chopped cilantro and sliced scallions or onions and toss again, but don't break the tofu cubes into bits.

Serve immediately, or cover and put away in the fridge for a few hours before serving. For an elegant look, use tongs to twist glazed soba noodles into little nests on the plates, then pile some spicy tofu into each nest and garnish with a sprig or two of cilantro.

Serves 4 to 6 as a vegan lunch in combination with noodles, or 6 to 8 as an appetizer

Ingredient Note . . .
Sambal oelek, a paste of red chiles in vinegar and salt, is the heat that ignites this pretty salad. It's used in Vietnamese and Thai food, and you can find it in the Asian section of your supermarket—or substitute any simple red chile paste.

recipe continues

COLD SOBA NOODLES WITH ORANGE-GINGER GLAZE

12 oz. soba noodles

½ cup fresh orange juice

1 Tbs. rice vinegar

1½ Tbs. finely grated fresh ginger

1 scant tsp. finely grated orange zest

¼ tsp. sea salt, plus more to taste

⅓ cup peanut oil

2 Tbs. black sesame seeds

Cook the noodles in boiling salted water according to package directions, probably 3 or 4 minutes. Drain them and immediately plunge them into a bowl of icewater to cool them, then drain again.

Whisk together the orange juice, vinegar, ginger, orange zest, sea salt, and peanut oil. Spoon 5 to 6 tablespoons of the mixture over the noodles and lift them gently with tongs or with your hands until they are evenly glazed. Taste, and adjust the seasoning by adding as much more of the glaze as you like, or another pinch of sea salt. (Reserve extra orange-ginger glaze to add to a stir-fry.) Sprinkle on the black sesame seeds, give the noodles a few more turns, and serve.

These noodles can be kept in the refrigerator, tightly covered, for several hours.

Serves 4 to 6

Spicy Tofu Salad *on Cold Soba Noodles with*
Orange-Ginger Glaze (p. 325)

FISH, FOWL, MEAT

FISH AND SEAFOOD

See also . . .

FOWL

Roast Turkey with Herbs; Turkey Giblet Sauce with Madeira   353

Roast Turkey Breast or Leg Quarters with Garlic and Herbs   356

Easiest Roast Chicken *stuffed with lemons*   357

Charcoal-Grilled Marinated Chicken   360

See also . . .

White Bean Chili *with chicken*   319

Black Bean Chili *with turkey*   316

Eight-Vegetable Cobbler *with chicken*   249

MEAT

See also...

THE OMNIVORE WAY . . .

You will see this note throughout the book, as I offer suggestions for garnishing vegan and vegetarian dishes, elaborating some, preparing others in two versions, or simply pairing a dish with the meat or seafood that suits it best.

Here is my approach to designing flexible meals and welcoming all tastes: I begin with the universal, something that *everyone* can eat and enjoy, whether vegan, vegetarian, or omnivore. That means something from the world of vegetables, grains, legumes, nuts, fruits. Then I add the cheeses, the eggs, the meats as they fit in, embracing all at my table. Examples of how to expand menus or elaborate recipes are included throughout the book. "The omnivore way" threads through every kind of dish, with the possible exception of dessert.

In some cases it is merely a suggestion to point you in the way of a good choice from among your own favorite dishes. Sometimes it is a word about a technique or flavor. And sometimes it is a recipe . . . which brings us here, to this collection, which has found its way into a book that is largely vegan and vegetarian in the recipes but that is really about hospitality, an invitation to everyone: let's sit down and have dinner together.

These are the dishes, drawn from many sources, that have worked best for me. Some are included in menus; others are simply mentioned in notes to recipes. Because they are dishes meant to accompany rather than to dominate, I have kept them simple. I hope that all of you who are experienced with cooking fish, fowl, and meat will indulge me, and will find in these ideas a way to connect to your own repertoire and your own traditions. And for you who are newer to the idea of putting a roast in the oven or a piece of fish in the pan, I hope you find simple and tasty ways to expand your meals to make everyone at the table feel loved. And I hope you have at least half the laughs I had in the kitchen while I was working on these recipes, cooking with my carnivore friends.

FISH AND SEAFOOD

STEAMED COD WITH MISO AND BOK CHOY

Ling cod is a delicate, flaky white fish, excellent for steaming. Other flaky fish can be steamed the same way for this lovely, easy dish. Sliced greens are quickly stir-fried, then the marinated fish is placed on top of them, covered, and steamed in the moisture of the greens for a few minutes. Sautéed oyster mushrooms make a perfect finish. It's a one-wok dish, but you need a large wok, with a lid for capturing the steam, or a very large sauté pan.

1 lb. ling cod fillet

6 Tbs. Miso Marinade (p. 93)

1¼ lbs. bok choy

8 oz. Napa cabbage

2 Tbs. extra-virgin olive oil

6 cloves garlic, chopped

12 oz. oyster mushrooms, cleaned and sliced

¾ tsp. sea salt

4 Tbs. mirin (rice wine)

2 Tbs. peanut oil

1 cup sliced green onions, white and green parts

2–3 Tbs. rice vinegar

1 cup roughly chopped fresh cilantro

Cut the ling cod into serving portions. Put the pieces of fish into a dish just large enough to hold them and drizzle the miso marinade over them, making sure they are all evenly coated. Cover the dish with plastic wrap and put it in the refrigerator for 2 hours, longer if you have the time.

Wash the bok choy and the Napa cabbage and slice both into thin strips. You should have 6 to 7 cups bok choy and 2 to 3 cups Napa cabbage.

Heat the olive oil in a medium nonstick skillet, add half the garlic, and sizzle it for less than a minute. Add the mushrooms and a pinch of salt and sauté, stirring over high heat for 5 to 6 minutes, until the liquid has cooked away. Let the mushrooms develop some golden brown color, then add 2 tablespoons mirin and stir over high heat for a few seconds as it forms a glaze. Keep the mushrooms warm, or quickly reheat them just before serving.

Heat the peanut oil in a large wok, add the remaining garlic, and stir over high heat for 30 seconds. Add the green onions and stir another 30 seconds. Add the sliced bok choy and Napa cabbage and ½ teaspoon salt and stir-fry for 2 to 3 minutes, until the vegetables are wilted. Add 2 tablespoons rice vinegar, lower the heat to medium, and cover the wok, leaving the vegetables to steam for 2 to 3 minutes, until they are tender but not yet soft.

Stir in the cilantro and the remaining 2 tablespoons mirin, and another tablespoon of vinegar if you like. Spread the vegetables evenly in the wok and place the portions of marinated cod on top of them. Drizzle the remaining marinade from the dish over the fish. Cover the wok and steam the fish over medium heat just until it flakes apart when the point of a knife is inserted in the thickest part, probably 6 to 8 minutes, but it depends on the thickness of the fish and the heat level.

To serve, slide a spatula under the vegetables and place each portion of fish, on its bed of vegetables, in a shallow bowl. Drizzle a little of the liquid from the bottom of the wok over each piece of fish, and top with a spoonful of sautéed oyster mushrooms.

Serves 6 if other stir-fries are served, or 4 as a substantial centerpiece dish

In a Mixed Menu . . .
Stir-Fry Is a Verb! (p. 293) is an elegant meal from simple components; this steamed fish follows a trio of vegan dishes, none complicated, all beautiful.

Ling Cod Steamed on Fennel and Onions (p. 337)

LING COD STEAMED ON FENNEL AND ONIONS

Here's a Mediterranean version of fish steamed in the moisture of vegetables. In this light dish the fish is perfumed with aromatic fennel and onion, lemon slices, and garlic. And it's easy—it's all cooked in one large sauté pan, and much of the preparation can be done in advance, making this workable for a dinner party.

1½ lbs. ling cod

6 Tbs. extra-virgin olive oil

1½ tsp. sea salt, plus more to taste

freshly ground black pepper

2 lemons

2 medium onions (12 oz.)

2 medium fennel bulbs (12 oz. trimmed)

8 Tbs. dry white wine

12 oz. spinach, washed and sliced into wide strips

2 tsp. chopped fresh oregano

5 cloves garlic, thinly sliced

5 Tbs. fresh lemon juice

Cut the fish into 6 pieces if you want substantial portions, or into 8 to 10 if you want small portions to accompany several other dishes in a festive meal.

Place the fish pieces in a glass dish, drizzle 1½ tablespoons of the olive oil over them, and turn them until all are well coated. Season the fish on both sides with 1 teaspoon salt and as much black pepper as you like. Cut the lemons into thin slices and place 2 or 3 lemon slices on top of each piece of fish. Cover the dish with plastic wrap and put the fish in the refrigerator if it is going to wait an hour or two, on the counter if less.

Cut the onions in half and slice them thinly. Trim the fennel bulbs, cut them in half lengthwise, and slice them thinly. Heat 1½ tablespoons olive oil in a large nonstick sauté pan and add the onions and fennel and ½ teaspoon salt. Toss the vegetables over high heat for 6 to 7 minutes, until they are soft and speckled with golden brown. Add 3 tablespoons of the white wine, lower the heat, and cook slowly for another 20 minutes, stirring occasionally. The vegetables should be tender but not mushy. (Everything can be prepared ahead to this point and held for a couple of hours. Bring the fennel and onions back to a simmer before proceeding.)

Add the spinach to the vegetables in the pan and toss until it is just wilted. Taste, and add a pinch more salt if needed. Add the remaining 5 tablespoons wine, give the vegetables a stir, and spread them evenly in the pan. Lay the fish on top of the vegetables in a single layer, leaving the lemon slices in place. Cover the pan, adjust the heat to medium, and steam the fish for 6 to 7 minutes.

recipe continues

While the fish is cooking, warm the remaining 3 tablespoons olive oil in a small pan and cook the garlic slices over medium-low heat until they are golden at their edges. Remove the pan from the heat and stir in the lemon juice and a pinch of sea salt.

After 6 or 7 minutes, check the fish by inserting the tip of a sharp knife in the thickest part of one piece. It is done when it flakes apart with just a bit of pressure. If not done, let it steam another minute or two. Exact cooking time for fish always depends on the thickness of the fish and its starting temperature.

Serve the fish as soon as it is done, using a wide spatula to lift a portion of vegetables with a piece of fish on top. I like to serve this in wide, shallow bowls, like risotto bowls. Drizzle a spoonful of the warm garlic and lemon oil on top of each serving.

Serves 6 as a substantial dish, more as part of a larger, more elaborate meal

---

In a Festive Mixed Menu . . .
Italian Style (p. 28) is a celebration: five courses, including an abundant antipasto and a robust pasta, followed by this delicate, fennel-perfumed ling cod.

OVEN-ROASTED GROUPER WITH MISO MARINADE
AND WASABI CRÈME FRAÎCHE

A fish that is marinated and baked, then drizzled with two sauces, seems like a fancy dish, and yet this is amazingly easy to do. Serve this roasted fish with any vegetable stir-fry meal to expand it elegantly for the omnivore crowd.

Grouper was the freshest fish in the market the day I first tried this, but if halibut looks better, or mahi mahi, buy that—the miso marinade is good with most mild-flavored white fish. I have also baked wild Alaskan salmon with this marinade, leaving it on its skin and using a lower oven temperature; the result was excellent, moist and flavorful. Oven time will have to be adjusted based on the type and thickness of the fish, but that's the way it is with all fish—it's done when it's done.

About 1½ lbs. grouper, halibut, or other firm-fleshed mild fish

1 recipe Miso Marinade (p. 93)

1–2 tsp. wasabi powder, to taste

½ cup crème fraiche

½ cup Miso Vinaigrette (p. 93)

Trim the fish, removing any small bones, and slice off the skin if you prefer. Cut it into 6 servings for substantial portions, more if you are serving several other dishes. Arrange the fish in a glass dish just large enough to hold all the pieces, pour a cup of miso marinade over it, and turn the pieces until they are coated. Cover the dish with plastic wrap and put it in the refrigerator for 2 hours, or as long as 6 hours.

Dissolve the wasabi powder in 1 to 2 tablespoons of water, then stir the wasabi paste into the crème fraiche. Cover the wasabi crème fraîche and keep it cold until ready to serve. Use the remaining miso marinade to make the miso vinaigrette.

Preheat the oven to 400°. Line a baking pan with aluminum foil, arrange the marinated fish pieces on it, and pour the marinade remaining in the dish over the fish. Bake the fish for 10 to 15 minutes, or until it just begins to flake apart when a sharp knife is inserted in the thick center. Baste the fish with the juices in the baking pan.

To serve, drizzle each piece of fish with a spoonful of the miso vinaigrette, and place a small spoonful of wasabi crème fraiche along one side.

Serves 6 to 10, depending on the number of vegetable dishes that are served

BLACK COD IN MISO MARINADE

Here's a very simple treatment using my favorite miso marinade. Black cod, also known as sablefish or butterfish, is a firm, mild-flavored white fish that cooks to a velvety texture when properly prepared—and that consists mainly of knowing when to stop cooking.

1½ lbs. black cod fillets

1 cup Miso Marinade (p. 93)

2 Tbs. peanut oil or vegetable oil for the pan

Cut the long fillets into portions about 4 ounces each. Place the fish in a glass dish just large enough to hold all the pieces in one layer, and pour the miso marinade over it. Turn the pieces over a few times, until all of them are well coated with the marinade, then leave them skin side up. Allow the fish to marinate for at least half an hour, or up to an hour if you have the time.

Preheat the oven to 400°. Heat the oil in a large ovenproof sauté pan. When it is shimmering but not yet smoking, place the fish slices in the pan, skin side up, and cover the pan with a spatter guard. Lower the heat to medium. After about a minute, lift the first piece and take a look—if it is well browned, quickly turn over all the pieces, and drizzle them with a few teaspoons of the marinade left in the dish.

Put the sauté pan into the hot oven and start checking the fish after 5 minutes. Exact cooking time will vary with the thickness of the fish, but it is done when the thick part of the fillet is just starting to flake.

Serves 6 as a substantial dish, more as a companion to a stir-fry or pilaf

PAN-SEARED HALIBUT WITH SAUTÉED TRUMPET MUSHROOMS

Delicate halibut pairs well with this simple sauté of mushrooms deglazed with white wine. I like king trumpet mushrooms, which are fat and dense, with a lovely mild flavor, but you can use any friendly fungus in this dish.

8 oz. king trumpet mushrooms

1 lb. halibut fillets

½ tsp. sea salt, plus more to taste

freshly ground black pepper

4 Tbs. extra-virgin olive oil, plus more to taste

1 medium shallot, chopped

1 clove garlic, chopped

1 Tbs. browned butter or plain butter

4–5 Tbs. dry white wine

¼ cup chopped fresh flat-leaf parsley

Clean the mushrooms with a brush or cloth and slice them; if they are large, cut them in half lengthwise first. Cut the halibut into 4 portions, more if you plan to serve this as a side dish, sprinkle each with salt and pepper, and set them aside.

Heat 2 tablespoons olive oil in a medium sauté pan and sizzle the shallot and garlic in it for a minute, then add the mushrooms, butter, and ¼ teaspoon salt. Toss the mushrooms over high heat until they release their water, 2 to 3 minutes. Lower the heat to medium and cook the mushrooms, stirring often, until they show golden brown edges, another 6 to 8 minutes. Add 4 tablespoons white wine, stir, cover the pan, and turn off the heat. Keep the mushrooms warm until you are ready to serve the fish, or reheat them just before serving.

Heat the remaining 2 tablespoons olive oil in a large nonstick sauté pan. When it is just shy of smoking, place the halibut pieces in the pan, salted side down. Sear the halibut for a minute over high heat, then carefully turn the pieces over. Lower the heat, cover the pan, and cook the halibut gently for 4 to 5 minutes, or until it tests done. Cooking time will vary with the thickness of the fillets, but check after 4 minutes: the fish should be opaque and begin to flake when prodded.

recipe continues

While the halibut is cooking, add the parsley to the mushrooms, as well as the remaining spoonful of wine if they seem dry, and toss them over medium heat for a minute. Serve the halibut with sautéed mushrooms spooned over the top.

Serves 4 as a substantial dish, more if served as an accompaniment to a hearty grain dish

---

Matchmaking for an Omnivore Meal . . .
Because it is quick and simple to prepare once the ingredients are ready, this dish can be an easy addition to a grain-based or vegetable-based meal. For a summertime supper, pair it with Summer Farro Salad with Tomatoes, Seared Onions, and Fennel (p. 107).

Or place a small piece of halibut and mushrooms on top of a serving of Spinach and Sorrel Risotto (p. 204), or on a wide bowl of Barlotto with Braised Greens, Currants, and Pine Nuts (p. 205)—the flavors go beautifully with all greens.

Pan-Seared Halibut with Sautéed Trumpet Mushrooms (p. 341), paired with Barlotto with Braised Greens, Currants, and Pine Nuts (p. 205)

GENTLY BAKED SALMON
WITH A PARSLEY PESTO COAT

This is an easy way to cook salmon and gives excellent results. The fish is baked at a low temperature, and the coat of pesto, that essential smear of something wet, keeps it from drying out. The result is an herb-infused fish that remains moist and tender, similar in texture to a poached salmon. And did I say *easy?* Serve it as an accompaniment to a grain- or vegetable-based meal, like any tabbouleh variation (pp. 116–17), or Summer Chop Salad with Corn and Pepper Salsa (p. 102)

See photo on p. 39.

1–1½ lbs. salmon fillet

extra-virgin olive oil

sea salt

freshly ground black pepper

½–¾ cup Parsley Pesto (p. 56), plus more for the table

Preheat the oven to 325°. Cut the salmon into 4-ounce pieces, or smaller ones as needed—or leave the fillet whole for a dramatic presentation. Pat the salmon dry with paper towels, rub it with a little olive oil, and season it with sea salt and black pepper. Arrange the salmon pieces in an oiled baking dish, skin side down, so they are not touching.

Spread each piece of salmon with a thick, even coat of fresh pesto, about 2 tablespoons per slice. Let the fish rest on the counter for about 20 minutes; this allows the pesto to infuse the fish with its flavor and lets the fish come to room temperature.

Bake the fish for 15 to 20 minutes, until it separates when a sharp knife or fork is inserted into the thickest part. Exact time will depend on the thickness of the fish and its temperature when it goes into the oven.

You can serve the fish on its skin, or slip a spatula between the fish and the skin and easily lift each piece off—a matter of taste. Drop a spoonful of pesto next to each serving, or pass a small bowl of pesto at the table.

Serves 4 to 6 as a substantial dish, more if served as an accompaniment to a hearty grain salad or pilaf or a garlicky pasta

In a Menu . . .
Easter Brunch (p. 36) includes this salmon in an array of springtime vegetables.

PAN-ROASTED SALMON WITH AGAVE VINAIGRETTE

An uncomplicated way with salmon, a dish that can be done almost at a moment's notice if you have a good fresh piece of fish. The simplicity of the treatment makes this an appropriate companion to many salads or pilafs with more complex flavors.

1 lb. salmon fillet, cut in serving portions, 2½–4 oz. each

6 Tbs. extra-virgin olive oil, plus more as needed

2 tsp. sea salt, plus more as needed

freshly ground black pepper

4–6 cloves garlic, finely chopped

4 Tbs. fresh lemon juice

2 Tbs. agave nectar

¼ cup chopped fresh flat-leaf parsley

Preheat the oven to 375°. Brush the salmon pieces with about 1 tablespoon olive oil and season them well with salt and pepper. Spread the chopped garlic evenly over the pieces of fish, pressing it down into the flesh.

Heat about 2 tablespoons olive oil in a large ovenproof nonstick sauté pan. When the oil is shimmering hot, place the salmon pieces in it skin side up and sear the side with the garlic for about a minute, or until you see the first signs of browning. Slide a spatula under each piece and turn it over onto its skin side. Immediately put the pan in the oven and roast the fish for 7 to 8 minutes, longer for very thick pieces. The centers should just be starting to flake when tried with a fork; if you are using a thermometer, look for an internal temperature of around 145°.

While the fish is in the oven, whisk together the lemon juice, the remaining 3 tablespoons olive oil, the agave nectar, and the remaining 1 teaspoon of sea salt to make the agave vinaigrette.

Arrange the pieces of salmon on a platter or on plates, skin side down, and drizzle each with some of the agave vinaigrette, then sprinkle with plenty of parsley.

Serves 4 as a substantial dish, more if served as a companion to a hearty pilaf or salad

Matchmaking . . .
Try this alongside Farro and Black Rice Pilaf (p. 212) and any roasted vegetables, or with Succotash with Scarlet Quinoa (p. 124).

Succotash with Scarlet Quinoa
(p. 124), paired with Pan-Grilled
Swordfish with Garlic (p. 347)

PAN-GRILLED SWORDFISH WITH GARLIC

This is a simple technique, and the result is a piece of fish that is excellent hot from the griddle or pan and also good when cooled and sliced into a salad.

12 oz.–1 lb. swordfish steak

sea salt

freshly ground black pepper

1½ Tbs. extra-virgin olive oil

3 cloves garlic, finely chopped

GARNISH:

lemon wedges

Rinse the fish, pat it dry, and sprinkle it with sea salt and black pepper on both sides.

Heat the olive oil in a medium nonstick pan, and when it is shimmering hot, sizzle the garlic in it for a few seconds. Push the garlic into the middle of the pan, put the swordfish down directly on top of it, cover the pan, and cook the fish over medium-high heat for about 3 minutes, then turn it over. Try to keep all the garlic under the fish, not out at the edges of the pan where it will scorch.

Cook the fish on the other side just until it begins to pull apart when a sharp knife is inserted in the middle and slightly turned. Exact cooking time depends on the thickness of the fish, so keep a close eye on it. Serve the fish the moment it is ready, with lemon wedges, or cool it and slice it to use with a salad.

Serves 3 to 4 as a substantial dish, more in a salad or in tacos

In Flexible Menus . . .
A Salad Supper for the Heat Wave (p. 104) is one of my favorite meals for the hot season; a juicy and complex salad is beautifully accompanied by slices of this quickly pan-grilled swordfish. And in Taco Night at Home (p. 312), Kimchee Tacos can be made with teriyaki grilled tofu or with this swordfish—see the recipe that follows.

FISH TACOS

They are the favorite taco of so many taco lovers, made with an endless variety of seafood, and in distinct styles. Some of my friends are devotees of the tacos made with deep-fried fish. Others stick with grilled. Some want mahi-mahi, some want cod, and so on. Here's my own current favorite.

12–18 corn tortillas

1 lb. Pan-Grilled Swordfish with Garlic (p. 347)

2 cups shredded cabbage

chopped fresh cilantro

Pico de Gallo (p. 76), or the hot chile salsa of your choice

OPTIONAL:

kimchee

Preheat the oven to 350°. Wrap the corn tortillas in foil, in packets of 6, and heat them in the oven for 5 or 6 minutes while you finish grilling the swordfish.

When the fish is done, slice it into 1-inch cubes. Serve everything at once and let everyone make their tacos the way they like them: start with a few pieces of fish in a warm tortilla—or 2 tortillas, overlapped, to catch all the salsa—shredded cabbage and cilantro on top of the fish, salsa to taste on everything, and kimchee for the fusionists.

Fold the tortilla, and lean over your plate to catch the drips!

Serves 4 to 6

PRAWNS SAUTÉED WITH GARLIC
GAMBAS À LA PLANCHA

Prawns sautéed in garlic is one of those classic, simple dishes found all over the Mediterranean, from the tapa bars of Spain to the *mezze* tables of the Middle East. You can sauté prawns or large shrimp in their shells, or you can peel them down to their tails, which makes them an easy finger food.

See photo on p. 200.

1 lb. large prawns (14–18)

2–3 Tbs. extra-virgin olive oil

4 large cloves garlic, finely chopped

2 Tbs. fresh lemon juice

½ cup coarsely chopped fresh cilantro

a pinch of sea salt

GARNISH:

lemon wedges

The prawns can be sautéed in their shells or peeled, depending on how you want to serve them. Sautéing in the shell keeps in a bit more flavor, but peeling the prawns makes them much easier to eat (and you don't need finger bowls). If peeling the prawns, leave the tails on and remove the dark veins.

Heat the olive oil in a large skillet, add the garlic, and add the prawns right on top of it. Cook the prawns over high heat for about a minute, until you see them starting to turn pink, then turn them over. Add the lemon juice and the chopped cilantro and cook another minute or so, just until the prawns have turned pink all over. Exact cooking time depends on the size of the prawns.

Sprinkle on a tiny bit of sea salt and serve the prawns with lemon wedges and crusty bread.

Serves 6 to 8 as a tapa, in a selection of *mezze*, or as a garnish for pasta. Easy to double.

In Flexible Menus . . .
Find these easy prawns in No One Eats *Mezze* Alone (p. 118), but don't stop there. Have them with Teddy's Fusion Arrabiata (p. 185) or with Lemon Risotto (p. 201) or Spaghetti with Garlic and Oil (p. 183).

STIR-FRIED SHRIMP WITH TATSOI

This is a subtle dish, with only a touch of chile and not much soy sauce. The flavor of the fresh shrimp and young greens should be enhanced, not dominated.

Tatsoi is a tasty Asian green with a tender white stem and a dark green top, a bit like a small chard leaf. The plant forms a spreading head, so young plants look like blossoms. I use the youngest greens I can find for stir-fry, but any size can be cut up. If you cannot find tatsoi, baby bok choy can be used instead.

1 lb. medium shrimp (about 25)

kosher salt or sea salt as needed

1 lb. baby tatsoi or bok choy

4–5 green onions, white and green parts

6 oz. baby mizuna

3½ Tbs. peanut oil or grapeseed oil

3–4 thin slices peeled fresh ginger

3 large cloves garlic, finely chopped

1 Tbs. rice vinegar

2 tsp. dark sesame oil

a pinch of crushed red chile

1 tsp. tamari or soy sauce, plus more for the table

Peel and devein the shrimp. Rinse them in a large bowl of cold salted water. Drain, and repeat the process with a fresh bowl of salted water. Blot the shrimp dry with paper towels.

Trim the tatsoi, keeping smaller leaves whole and slicing large ones on a slant. Slice the green onions, also on a slant. Cut the mizuna in 1-inch-wide pieces. Measure out all the ingredients and line them up.

Heat 2 tablespoons of the oil in a large wok, add the ginger slices and half the chopped garlic, and stir for a few seconds. Add the shrimp and stir-fry over high heat until they are pink and opaque, about 2 minutes. Use a slotted spoon to remove the shrimp to a plate lined with paper towels, and blot the excess oil.

Wipe the wok, heat the remaining 1½ tablespoons oil, and add the remaining garlic. Stir a few seconds, then add the tatsoi and green onions and stir-fry for 2 to 3 minutes, until they begin to go limp. Add the mizuna, stir-fry another minute or two, then add the remaining ingredients and stir again, just until the thicker stems of tatsoi are tender-crisp.

Add back the shrimp, which should still be warm, stir for 10 to 15 seconds, and serve. Have tamari or soy sauce on the table for those who might want more.

Serves 4 to 8, depending on the number of other dishes

TUNA IN OLIVE OIL AND CAPERS

In the category of "simplest is best," here's tuna the way we often find it on a good antipasto table: chunks of tuna in a good olive oil, with the piquant pop of capers and a touch of lemon. The tuna might be keeping company with plump, creamy cannellini beans. I serve the two separately, side by side.

Tuna packed in olive oil is generally available in 5- or 6-ounce cans. You can also drain tuna that is packed in water and marinate it in your own extra-virgin olive oil. As for capers, any capers will work, but if you have access to salt-cured capers, which can be found in some gourmet shops, grab them.

10–12 oz. canned tuna packed in olive oil

3 Tbs. capers, drained

1 Tbs. fresh lemon juice, plus more to taste

freshly ground black pepper

a pinch of sea salt, if needed

Do not drain the tuna, just gently break it apart into chunks as you transfer it from the cans to a bowl. If you do not have tuna packed in olive oil, use solid water-packed tuna; drain it well, break it apart gently, and mix it with 2 to 3 tablespoons of olive oil.

Add the capers, the lemon juice, and lots of freshly ground black pepper. Gently lift and turn the pieces of tuna to combine the ingredients, but do not overmix. Taste the tuna and decide if you want to add a little more lemon juice or a pinch of salt.

Serve the tuna alongside Marinated Cannellini with Olives and Roasted Peppers (p. 132) and a good focaccia. The tuna can be spooned on top of a serving of the cannellini as a garnish, or mixed into the beans for a classic Italian salad.

Serves 6 as an appetizer, more as part of the antipasto table

---

In a Flexible Menu . . .
Risotto as You Like It (p. 198) is a menu that offers the option of a traditional Italian cannellini salad two ways, with or without the tuna.

FOWL

ROAST TURKEY
WITH HERBS

A straightforward method for roasting a moist and aromatic turkey—here it is, summed up: butter and herbs. There is no stuffing to confuse the cooking time; instead, the cavity is filled with fresh herbs to perfume the turkey, and the bird is rubbed lavishly with butter. Then, don't overcook it. Use a meat thermometer, the only truly reliable method to know when the turkey is done. And please buy an organic turkey if you can, one that hasn't been fed hormones and has not been injected with flavorings.

a 12–14-lb. turkey, fresh if possible

1 lemon

3–4 tsp. sea salt

1 head garlic, separated into cloves and peeled

8 Tbs. butter, softened, plus more to taste

freshly ground black pepper

1 Tbs. chopped fresh thyme

4 branches fresh sage (7–8 inches long)

4 branches fresh rosemary (6–7 inches long)

a handful of celery leaves

Turkey Giblet Sauce with Madeira (recipe follows)

EQUIPMENT:

large roasting pan, rack, kitchen twine, trussing pins, baster, meat thermometer, fat separator, aluminum foil

If the turkey is frozen, defrost it according to the directions on the package. As a general guide, a 14-pound turkey will take up to 3 days to defrost in the refrigerator and up to 8 hours in a sink full of water. When the bird is defrosted, pull out the giblets and set them aside. Trim off any loose knobs of fat. Wash the turkey thoroughly inside and out, in several changes of water, and pat it dry with paper towels. The turkey must be dry, or you will not be able to rub it with butter. Cut the lemon in half and rub the inside of the cavities with it, and sprinkle them well with 1 teaspoon salt. Slice 2 or 3 cloves of garlic and push some garlic slices between the skin and the breast, being careful not to break the skin.

Mix the softened butter with 2 teaspoons salt, some freshly ground black pepper, and the chopped thyme. Put half the thyme butter into the main cavity of the turkey and spread it around. Push in 3 branches of sage, 3 branches of rosemary, the celery leaves, and about three-quarters of the remaining garlic cloves. Close up the cavity with a couple of trussing pins, or sew it shut if you are ambitious. Push the last bit of sage and rosemary into the smaller cavity, along with a couple of garlic cloves, and close up that one by pulling the loose skin over the opening.

Preheat the oven to 325°. Truss the turkey. Use any method you prefer, but here is my easy (lazy) trussing method: Cut a long piece of kitchen twine. Pull the turkey's legs together, cross them, and tie them securely with the twine, then pull the two ends of the twine underneath the bird, cross in one big *X*, and pull the ends up over the wings. Tie it off and you're done. A turkey that is not stuffed is pretty easy to truss!

recipe continues

Rub half the remaining thyme butter over one side of the turkey, then place the turkey on the rack, buttered side up, and put it in the oven. Roast the bird this way for 1 hour, then turn it over, spread the remaining thyme butter over the other side, sprinkle on a little additional salt, and roast for another hour. Now turn the turkey breast side up, baste it with the pan juices, roast for another 30 minutes, then baste again. If you see it becoming too dark on top, cover it loosely with a piece of foil.

After 2½ to 3 hours, when the turkey is well browned and has released juices into the roasting pan, start testing the temperature. A turkey should never be undercooked, but don't overcook it either, as it easily dries out; using a meat thermometer is a reliable way to have a perfectly cooked turkey and a stress-free afternoon. Insert the thermometer into the thickest part of the thigh or the breast, but do not let it touch bone or gristle. Optimum temperature for the breast is between 165° and 170°; for the thigh it's about 175°. Since the thigh is usually smaller than the breast and you roast your turkey on its sides for the first 2 hours, there's a good chance of hitting this just right.

When the turkey tests done, take it out of the oven and let it rest for 30 to 45 minutes before carving. You can cover it with a tent of foil to help retain heat, but a turkey holds its heat for quite a while. (If you need to hold the turkey longer before serving, you can return it to a 250° oven for about 15 minutes to keep it warm.) When ready to serve, remove the turkey to a carving board or a platter and finish the sauce.

Serves 10 to 12, with a good probability of some leftovers

In a Flexible Thanksgiving Menu . . .
Thanksgiving for Everyone (p. 20) is the meal where this excellent roast turkey shares the stage with a beautiful polenta torta and an array of vegetables.

TURKEY GIBLET SAUCE WITH MADEIRA

3 Tbs. extra-virgin olive oil

neck and giblets from a 12–14-lb. turkey, cut in small pieces

sea salt

1 large onion, chopped

2 medium carrots, chopped

2 large stalks celery, chopped

4 cloves garlic, chopped

1 bay leaf

2–3 fresh or dried sage leaves

1 small sprig fresh rosemary or 1 tsp. dried

3–4 branches fresh flat-leaf parsley

2–3 cups vegetable or chicken broth

1 cup Madeira, sherry, or other fortified wine

Heat 2 tablespoons olive oil in a sauté pan and sauté the neck and giblets with a pinch of salt over medium-high heat, stirring, until they are well browned, 9 to 10 minutes. Remove the neck and giblets from the pan with a slotted spoon and add the onion, carrots, celery, garlic, bay leaf, and at least ¼ teaspoon salt. Sauté the vegetables, stirring often, until browned, 8 to 9 minutes. Return the neck and giblets to the pan, along with the sage, rosemary, and parsley.

Add 1½ cups water, 2 cups of the vegetable or chicken broth, and the Madeira or other fortified wine. Bring the liquid to a boil, then lower the heat and simmer the broth gently, covered, for 2 to 2½ hours. It should reduce, but not drastically. If the liquid level drops enough to expose the meat or vegetables, add a little water or more broth. Strain the broth through a fine sieve and set it aside until the turkey is out of the oven.

When you remove the turkey from its roasting pan, stir up the pan drippings, pour them through the same sieve, and add them to the strained giblet broth. Pour all the sauce into a fat separator (a beaker with a long spout that pours from the bottom) while it is hot. Wait a minute until the fat has risen to the top and is distinct from the broth, then pour the broth slowly into a clean pot until you see the layer of fat touching the spout bottom.

Heat the defatted sauce back to a simmer, taste it, and correct the seasoning; add a pinch of salt if needed, or add a tiny bit of water if the sauce tastes too concentrated and salty. Pour the hot, clear sauce into a sauceboat.

You should have 3 to 3½ cups of intensely flavored sauce

ROAST TURKEY BREAST OR LEG QUARTERS WITH GARLIC AND HERBS

When you want to keep it simpler, or when you don't have a crowd, putting a turkey breast or a pair of leg quarters in the oven is a good option. This method, with the turkey breast sitting on a bed of vegetables, is not much work and produces moist roast turkey infused with the perfume of garlic, herbs, and apples.

1 whole turkey breast or 1 large half breast, or two legs and thighs (5–7 lbs.)

6 cloves garlic, peeled and thinly sliced

1½ tsp. sea salt, plus more to taste

freshly ground black pepper

4 Tbs. butter, softened

2 Tbs. herbes de Provence

3 Fuji apples or other dense, juicy apples, cored and cut into 1-inch dice

4 small turnips, peeled and cut into 1-inch dice

1 yellow onion, peeled and cut into 1-inch dice

1 small celery root, peeled and cut into ½-inch dice

1 cup chicken broth, if needed

OPTIONAL:

¼ cup Madeira or Marsala

Wash the turkey breast or legs in several changes of water and pat dry with paper towels. Push the slices of garlic (the more, the better!) in between the skin and the meat, being careful not to break the skin. Sprinkle the turkey all over with at least 1 teaspoon salt, more if it is large, and grind on plenty of black pepper. Mix 3 tablespoons of the softened butter with the herbes de Provence and smear the mixture over the top of the turkey breast or the thighs and legs.

Preheat the oven to 400°. Mix together the apples, turnips, onion, and celery root and toss with ½ teaspoon salt and some pepper. Spread the vegetables in the bottom of an ample baking dish, drizzle with a little bit of the chicken broth, and the Madeira or Marsala if you wish, and place the prepared turkey on top of the vegetables.

Roast the turkey for 30 minutes, then turn the oven down to 325°, let the remaining butter melt over the turkey, and roast for another 1½ to 2½ hours, depending on size, basting every 30 minutes or so with the juices that form in the bottom of the pan. If the butter and juices are not giving you enough liquid for easy basting, add more chicken broth.

The turkey is ready when a meat thermometer inserted in the thickest part of the breast reads 165° or the thickest part of a thigh reads 175°. Your turkey should be well browned, but if it seems to be getting too dark, cover it loosely with foil. Allow the turkey breast or leg pieces to rest on the counter for 15 to 20 minutes before slicing.

Serves 5 to 6, with the possibility of some leftovers

In a Flexible Holiday Menu . . .
The Great Pumpkin (p. 22) is a different take on the harvest festival but perfectly embraces this more modest verison of roasted turkey.

EASIEST ROAST CHICKEN
STUFFED WITH LEMONS

It could also be called Perfect Roast Chicken, because the results are superb: a moist, tender, and flavorful chicken. But it really is easy. My friend Lena and I were in a quest to find the simplest method for achieving an excellent roast chicken. The bird was there, waiting: a plump 5-pound organic chicken. We discussed several roasting methods—high temperature, low temperature, turning, no turning—and decided to see what our favorite food writers had to say.

Oh my. So much information. Pages on brining and seasoning, pages about trussing, twelve photographs to make it clear, more pages about stuffing, turning, basting . . . I'm sure each method has resulted in superb roasted chickens. But we kept shaking our heads. Too complicated, don't want to do all that . . . In the end we went with simplicity and intuition, but we did take a piece of advice from the great Julia Child. She was a scientist in the kitchen when it came to timing a bird in the oven, and her formula worked perfectly: 45 minutes, plus 7 minutes per pound (allowing a buffer of 10 to 30 minutes more, depending on the size of the bird). When it came to trussing, though, we used my 20-second method.

a 5-lb. organic roasting chicken, at room temperature

1 tsp. sea salt, plus more to taste

freshly ground black pepper

2 medium lemons, scrubbed

2 small branches fresh rosemary, cut in 3-inch pieces

7–8 cloves garlic, peeled

1½ Tbs. butter, softened

3–4 Tbs. extra-virgin olive oil

EQUIPMENT:

a yard of kitchen string or twine, a meat thermometer

Preheat the oven to 425°. Remove the package of giblets from inside the chicken (you may want to set these aside to use in a stock). Trim off any loose pieces of fat that you see and discard them. Wash the chicken thoroughly, submerging it in several changes of warm water. Pat the chicken dry inside and out with paper towels.

Salt the inside of both the cavities and all over the outside of the chicken, and grind some pepper into the cavities. Cut the lemons in quarters. Put the rosemary, garlic cloves, and lemon pieces inside the large cavity of the chicken. Rub the outside of the chicken with the softened butter.

Truss the chicken: take your piece of kitchen string, lay it across the top of the chicken, and pull down both ends over the wings, then flip the chicken over, cross the string under it, flip the chicken again, bring the ends of the string together over the legs, and tie a firm knot. Basically, you are just tying it up like a package. This works, and it takes less time to do it than to read about it.

recipe continues

Place the chicken breast side up on a rack in a roasting pan that is just large enough to hold it. Drizzle a little olive oil on it and roast it for 15 minutes. Take the chicken out and use wads of paper towels or clean oven mitts to turn it over, breast side down. Drizzle on a bit more olive oil and give it 15 minutes more in the hot oven, then turn it once more, breast side up again. Baste the chicken with the fat and juices that are beginning to accumulate in the pan and roast it another 15 minutes, still at 425°.

Turn the oven down to 350°. Baste the chicken every 15 minutes, and after 35 minutes more check its temperature with a meat thermometer. Insert the thermometer into the thickest part of the thigh, and be sure you are not touching bone. A temperature of around 170° means you are done. Check both sides of the chicken to be sure. If you can't find your meat thermometer, don't despair. You can test the chicken by moving the drumstick, which should swivel easily in its socket, and when you pierce the chicken at a joint, look for juices running clear, not pink.

Take the chicken out of the oven, remove it to a platter or cutting board, cover it loosely with a foil tent, and let it rest for about 20 minutes before you carve it.

If you want to use the pan juices for a quick sauce, add a cup or so of either chicken stock or vegetable broth to the drippings and boil the liquid as you scrape up any bits that are stuck to the pan. After about 5 minutes, pour the pan juices into a defatting beaker and let the fat settle at the top, then pour the juices out through a strainer.

I have eaten roast chicken hot, warm, and at room temperature. You really can let that chicken sit on the counter for an hour or so, covered with its tent, and it will be just fine, so no need to stress about having everything done at exactly the same moment.

Serves 6 as a substantial dish, more when served alongside a centerpiece salad or a hearty pilaf and vegetable combination

---

In a Flexible Menu . . .
Sunday Dinner Comfort Food (p. 279) offers this lemon-scented roast chicken as an accompaniment to Fresh Corn Polenta and Farmhouse Mushroom Ragout.

Easiest Roast Chicken *stuffed with lemons* (p. 357), paired with Kabocha Squash
and Tuscan Kale Salad with Mixed Grains (p. 122)

CHARCOAL-GRILLED MARINATED CHICKEN

Here is the most straightforward summer chicken dish—an easy, herb-infused marinade and 15 minutes on the grill. Add sliced grilled chicken to a center-of-the-plate grain salad, like Summer Farro Salad with Tomatoes, Seared Onions, and Fennel (p. 107), to make it an omnivore meal.

¼ cup extra-virgin olive oil

½ cup balsamic vinegar

1 tsp. sea salt

2 Tbs. chopped fresh flat-leaf parsley

2 tsp. finely chopped fresh rosemary

2 tsp. chopped fresh thyme

1 tsp. crumbled dried sage

3 cloves garlic, finely chopped

freshly ground black pepper to taste

1½–2 lbs. boneless chicken, breasts, thighs, or both, with or without skin

Whisk together all the ingredients except the chicken, or pulse briefly in a blender. Wash the chicken well, pat the pieces dry with paper towels, and arrange them in a glass or ceramic baking dish. Pour the marinade over the chicken and turn the pieces over until all of them are well coated. If you like, you can score the thickest parts with a sharp knife to allow the chicken to absorb more of the marinade.

Cover the dish and leave the chicken to marinate in the refrigerator for 2 hours, or longer if you have plenty of time; as long as overnight is fine.

Fire up the coals, and when the grill is hot, cook the chicken about 6 to 8 minutes on a side, or until it tests done.

Serves 4 to 6, more if used in conjunction with a hearty salad, pilaf, or other substantial dish

---

To bone or not to bone . . .
It is easier to grill chicken that has been taken off the bone, but if you prefer to keep it on the bone, you can certainly do that; watch it more closely when it's on the grill, as it is less pliable, and the pieces must be moved to catch more heat on the thicker parts, less on the thinner, in order to cook through evenly.

MEAT

PAN-ROASTED PORK TENDERLOIN

Pan roasting is an easy way to cook a pork tenderloin: rub it with a garlicky pesto, sear it in a pan, and finish it in the oven in the same pan. It can then be used in any number of ways. Slice it into thin medallions to serve as a warm side with a hearty pilaf—Red Quinoa and Pumpkin-Seed Pilaf (p. 214), for example—or cut leftovers into strips as a garnish for the kale salad variation with nectarines (p. 101).

Pork tenderloins are generally sold two to a package; double this recipe to cook both at once, which will be enough for a larger dinner party, or put one in the freezer.

1 pork tenderloin (about 1 lb.)

¼ cup finely chopped fresh flat-leaf parsley

3 cloves garlic, finely chopped

2½ Tbs. extra-virgin olive oil

freshly ground black pepper

sea salt

Cut the tenderloin in half, making two shorter pieces for easier handling in the pan.

Mix together the parsley, garlic, 1½ tablespoons olive oil, and a good amount of freshly ground black pepper. Smear this rough pesto over the pieces of meat until they are well coated all over.

Preheat the oven to 375°. In a heavy ovenproof sauté pan, heat the remaining 1 tablespoon oil until it is shimmering but not smoking, then salt the tenderloin pieces generously and sauté them over high heat. Turn the meat after about 2 minutes, then keep turning from time to time until both pieces are nicely browned all over, 5 to 6 minutes total.

Roast the tenderloin in the hot oven, uncovered, for about 20 minutes, or until it tests done. An instant-read thermometer should read 145° to 150°. Cover the meat loosely with a piece of foil and let it stand on the counter for about 10 minutes before slicing.

Serves 4 to 6, more when paired with pilafs or grain salads

Other Flavor Ways . . .
Garlic and parsley pesto is a great aromatic, but the pork can be seasoned with a spice rub and cooked the same way. Try garlic with crushed chile and cumin, for example. Or use any commercial spice mixture that you love. The citrus marinade that is used for Citrus-Glazed Roasted Root Vegetables (p. 271) is another flavor option: marinate the pork in the citrus mixture and spoon more of it over the meat as it cooks.

MINT-SCENTED PORK AND PINE NUT MEATBALLS

Plenty of mint and parsley combine with garlic and a hint of green chile to spice up these lean pork and pine nut meatballs. They're small—the size of large walnuts—and that makes them easy to use as a garnish in a minestrone soup or a main-dish pilaf.

See photo on p. 35.

3 Tbs. chicken broth, vegetable broth, or water

1 egg

4 Tbs. dry breadcrumbs

3 Tbs. finely chopped fresh mint leaves

3 Tbs. finely chopped fresh flat-leaf parsley

3 Tbs. coarsely chopped pine nuts

2 large cloves garlic, minced

1 tsp. finely chopped fresh green serrano chile

1¼ tsp. sea salt

freshly ground black pepper to taste

1 lb. lean ground pork

2 Tbs. extra-virgin olive oil

Whisk together the broth or water, egg, and breadcrumbs. Add the chopped mint, parsley, pine nuts, garlic, chile, salt, and pepper and stir well. Mix the ground pork with the seasoning mixture, using your clean hands or a large fork to combine everything thoroughly.

Scoop out rounded tablespoons of the mixture and use your damp hands to shape them into balls. You should have 32 to 35 meatballs, roughly the size of big walnuts.

Heat the olive oil in a large nonstick pan and add as many of the meatballs as fit without crowding; a medium pan might mean 2 batches, a large one might handle them all at once. Sauté the meatballs in the hot oil, using a pair of forks to turn them frequently until they are browned all over, 10 to 12 minutes. Use a slotted spoon to remove the cooked meatballs onto a plate lined with several paper towels, and roll them around to blot the excess fat. Add any remaining meatballs to the pan and sauté them the same way.

Makes 32 to 35 small meatballs, enough to serve 6 to 10

Use the Freezer . . .
These meatballs can be frozen, then defrosted in the refrigerator or on the counter and reheated. To reheat, arrange them in a single, uncrowded layer on a baking sheet and place them in a 400° oven for 5 to 6 minutes, or until starting to sizzle.

In a Festive Mixed Menu . . .
These savory pork tidbits join the fun with Cocktails on New Year's Eve (p. 32).

CARNITAS
CHILE-SEASONED PORK FOR
TACOS OR BURRITOS

Carnitas is the affectionate name given to slow-cooked, chile-seasoned pork that is torn into shreds for tacos, enchiladas, and burritos. "Too easy to call it a recipe," said my friend as we made this, but here's his method.

4½ lbs. pork shoulder, bone-in

1 large dried guajillo chile

2 tsp. cumin seeds

½ tsp. ground cinnamon

1 tsp. smoked Spanish paprika

1 Tbs. light or dark brown sugar

1 Tbs. kosher or sea salt

4 Tbs. canola oil

1 onion, roughly chopped

4 cloves garlic, peeled and
   smashed

Trim the pork shoulder, cutting away large slabs of fat but leaving some smaller bits. Cut it into 2- or 3-inch pieces, and leave the bone. Pull the stem out of the chile pod, shake out the seeds, and snip the chile into strips. Toast the cumin seeds over high heat in a dry skillet for 2 to 3 minutes, until they give off a heavenly fragrance. Grind the chile and the cumin seeds in a *molcajete* or a spice grinder, until the seeds are pulverized. Don't worry about the pieces of chile pod—some will shred, some won't. Add the cinnamon, paprika, brown sugar, and salt.

Preheat the oven to 350°. Combine the pork with 1 tablespoon canola oil and the spice mixture and toss until all the meat is coated. Put the spiced meat into a Dutch oven or a large, heavy pot and add enough water to nearly cover it. Add the onion and garlic. Cover the pot with a good-fitting lid and cook the pork in the oven for about 3 hours.

Use a slotted spoon or tongs to lift the pieces of pork out of their broth; the meat should be very tender. Heat the remaining 3 tablespoons oil in a large sauté pan and add the pork, as well as any bits of onion or chile that you can capture out of the liquid in the pot. Sauté the pork, turning often, until you see some brown edges developing and the meat is falling apart, about 15 minutes. Moisten the meat with a little bit of the liquid from the pot and pull it apart into bite-sized pieces, removing the bone and any gristle.

Makes 4 to 5 cups, enough to fill 16 to 18 tacos

Lazy Carnitas . . .

If you don't have guajillo chiles on hand or don't feel like mixing spices, you can throw a couple tablespoons of a good chili powder onto the pork along with the onion, garlic, and salt, and proceed as described.

In a Flexible Menu . . .

Taco Night at Home (p. 312) is a casual DIY feast in which various fillings, including carnitas, are combined in tempting ways and everyone gets the taco of his or her dreams.

BAKED KIBBEH WEDGES

Kibbeh is a *mezze* player that comes in so many variations that it's difficult to define. Basically, it is a mixture of ground meat with bulgur and spices. But sometimes it's raw, sometimes cooked, sometimes layered, sometimes formed into small meatballs or oval croquettes. I've seen vegetarian kibbeh, too, made with squash, potato, or eggplant. What they all seem to have in common is that they are labor-intensive. But the great Claudia Roden discovered an easy kibbeh, and here is my spin on it. The lamb and bulgur mixture is baked in one dish, like a flat cake, and cut into wedges, then served with a pile of gorgeous seared onions on top. Thank you, Claudia.
See photo on p. 121.

¾ cup fine- or medium-grain bulgur

2 lbs. yellow onions

4 cloves garlic

1½ tsp. sea salt

freshly ground black pepper

⅛ tsp. cayenne, plus more to taste

1 tsp. ground cinnamon

1 lb. ground lamb

¼ cup chopped fresh flat-leaf parsley

2 Tbs. chopped fresh mint

4 Tbs. extra-virgin olive oil, plus more for oiling the pan

¼ cup pine nuts

2–3 Tbs. raisins

¼ tsp. crushed red chiles

2 Tbs. red wine vinegar

Combine the bulgur in a bowl with ¾ cup boiling water and leave it to soak for 5 minutes. If there is any liquid left, drain the bulgur in a sieve.

Peel 1 medium onion, cut it into pieces, and put it in the food processor with the garlic, 1 teaspoon salt, some freshly ground black pepper, the cayenne, and the cinnamon. Process until the onion is finely chopped, scraping down the sides of the container as needed. Add the bulgur and process again, to a rough paste. Add the ground lamb and pulse until everything is well combined, scraping down the sides again. Add the fresh herbs and give it a final spin.

Preheat the oven to 375°. Liberally oil a 12-inch tart pan or gratin dish and spread the thick lamb and bulgur mixture in it evenly, pushing it down with a spoon or with your fingers. Spread about 2 tablespoons olive oil over the top of it. With a sharp knife, cut the raw lamb mixture into 8 wedges, and then run the knife around the edge to loosen it slightly. Alternately, if you plan to serve the kibbeh as part of a *mezze* table, you can press the lamb and bulgur mixture into an oiled 8-by-11-inch baking pan and cut it into small squares instead of wedges.

Bake the kibbeh for 35 to 40 minutes. It will be just a little crusty at the edges, and the wedges or squares will separate easily when you run a knife through again.

Make the topping: Peel, quarter, and slice the remaining onions. Heat the remaining 2 tablespoons olive oil in a large nonstick pan and sear the onions in it with the remaining ½ teaspoon salt, stirring over high heat for 7 to 8 minutes, until they show some dark brown spots here and there. Lower the heat, cover the pan, and cook the onions very gently for 45 minutes, stirring occasionally.

Add the pine nuts, raisins, and crushed red chiles to the onions, then raise the heat to high again and after a moment add the wine vinegar. Stir as the vinegar cooks away, just a minute or two, and remove from the heat.

The kibbeh can be served hot, warm, or at room temperature. Arrange the wedges or squares on a platter and spoon the onion topping over them.

Serves 6 to 8, more if part of a large *mezze* table

In a Mixed Menu . . .
No One Eats *Mezze* Alone (p. 118): a tableful of favorites from this Middle Eastern tradition, including this not-so-laborious kibbeh.

HERB-RUBBED, PAN-ROASTED FLANK STEAK

Garlic, parsley, and olive oil—the go-to troika of seasonings for so many things—impart their savory goodness to this straightforward preparation. For a spicier piece of meat, crushed chiles or smoky hot paprika can be added to the rub.

1 lb. flank steak

3–4 Tbs. finely chopped fresh
    flat-leaf parsley

4 cloves garlic, finely chopped

3 Tbs. extra-virgin olive oil

freshly ground black pepper

sea salt

OPTIONAL:

crushed red chiles or spicy
    smoked paprika such as
    pimentón de la Vera

A flank steak is a long piece of meat, and you may want to cut it into 2 pieces for ease of handling in the pan.

Combine the parsley, chopped garlic, half the olive oil, and a big blast of freshly ground black pepper in a bowl and whisk together with a fork. If you like, add a pinch (more if you are a chile-head) of crushed red chiles or pimentón. Rub the steak all over with this mixture and let it rest for 15 or 20 minutes.

Preheat the oven to 375°. Heat the remaining 1½ tablespoons olive oil in a heavy ovenproof sauté pan until it is shimmering. Salt the steak well all over and sauté it over high heat for about a minute on each side, or just enough to sear the garlic-crusted meat. Put the pan in the oven for 5 to 6 minutes, or until the internal temperature reads about 140° on an instant-read meat thermometer.

Allow the meat to rest for a few minutes, then cut it on a diagonal, against the grain, in thin slices.

Serves 4 to 6 when combined with a pilaf or salad

GARLIC-AND-HERB-RUBBED LAMB CHOPS

My pals call these "lamb pops," because once the bones are neatly trimmed they look like meat lollipops. A quick garlicky herb paste spiked with mint and green chile coats the chops, giving them a bright flavor. Garnish a plate of Middle Eastern pilaf or tabbouleh with a couple of these pops for the omnivores. Ask the butcher for a small, or New Zealand, rack of lamb (there should be 8 bones in a small rack) and say you would like it frenched, with all the fat trimmed.

8 lamb rib chops (about 1½ lbs.)

2½ Tbs. extra-virgin olive oil, divided

2 Tbs. chopped fresh mint

2 Tbs. chopped fresh flat-leaf parsley

2 Tbs. chopped fresh cilantro

1 tsp. finely chopped fresh green serrano chile, plus more to taste

2 large cloves garlic, minced

sea salt

If your butcher has frenched the lamb chops for you, you're ahead. A New Zealand rack might be partially trimmed, with a big layer of fat left. Cut the rack in half, making 2 smaller racks for ease of handling, then cut almost all the fat from the bone, as well as the excess fat from around the meat; leave just a little for flavor.

Make the herb paste, using 1½ tablespoons of the olive oil, the mint, parsley, cilantro, chile, and garlic. Pulse everything in a mini food processor, or hand-chop and whisk it together with a fork. Rub the paste on the lamb, coating all sides well. Leave the lamb for about 30 minutes to absorb the flavors of the herbs.

Preheat the oven to 400°. Salt the lamb chops well. Heat the remaining 1 tablespoon olive oil in an ovenproof pan until it shimmers and sear the lamb over high heat, turning frequently, until all sides are nicely browned, 2 to 3 minutes. Put the pan in the oven and roast the chops for about 10 minutes or until done to your taste. Let them rest 5 minutes, then slice through between the bones to separate the chops.

Serves 4 as a garnish to a hearty pilaf or grain salad

Another Flavor Way . . .
Mix 3 tablespoons Dijon mustard with 3 tablespoons very finely chopped nuts and smear this mixture liberally all over the chops, then proceed as described.

In a Flexible Pilaf Menu . . .
Vegetables in the Center (p. 265) suggests these chops as a side to Ratatouille from the Charcoal Grill and Farro and Black Rice Pilaf.

SPICY LAMB MEATBALLS

Little meatballs, slightly spicy and full of the Middle Eastern flavors of cinnamon, mint, garlic, and cumin, are just the right omnivore garnish for that pilaf or couscous or bulgur salad. And you can make these spicier. I've kept the seasoning fairly tame, but feel free to add a big pinch of crushed red chiles, or increase the amount of serrano chile.

3 large cloves garlic

¼ cup packed fresh mint leaves

2 tsp. chopped fresh marjoram

2–3 tsp. chopped fresh green
   serrano chile

1 large onion (8 oz.), cut in pieces

1 tsp. ground cinnamon

1 tsp. toasted and ground cumin
   seeds

1 tsp. ground coriander

½ tsp. allspice

1¾ lbs. ground lamb

1 cup pine nuts

1¼ tsp. sea salt

plenty of freshly ground black
   pepper

2–3 Tbs. extra-virgin olive oil

In a food processor, pulse the garlic, mint leaves, marjoram, and green chile until everything is minced. Add the onion and all the spices and pulse until the onion is finely chopped. Add the lamb, pine nuts, salt, and pepper and pulse again to combine. Some pine nuts may remain whole, and that's fine. Remove the mixture to a bowl.

Form a small meatball by taking a rounded tablespoon of the lamb mixture and rolling it between the palms of your hands. Repeat until all the mixture is used. Pour 2 tablespoons olive oil into a wide bowl or pie dish and roll the meatballs in it gently until they are well coated.

To cook these meatballs on the stovetop, heat the remaining 1 tablespoon olive oil in a nonstick pan and place about a dozen meatballs in it over medium-high heat. After 2 minutes, start turning them with tongs; turn and roll them until they are browned all over, 6 to 7 minutes. Remove them to a plate lined with paper towels to blot excess fat. Alternately, arrange the meatballs on a large baking sheet and cook them in a preheated 425° oven for 20 to 22 minutes, turning them several times during their cooking time. They should be browned all over, but won't get as dark as they will in a pan.

Makes about 40 small meatballs

In a Flexible Meal . . .
Vegetables in the Center (p. 265) suggests grilled lamb sausage as a possible accompaniment to Ratatouille from the Grill, but why not Spicy Lamb Meatballs?

Spicy Lamb Meatballs (p. 370)

DANA'S BACON AND GARLIC CRISPS

Crisp, crumbled bacon is a favorite salad topping of many cooks, and many diners. My friend Dana invented this easy version: bacon bits with an upgrade. He uses it on soups, vegetables, and salads. The garlic, rosemary, and pepper marry perfectly with the smoky bacon.

1 lb. thick-cut bacon

8–10 cloves garlic

3 Tbs. finely chopped fresh
   rosemary

freshly ground black pepper

Preheat the oven to 400°. Line a baking pan with parchment paper and spread the bacon on it in 1 layer. Slice the garlic cloves paper-thin and scatter the slices over the bacon strips. Be sure all the garlic is on the bacon; garlic left on the pan will burn. Scatter the chopped rosemary over the bacon, and grind on plenty of coarse black pepper. I mean plenty.

Roast the seasoned bacon until it is rippled and browned and has rendered most of its fat, anywhere from 20 to 35 minutes, depending on the thickness of the bacon. Remove the bacon from the oven and use tongs to transfer the strips to a plate lined with several layers of paper towels. Let the bacon cool completely on the paper towels—it will crisp up as it cools—then cut it into ½-inch chunks.

Makes a little over 1 cup

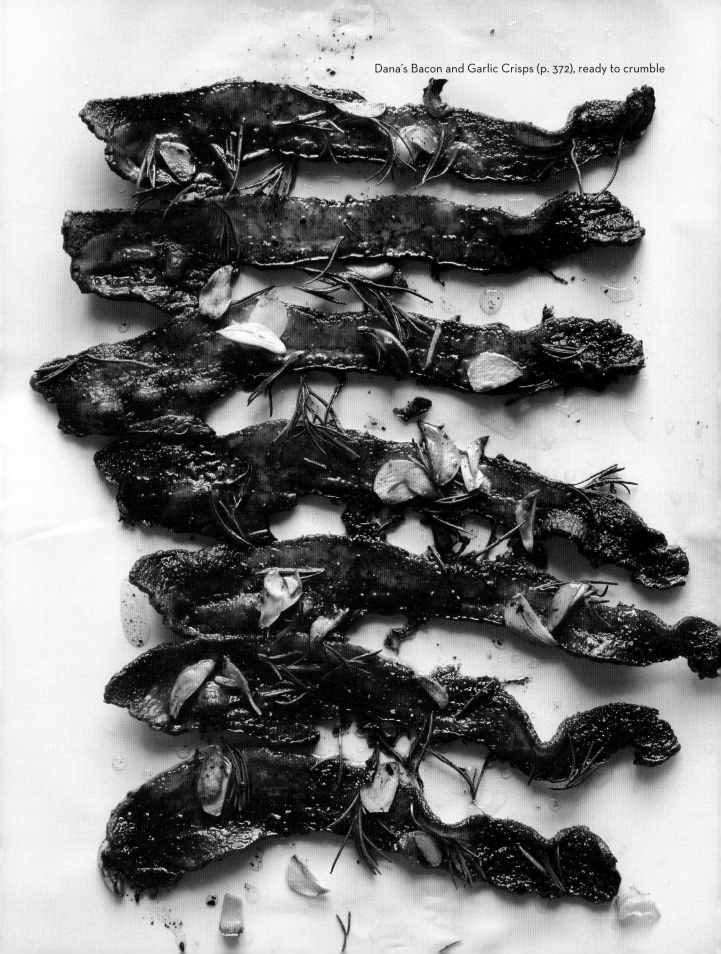

Dana's Bacon and Garlic Crisps (p. 372), ready to crumble

FRUIT COMPOTES AND SORBETS

Chilled Orange Slices in Orange Caramel   378

Basil-Scented Apple Compote   380

Gaviota Strawberries and Tangerines in Agave Nectar   381

Sliced Peaches in Lemon-Basil Syrup   382

Citrus and Spice Caramel Sauce   383

Lemon Sorbet   384

Pear and Rosemary Sorbet   385

Peach and Basil Sorbet   386

Lime and Coconut Sorbet   388

TARTS, CAKES, PUDDINGS, AND A CHOCOLATE BARK

Apricot and Cherry Galette; Vegan Pie Pastry   390

Winter Fruit Crumble with Gingersnap Topping; Apple and Blackberry Crumble;
Apple Cranberry Crumble   393

Apple Pecan Crisp   394

Galician Almond Cake   395

Carrot and Walnut Cake   396

Pumpkin Gingerbread   398

Coconut Rice Pudding with Cardamom   399

Dark Chocolate Almond Bark *with cherries and ginger*   400

DESSERTS

THE SWEET SPOT

"A perfect peach," mused Julia Child, holding out her cupped hand and looking at the peach in her memory's eye. "You can give that to the queen."

We were talking about desserts. She, of course, had made more than her share of spectacular creations. But she knew that beautiful fruit, in the prime of its season and the moment of its ripeness, is a dessert that can hardly be improved upon. Many of the menus in this book suggest seasonal fruit as a dessert for that reason.

And yet, while the "perfect peach" cannot be improved, it can be varied. There are times when we come to the sweet moment of the meal and we want to celebrate with something traditional or fancy—something Julia might have made. On our big holidays, we look forward to Grandma's special cookies or to a buttery tart with joyful anticipation.

We can have it all. This collection ranges from light fruit compotes to old-fashioned galettes, crumbles, and cakes. But my emphasis is on desserts that everyone can eat. Although you'll find butter and eggs in the pages ahead, you will also find a suite of bright fruit sorbets, and pastries that can be made two ways, with or without dairy products. You'll even find a couple of marvelous vegan cakes. I've emphasized the dairy-free choices because I know that anyone who bakes already has a collection of butter- and cream-based confections available to them; finding recipes for desserts that *everyone* can

eat—and that everyone *wants* to eat—is still a little more challenging.

Creating the recipes was a journey of happy discovery for me. All summer long I made sorbets. Finally I had to stop myself; the freezer was crammed with temptation. And the day I made a vegan carrot and walnut cake that no one could stop eating was a day of sweet triumph. Since flexibility is my goal, many of these desserts are designed to work in combinations. The sorbets can be combined with a scoop of ice cream. The compote can be served with biscotti or without. The apple crisp or the orange slices in spicy caramel can be enhanced with a spoonful of whipped cream, or not.

Other sweets can be made in two versions, the traditional butter-based way and a vegan version. I've made Apricot and Cherry Galette that way, and juicy-crunchy Winter Fruit Crumble with Gingersnap Topping. If you have a big group coming for a holiday meal, make two, one each way. The big holidays, like Thanksgiving and Christmas, are actually easier to handle for a mixed group. I cannot recall a Christmas when I served only one dessert, can you? So go ahead and make a big batch of your mom's shortbread cookies, or the Yule log constructed of chocolate buttercream, and add a vegan Pumpkin Gingerbread and a tray of Dark Chocolate Almond Bark to that dessert table.

Enough sugar rush for all, and then some.

FRUIT COMPOTES
AND SORBETS

CHILLED ORANGE SLICES IN ORANGE CARAMEL

VEGAN

These simple chilled orange slices are bathed in a delicate syrup that derives its haunting flavor from caramelized sugar and vanilla bean. It's an elegant and refreshing finish to the rich meals we like in winter.

9–10 large sweet navel oranges

a 1-inch piece of vanilla bean

1¼ cups sugar

Using a sharp, thin knife, cut away the peel and all the white pith from 6 or 7 of the oranges. Cut the peeled oranges crosswise into even slices ¼-inch thick. Stack the orange slices in a bowl, cover them with plastic wrap, and put them in the refrigerator to chill.

Using a microplane or fine grater, shave the zest from one of the remaining oranges, being careful to take only the orange part. Juice the remaining oranges and strain the fresh juice through a sieve. You should have at least 1½ cups juice. Slice the vanilla bean in half lengthwise and scrape out the soft pulp with the edge of the knife.

In a clean medium-sized pan, combine the sugar, the vanilla bean pulp and pod, and ¼ cup orange juice. Stir the mixture over low heat, washing the crystals down from the sides of the pan with a pastry brush dipped in water, until the sugar dissolves and begins to bubble. Allow the syrup to boil gently, undisturbed, until it is an even, deep golden brown.

Remove the pan from the heat, and carefully add the remaining 1¼ cups orange juice and the grated zest. The syrup will bubble up and the caramel thicken, but don't worry. Return the pan to the heat and stir gently over medium heat until the caramel has completely dissolved, then simmer another 5 minutes.

Strain the syrup through a sieve and discard the vanilla bean and the zest. You'll have an amber syrup with tiny dark flecks in it from the vanilla bean pulp. Chill the syrup.

To serve, arrange 5 or 6 orange slices in each wide, shallow dessert bowl and spoon some of the syrup over the slices. A sprig of mint or an edible flower can be used as a garnish if you want to be fancy, and a scoop of vanilla ice cream can be added if you like.

Serves 6 to 8

Chilled Orange Slices in Orange Caramel
(p. 378)

BASIL-SCENTED APPLE COMPOTE

VEGAN

The last basil in the garden meets the new apples in this cooling, delicious compote for early fall. It's lovely on its own or poured around a scoop of vanilla ice cream.

6–8 firm-textured apples (6 cups sliced)

1 cup sugar

8–12 large basil leaves

juice and zest of 1 lemon, zest cut in thin strips

Peel the apples, quarter and core them, and slice the quarters crosswise. Combine the sugar with 1⅓ cups water in a medium skillet and heat gently until the sugar dissolves. Add the apple slices, basil leaves, and lemon zest. Bring the liquid to a boil, then lower the heat and let it simmer 6 to 8 minutes, until the apples are just tender. Remove the apples and cook down the syrup for 5 to 6 minutes more, then allow it to cool.

Pour the cooled syrup back over the apples and add the lemon juice, a bit at a time, until sweet and tart are balanced. Chill the compote for several hours, allowing the flavors to develop. If you like, you can remove the strips of lemon zest and the basil leaves before serving—but I leave them in.

Serves 6

GAVIOTA STRAWBERRIES AND TANGERINES IN AGAVE NECTAR

VEGAN

The best fruit dessert is made from local fruit in its perfect season. In Ojai we are blessed with Gaviota strawberries—intense, sweet, slightly tart strawberry heaven. And the tangerines my friends Jim Churchill and Lisa Brenneis grow are another wonder.

But that's my neighborhood; you should look for the strawberries that are special to your area and pair them with the best tangerines or oranges you can find. Then do very little else—a drop of lemon and agave, a sprinkle of herbs. Spoon the fruit over ice cream. Pour it around a sponge cake. Have it all by itself.

6 cups Gaviota strawberries or your best local strawberries (about 2 lbs.)

1 lb. large, sweet tangerines, any seedless variety

2 Tbs. fresh lemon juice, plus more to taste

2 Tbs. agave nectar, plus more to taste

a pinch of sea salt

3–4 Tbs. thinly sliced basil leaves or mint leaves, or both

Trim and rinse the strawberries and cut larger ones in half. Peel the tangerines, section them, and remove any pith from the sections.

Combine all the ingredients in a bowl and mix gently, being careful not to bruise or break the fruit. Leave the fruit to macerate for about 30 minutes, and after 15 minutes taste and adjust the lemon and agave slightly if needed. The acidity of these fruits will vary with variety and weather, so you will need to use your taste buds to find the right balance.

Serve in dessert bowls, with whipped cream or ice cream or—my favorite way—spooned around a wedge of Galician Almond Cake (p. 395) in place of the Citrus and Spice Caramel Sauce.

Serves 6 to 8

SLICED PEACHES IN LEMON-BASIL SYRUP

VEGAN

Aromatic infused syrups are easy to make and turn any bowl of seasonal, slightly tart fruit into a special dessert. The lemon-basil syrup that you make for this simple fruit dessert can also be used to sweeten iced tea or to make your own flavored soda.

1½ cups (11 oz.) sugar

1¼ cups water

a pinch of sea salt

2 Tbs. chopped fresh basil plus sliced basil leaves for garnish

1 tsp. finely grated lemon zest (from 1 medium lemon)

4 Tbs. fresh lemon juice

5–6 large yellow peaches

Combine the sugar and water in a medium saucepan and stir gently over low heat until the sugar is dissolved. Add the salt and the chopped basil and simmer the mixture for 5 minutes. Add the grated lemon zest and 2 tablespoons lemon juice and allow the mixture to cool completely. Strain the syrup through a fine sieve, and keep it in a covered container in the refrigerator until you are ready to use it.

Peel the peaches and slice them in thin wedges, tossing them in a bowl with the remaining 2 tablespoons lemon juice to keep them looking gorgeous. Add ½ cup syrup and gently mix until all the peaches are coated. Taste, and add as much more syrup as you like; this will depend on the sweetness of the peaches and your own preference. Chill the peaches and syrup.

To serve, spoon a cup or so of peach slices with some syrup into each dessert plate, scatter slivers of basil leaves over the peaches, and pass additional syrup at the table.

Serves 6

CITRUS AND SPICE CARAMEL SAUCE

VEGAN

Gently spiced citrus juice and caramel combine for a sauce that makes a bowl of ice cream, a piece of sponge cake, or sliced fruit into an alluring dessert. I love this syrup with Galician Almond Cake (p. 395). And remember, the longer you let the syrup sit with the aromatics before straining, the spicier it will be.

1¼ cups sugar

2 Tbs. fresh lemon juice

1½ cups fresh orange or tangerine juice, strained

grated zest of 1 orange (about 1½ tsp.)

a pinch of sea salt

3–4 whole cloves

a ½-inch piece of cinnamon stick

OPTIONAL:

¼ tsp. pure vanilla extract

In a medium stainless steel sauté pan, combine the sugar, lemon juice, and 2 tablespoons orange or tangerine juice. Stir until the sugar is partly dissolved, then heat gently, washing the crystals down from the sides of the pan with a pastry brush dipped in water, until all the sugar dissolves and begins to bubble. Allow the syrup to boil gently over medium-low heat, undisturbed, until it is an even, deep golden brown, about 10 minutes.

Remove the pan from the heat and carefully add the remaining orange or tangerine juice, the orange zest, and the salt. The syrup will bubble up and the caramel thicken, but don't worry. Return the pan to the heat and stir gently over medium heat until the caramel has dissolved. Add the cloves and cinnamon stick, and the vanilla if you are using it, and simmer another 5 minutes. Allow the syrup to cool completely.

Strain the syrup through a sieve and discard the zest and whole spices. Keep the syrup in a closed container in the refrigerator until ready to use.

Makes about 1¾ cups

I love sorbets for their refreshing, bright flavors. And they are such flexible players for dessert. These four very different sorbets are all vegan, but it's easy to do two-way desserts: pair a scoop of sorbet with a scoop of vanilla ice cream, or serve the sorbet with biscotti or butter cookies on the side. Or stay light and serve your sorbet with an accompaniment of fresh berries or chilled sliced fruit.

LEMON SORBET

VEGAN

Here it is: the pure lemon ice that brings refreshment in the heat of summer, the one you would choose if you could have only one sorbet on the desert island. I like it on the tart side, but you can tune the tart-sweet balance—your taste buds will speak to you.

2 cups (15 oz.) sugar

1 Tbs. plus 1 tsp. finely grated lemon zest (lightly packed)

1 cup fresh lemon juice, strained, plus more to taste

sea salt

Combine the sugar and 2 cups water in a pot and stir over low heat until the sugar is dissolved. Simmer for 5 minutes, then stir in the lemon zest and cool the syrup completely.

Stir in the lemon juice and a pinch of sea salt and taste. The mixture should be intensely lemony and tart-sweet. If you want a less sugary sorbet, add more lemon juice, a spoonful at a time, but remember that the sweetness will be less apparent once the sorbet is frozen. If the flavor seems too intense, add a spoonful of water.

Chill the mixture thoroughly, then freeze it in an ice cream maker according to the manufacturer's instructions. Pack the sorbet into a chilled container with a tight-fitting lid and leave it in the freezer for at least 4 hours before serving.

Makes about 1 quart, enough for 6 to 8 servings

PEAR AND ROSEMARY SOREBET

VEGAN

Rosemary brings a whiff of piney freshness to the sweetness of ripe autumn pears. This is a beautiful sorbet for a warm fall evening. Serve it with an almond cookie or biscotti.

1 cup sugar

1 small sprig fresh rosemary or
   ½ Tbs. dried rosemary

sea salt

2 lbs. ripe Anjou pears

1 Tbs. cider vinegar

freshly ground black pepper to
   taste

1–2 Tbs. agave nectar or mild
   honey, if needed

Combine the sugar and 1 cup water in a small saucepan and stir over low heat until the sugar is dissolved. Add the rosemary and a pinch of sea salt and simmer the syrup for 5 minutes. Allow the syrup to cool completely, then strain out the rosemary.

Meanwhile, peel and core the pears and trim out any bruises or bad spots. In a blender, combine the pears, syrup, vinegar, and pepper and process to a smooth puree. Taste, and add a bit of agave nectar or honey if needed; it will depend on the sweetness of the pears.

Chill the mixture well, then freeze it in an ice cream maker according to the manufacturer's directions. Pack the sorbet into a chilled container, cover tightly, and put it in the freezer for a few hours before serving.

Makes a little less than 1 quart, enough for 6 to 7 servings

PEACH AND BASIL SORBET

VEGAN

The perfect summer dessert: a sweet chill with a peppery spike of herbal excitement . . . The basil is subtle but important, and the peaches must be the ripe golden beauties of July or August.

1 cup sugar

¼ cup (½ oz.) packed sliced or chopped fresh basil leaves, plus more to taste

sea salt or kosher salt

2½ lbs. ripe yellow peaches, peeled and cut up (about 4 cups)

3 Tbs. fresh lemon juice

Combine the sugar and 1 cup water in a small stainless steel pot and heat it gently, stirring, until the sugar is dissolved. Add the basil and a pinch of salt and simmer gently for 10 minutes. Turn off the heat and let the syrup cool completely. Strain the syrup and reserve the basil. You should have 1¼ cups syrup.

Put the peaches in a blender, add the cooled syrup and the lemon juice, and puree. Add about 1 teaspoon of the reserved basil and pulse a few times, just until the basil makes green flecks in the peach puree. For a more pronounced basil flavor, add a teaspoon or so of finely chopped raw basil.

Chill the mixture well, then freeze it in an ice cream maker, following the manufacturer's instructions. Transfer the sorbet to a chilled container, cover tightly, and put it in the freezer for about 2 hours to firm up.

Makes a little more than 1 quart, enough for 6 to 8 servings

Peach and Basil Sorbet (p. 386)

LIME AND COCONUT SORBET

Sweet and tart, creamy and light—this is one of those perfect combinations.

1⅓ cups sugar

sea salt

1 Tbs. finely grated lime zest (from 2 limes)

¾ cup fresh lime juice

1 cup full-fat unsweetened coconut milk

½ cup unsweetened shredded coconut

Combine the sugar with 1⅓ cups water and a pinch of salt in a stainless steel pot and stir over low heat until the sugar is dissolved. Simmer the syrup for 5 minutes, then turn off the heat and whisk in the grated lime zest, ⅔ cup of the lime juice, and the coconut milk. Whisk gently until the coconut milk is incorporated, with no lumps to be seen. Taste, and add more lime juice, a spoonful at a time, until you have the perfect sweet-tart balance. Stir in the shredded coconut.

Chill the mixture well, then freeze it in an ice-cream maker according to the manufacturer's directions. Pack the sorbet into a chilled container, cover tightly, and put it in the freezer for at least 3 hours before serving.

Makes just under 1 quart, enough for 6 to 7 servings

TARTS, CAKES, PUDDINGS, AND A CHOCOLATE BARK

APRICOT AND CHERRY GALETTE

VEGETARIAN OR VEGAN

There is something so appealing about the look of a rustic tart, casually shaped by folding the untrimmed pastry edge over the filling in loose pleats and leaving the fruit in the center exposed. This one combines two of the great flavors of early summer.

FOR THE PASTRY:

1²/3 cups unbleached all-purpose flour

2 tsp. sugar

¾ tsp. sea salt

10 Tbs. unsalted butter

4–5 Tbs. icewater

FOR THE FILLING:

1½ lbs. firm, tart apricots

1½ lbs. sweet red cherries

¾ cup fine sugar

1½ Tbs. cornstarch

a dash of ground cinnamon

½ tsp. almond extract

½ cup (2 oz.) chopped walnuts

3 Tbs. unbleached all-purpose flour

OPTIONAL GLAZE:

½ cup apricot jam or apple jelly, melted and strained

Make the pastry: Put the flour, sugar, and salt into the container of a food processor and add the cold butter, cut into bits. Process briefly, until the mixture resembles coarse meal. Sprinkle in icewater while running the processor, just until the pastry starts to hold together. Remove the pastry, form it into a ball, wrap it in plastic wrap, and put it in the refrigerator to rest for about 30 minutes.

Make the filling: Slice the apricots off their stones and leave them in halves, or cut them in quarters if large. Stem and pit the cherries. Whisk together ½ cup sugar, the cornstarch, and the cinnamon. In a bowl, toss the prepared fruit with the sugar mixture and the almond extract. Combine the walnuts, the remaining ¼ cup sugar, and the flour in a food processor and process briefly, until the nuts are ground to a meal.

On a lightly floured board, roll out the pastry to a circle about 18 inches across, and don't worry about the rough edges; just be sure the pastry is not split too far into the center, or the filling will leak. Drape the pastry over the rolling pin and transfer it to a baking sheet lined with parchment, allowing the excess to hang over the sides. Preheat the oven to 425°.

Spread the walnut mixture in the center of the pastry, leaving a 2-inch border all around. Pile the fruit on top of the walnut layer, making sure the apricots and cherries are more or less evenly distributed and look nice on top. Fold the border of the pastry circle up over the fruit, gathering it in loose pleats. Remember, you're going for a rustic look.

Bake the galette for 20 minutes, loosely covered with a sheet of aluminum foil, then lower the temperature to 375° and bake for another 40 minutes. Remove the foil for the last 10 minutes or so to brown the crust.

Allow the galette to cool, and brush the exposed fruit with melted jam or jelly if you wish to make it shiny. Use two long spatulas to help slide the galette onto a serving platter.

Serves 8

And the Vegan Way . . . Vegan Pie Pastry

The filling is already vegan, and the pastry crusts I have made with the following nondairy formula have been delicate and tasty. Vegan pastry is a bit more fragile than traditional pastry, but a sheet of parchment is the piece of magic that makes it easy. And using liquor to moisten the pastry dough instead of water is a neat trick: the alcohol cooks away, resulting in a pastry with the light, dry texture of a shortbread cookie.

2 cups (10½ oz.) unbleached all-purpose flour, plus more for dusting

2 tsp. sugar

½ tsp. sea salt

6 oz. vegan butter (such as Earth Balance), chilled and cut in pieces

1 tsp. finely grated lemon zest

1 Tbs. vodka, Calvados, or pear eau de vie

Put the flour, sugar, and salt into the container of a food processor and add the cold vegan butter and the lemon zest. Process briefly, until the mixture resembles coarse meal. Sprinkle in the liquor and pulse just until the pastry starts to hold together. Remove the pastry, form it into a 6-inch disk, wrap it well, and chill it for 30 minutes.

Place a large piece of parchment on a board, dust it lightly with flour, and roll the pastry out into a circle 16 to 18 inches across. Rolling vegan pastry requires some care, so go slowly, patch cracks, and dust a little more flour on top of the pastry if you need to. And remember that this is a rustic galette, so you will not be trimming the edges of the pastry; the edge can be rough, but it must not be split too far into the center or the filling will leak.

Slide the parchment, with the pastry circle on it, onto a large baking sheet. Now proceed to spread the walnut mixture over the pastry, and then the fruit filling, as instructed in the recipe above. When you have folded the border over the filling in loose pleats, you can brush the top of the pastry with soymilk or almond milk and sprinkle coarse sugar over it. Before baking, trim the parchment with scissors so it does not overhang the pan. Once the galette is baked, it is very easy to slide it off the parchment onto its serving platter.

Winter Fruit Crumble
with Gingersnap
Topping (p. 393), the
summer variation, with
vanilla ice cream

WINTER FRUIT CRUMBLE WITH GINGERSNAP TOPPING

VEGETARIAN OR VEGAN

The flavors of two wonderful old-fashioned desserts are combined here, the apples and pears of autumn pies and the spicy snap of ginger cookies in the crumble topping.

FOR THE TOPPING:

1 cup (3½ oz.) rolled oats

²/3 cup unbleached all-purpose flour (3¼ oz.)

¾ cup (5½ oz.) dark brown sugar, packed

a pinch of sea salt

1 tsp. ground cinnamon

¼ tsp. ground nutmeg

1 tsp. ground ginger

a pinch of cloves

freshly ground black pepper to taste

6 Tbs. butter, chilled and cut in pieces

1 Tbs. molasses

FOR THE FILLING:

1½ lbs. firm ripe pears, such as Bartlett

1½ lbs. tart apples, such as Pippin or Granny Smith

2 Tbs. fresh lemon juice

1/3 cup (2½ oz.) sugar

1/3 cup (1½ oz.) raisins

1 tsp. ground cinnamon

¼ tsp. ground nutmeg

Make the topping: In the container of a food processor, combine the oats, flour, brown sugar, salt, and spices. Pulse until the oats are broken up. Add the cut-up butter and pulse until the mixture looks like coarse meal. Add the molasses and pulse again. If the mixture is not starting to clump together, add 1 tablespoon icewater and process only until it does start to pull together. Chill the topping for 10 to 15 minutes. Preheat the oven to 375°.

Make the filling: Peel the pears and apples and cut them in thick slices; about 7 cups. Toss the fruit with the lemon juice. Stir in the sugar, raisins, cinnamon, and nutmeg. Spoon the filling into a medium gratin dish.

Pinch off pieces of the topping and scatter them all over the fruit, building up a rough, rustic crust. Bake the crumble for 40 to 45 minutes; the top should be crisp and browning, the fruit bubbling. Serve the crumble hot or cool, and spoon some of the juices into each bowl.

Serves 6 to 8

The Vegan Way . . .
The gingersnap topping can be made with a top-quality vegan margarine, such as Earth Balance, in place of the butter.

The Summer Way . . . Apple and Blackberry Crumble
In summer, blackberries or boysenberries make a wonderful addition. Replace the pears with about 4 cups of berries and drop the raisins.

And Still Another Way . . . Apple Cranberry Crumble
Around the winter holidays, I like this cheery version: use 4½ pounds apples, drop the lemon juice, and add 1½ cups fresh, cleaned cranberries to the mix.

APPLE PECAN CRISP

VEGETARIAN OR VEGAN

Tart, snappy apples and a topping like a shortbread cookie with pecans—who could say no to that? For the vegan way, use a high-quality vegan margarine, such as Earth Balance, in place of the butter.

FOR THE FILLING:

3 lbs. tart apples, peeled and sliced

2 Tbs. lemon juice

1/3 cup (2 1/2 oz.) sugar

1 tsp. ground cinnamon

1/4 tsp. nutmeg

2 tsp. finely grated lemon zest

FOR THE TOPPING:

1 1/2 cups (6 1/2 oz.) unbleached all-purpose flour

1/2 cup light or dark brown sugar, packed

1/4 cup granulated sugar

1 tsp. ground cinnamon

1/4 tsp. sea salt

2 Tbs. cold, unsalted butter, sliced

1 cup (3 1/2 oz.) pecans, lightly toasted and chopped

Mix together all the filling ingredients and spoon the filling into a medium gratin dish. Preheat the oven to 375°.

For the topping, combine the flour, sugars, cinnamon, and salt in a food processor and pulse briefly. Add the sliced butter and process until the mixture starts holding together. Remove the mixture to a bowl and add the chopped pecans, working them in with your hands. Crumble the topping evenly over the apples. Bake the crisp for 50 to 60 minutes, but check it at 40 minutes; if the top looks dark, cover the crisp loosely with foil. Allow the crisp to cool slightly before serving.

Serves 6 to 8

GALICIAN ALMOND CAKE

VEGETARIAN

Tarta de Santiago: I ate more than my share of this almond cake some years ago when my friend Cecilia and I walked the Camino de Santiago, the ancient pilgrimage route in Spain. Simple, dense, moist, it's the kind of cake I love best. The lemon zest is my addition to the traditional recipe. Serve this with a spoonful of Citrus and Spice Caramel Sauce on the plate around it—so good.

1¼ cups (6½ oz.) blanched almonds

⅞ cup (7 oz.) granulated sugar

3 large eggs (6½ oz.), at room temperature

1 tsp. finely grated lemon zest

¼ tsp. almond extract

6 Tbs. (1¾ oz.) unbleached all-purpose flour

¼ cup powdered sugar

GARNISH:

Citrus and Spice Caramel Sauce (p. 383)

Butter a 9-inch springform pan, put a round of parchment on the bottom, and butter the parchment. Preheat the oven to 350°.

Chop ⅓ cup of the almonds medium-fine and set aside. Combine the remaining ⅞ cup almonds with ⅓ cup of the granulated sugar in the container of a food processor and process them to a fine sandlike meal. Combine the chopped almonds with the processed ones.

Beat the eggs until they are foamy and light, then add the remaining ½ cup granulated sugar and beat until the mixture is pale and thick. Add the lemon zest and almond extract, then beat in the flour and the almond mixture.

Pour the batter into the prepared springform pan and bake for 35 to 40 minutes, until the top of the cake is pale gold and a toothpick inserted near the center comes out clean.

Let the cake cool for a few minutes, then remove the sides of the pan. Slip a long spatula between the parchment and the bottom of the pan and slide the cake, with its parchment, onto a cooling rack. Sift the powdered sugar over it while it is still warm, then transfer the cake to a serving plate. When serving, drizzle a few spoonfuls of Citrus and Spice Caramel Sauce over or around each wedge of cake.

Serves 6 to 8

CARROT AND WALNUT CAKE

VEGAN

The fresh crop of walnuts in the fall is a good excuse to bake this moist, dense, and spicy cake. I've tried many carrot cakes and find most of them too heavy and oily. This one delivers all the flavor and feels just right.

2⅓ cups (9½ oz.) unbleached all-purpose flour

1 Tbs. baking powder

1 tsp. baking soda

¾ tsp. sea salt

2 tsp. ground cinnamon

½ tsp. ground nutmeg

½ tsp. ground cloves

1 cup fresh orange juice

1½ tsp. grated orange zest

½ cup canola oil

¾ cup (5½ oz.) granulated sugar

½ cup (3 oz.) dark brown sugar

2 tsp. vanilla extract

1 cup (4½ oz.) finely chopped walnuts

¼ cup (1½ oz.) candied ginger, finely chopped

2 cups (8 oz.) grated carrots

½ cup (2½ oz.) raisins

FOR THE SUGAR GLAZE:

1 cup powdered sugar

1 tsp. vodka

3–4 tsp. strained orange juice

¼ tsp. almond extract

Sift together the flour, baking powder, baking soda, salt, cinnamon, nutmeg, and cloves. In another bowl, whisk together the orange juice, zest, canola oil, sugars, and vanilla extract. Add the dry ingredients to the wet mixture in 2 or 3 batches, beating with an electric mixer until just combined. Stir in the finely chopped walnuts, ginger, grated carrots, and raisins. Preheat the oven to 350°.

Oil two round cake pans and line the bottoms with oiled parchment. Spoon the batter evenly into the pans and bake the cakes for 40 to 45 minutes, or until a toothpick inserted in the center comes out clean. Cool the cakes before removing them from the pans.

Combine the powdered sugar in a bowl with the vodka, 3 teaspoons orange juice, and the almond extract. Stir until the sugar is dissolved. If the mixture is more a paste than a sauce, add more orange juice. You should have a smooth glaze that pours slowly from a spoon. This amount is sufficient to glaze 1 cake generously or to make light swirls over 2 cakes. Drizzle the glaze over the cakes, letting it drip down the sides. Allow the glaze to dry before covering the cakes.

My favorite way to finish these cakes is with that citrusy sugar glaze. But the cakes can also be dusted with powdered sugar or garnished with a spoonful of crème fraîche. Or you can make your favorite frosting and put together a layer cake.

Even though this moist cake keeps well for several days if covered tightly with plastic wrap, you will have a hard time keeping it that long.

Makes 2 small cakes or 1 layer cake, enough for 12 servings

Carrot and Walnut Cake (p. 396)

PUMPKIN GINGERBREAD

VEGAN

A pan of fresh homemade gingerbread: pure comfort food. This one is based on an old favorite recipe, with pumpkin puree added and the oil slightly reduced. The result is a rich-tasting cake that stays moist for days. It's a homey treat by itself, and a fancy dessert when served with vanilla ice cream, or with Citrus and Spice Caramel Sauce (p. 383).

1 cup (7½ oz.) sugar

½ cup canola oil

1 cup dark molasses

2 tsp. baking soda

1 cup (8 oz.) pureed pumpkin

1½ Tbs. minced fresh ginger

2¾ cups unbleached all-purpose flour

½ tsp. sea salt

½ tsp. baking powder

1 tsp. ground ginger

¾ tsp. ground cinnamon

½ tsp. ground cloves

Oil a 9-by-12-inch baking pan, line the bottom with parchment, and oil the parchment. Preheat the oven to 350°.

Combine the sugar, oil, and molasses in a large mixing bowl. Dissolve the baking soda in a cup of boiling water and stir it into the sugar mixture, then stir in the pureed pumpkin and minced ginger. In another bowl, sift together the flour, salt, baking powder, and all the spices. Stir the dry mixture into the wet. Use a whisk or the low setting of an electric mixer to beat the batter just until everything is combined and there are no lumps.

Pour the batter into the prepared baking pan. Bake for about 45 minutes, or until a toothpick inserted near the center comes out clean. Allow the gingerbread to cool slightly before cutting.

Makes 1 cake, enough for 10 to 12 servings

COCONUT RICE PUDDING WITH CARDAMOM

VEGAN

A sweet, milky risotto made with coconut milk, an aromatic touch of cardamom, and fresh lemon zest—simple and perfect. For a richer dessert, use full-fat coconut milk.

2 cups light coconut milk

2 cups almond milk

3/4 cup Arborio rice

1/3 cup sugar

a pinch of sea salt

1/4 tsp. ground cloves

4-5 cardamom pods

1/2 cup raisins

finely grated zest of 1 lemon

Combine the milks, rice, sugar, salt, and cloves in a medium heavy-bottomed saucepan. Split open the cardamom pods, remove the seeds, and crush them slightly in a mortar or on a board, using the flat side of a chef's knife. Add the crushed cardamom seeds to the saucepan. Bring the mixture to a boil, then lower the heat and let it simmer for about 40 minutes, adding the raisins about halfway through and stirring often toward the end of the cooking time. Stir in the lemon zest and taste. The rice should be tender and the liquid thick.

The rice pudding can be served warm or cool. It will thicken further as it cools, so if you are serving it cold, you may want to stir in a little more milk to regain the moist texture.

Serves 4 to 5

Another way . . .
Add diced mango to the pudding instead of raisins; mango and coconut are a great pair. Stir in the fruit a few minutes before the pudding is finished.

DARK CHOCOLATE ALMOND BARK
WITH CHERRIES AND GINGER

VEGAN

I could not end without a taste of fine dark chocolate.

Toasted almonds, tart cherries, and a zippy touch of ginger give this simple bark a complex flavor. A plate of these dark, shiny shards of chocolate can be served with a cup of coffee for a minimalist dessert, or a few jagged pieces can elevate any scoop of ice cream or bowl of pudding. Use only the highest-quality dark chocolate; chocolate with at least 65 percent cocoa is best.

1 lb. top-quality bittersweet chocolate

2/3 cup lightly toasted almonds

2/3 cup dried tart cherries

3 Tbs. finely chopped candied ginger

Line a large baking sheet with parchment or a Silpat. Break the chocolate into pieces. Coarsely chop half the almonds.

Use a double boiler, or rig one: Put an inch or 2 of water into a medium saucepan and bring the water to a boil, then lower to a simmer. Set a large, heatproof bowl over the saucepan, making sure the water doesn't touch the bottom of the bowl. Put the chocolate into the bowl and melt it slowly, stirring constantly.

When the chocolate is completely melted, remove the bowl to the counter and stir in the chopped almonds, most of the cherries, and the ginger. Spoon the mixture onto the parchment-lined pan and use a rubber spatula to spread it into a fairly thin sheet, about 10 by 14 inches, distributing the almonds and fruit throughout the sheet.

Sprinkle the whole toasted almonds and the remaining cherries over the top, pressing down on them lightly to make sure they stick.

Put the pan in the refrigerator and allow the chocolate to cool until it hardens completely, at least 1 hour and possibly longer, depending on thickness. Break the sheet of chocolate bark into random pieces, and keep the pieces cold in a parchment-lined container until ready to serve.

Makes 20 to 24 generous pieces

Dark Chocolate Almond Bark *with cherries and ginger* (p. 400)

SINCERE THANKS

By now I should know that it might be a long journey to write a book, and yet it always takes me by surprise. This one took a few years, and I didn't travel alone. Thanks to those who kept me on the road!

First, thanks to my brilliant editor at W. W. Norton, Maria Guarnaschelli, who saw this idea from the very start, and held on to the vision faithfully through every bump and pothole in its path as it grew into a book.

And thanks to the whole, excellent team at Norton, where I felt supported at every step: thanks especially to Susan Sanfrey, the calm and thoughtful project editor who was able to see the big picture and the tiniest detail at once . . . thanks also to Sophie Duvernoy, who followed up every question with patience and admirable organization . . . and many thanks to Liz Duvall, the best copy editor on the planet, who sifted endlessly through the words and numbers, the dots and dashes, until it all made sense.

A loud shout-out of thanks to Kris Dahl, my enormously supportive agent (and sometimes therapist), who steered the deal through and kept it on track with unfailing good humor.

And a very special thank you to my friend and fellow denizen of Ojai, the genius photographer Victoria Pearson. Vicki, I feel so lucky to have your gorgeous images in my book!

Slow food and fast friends . . .

This book took me into some new territory, which was exciting but also challenging. I could not have done it without the happy, generous help of my kitchen friends, fellow cooks who marched into my kitchen and made themselves right at home, cooking with me through many adventurous menus, many hilarious afternoons of experiments, many delicious evenings of tastings:

Dana Fulmer, the chef who showed up with his knives and his apron and his lovely wife, Lori, shared so much of his deep culinary knowledge, and became a dear friend . . .

Larry Yee, my brother from another mother, and one of the finest intuitive cooks and most generous spirits I know . . .

Lisa Cervantes, the matchmaker and organizer, always ready with books and ideas and emergency cocktails . . .

Cindy Pitou Burton, who would zoom by at the drop of a text to taste and to document the experiments for the website . . .

And Haigaz Faragian, who shared his mother's recipe for the addictive black lentil puree, and Jeri Oshima, an artist in her kitchen and mine, and Lena Muniz, who didn't mind driving up from LA just to roast a chicken.

And of course—I'm thankful for all the friends who gathered at those raucous tasting dinners on the terrace.

I feel a deep gratitude for the unique food community of the Ojai Valley: The farmers who bring their bounty to our Sunday market and make it easy to be a good cook here; the home cooks who are always ready to share; the folks who keep those large and small roadside stands alive; Kate, the great bread baker with her bakery in the woods; Adam, our world-class winemaker, and Henry, the distiller who makes gin infused with wild sage from the mountainsides where we hike; the many other food artisans who pour love into their cheeses, teas, olive oils, salsas and preserves; and all the neighbors who share backyard fruit and leave surprise pumpkins on my kitchen counter. In this mix of slow food and fast friends, hospitality feels as easy as breathing.

And deeply felt thanks to my Christmas Eve family . . . the group of dear friends and relatives who have gathered at my Ojai table for decades now, honoring old traditions and creating a new one. Sitting at one big table we watched our children grow up, and we saw hospitality become community, and community become family. I love you all—and thanks, Emery Mitchem, for coining the name!

And finally, a grateful embrace to my two sons, Christopher and Teddy Nava, who cook and eat with such gusto and flair, and are still my two favorite mouths to feed.

INDEX

Note: Page numbers in *italics* refer to illustrations; (var.) indicates a recipe variation.

ABOUT THE AUTHOR

Anna Thomas wrote her first cookbook while she was a film student at UCLA; *The Vegetarian Epicure* revolutionized the landscape of American cooking and remains a classic, widely acknowledged as the book that brought pleasure to vegetarian cuisine. She has developed a devoted following through her books, which include the recent James Beard Award-winning cookbook *Love Soup*, as well as *The Vegetarian Epicure, Book Two*, and *The New Vegetarian Epicure*. Anna is also an Academy Award-nominated screenwriter, as well as a producer and director, and has served on the faculty of the American Film Institute since 2001. She divides her time between Los Angeles and Ojai, California.